A Social Constructivist Approach to Translator Education

Empowerment from Theory to Practice

Don Kiraly

St. Jerome Publishing
Manchester, UK & Northampton MA

Published by

St. Jerome Publishing
2 Maple Road West, Brooklands
Manchester, M23 9HH, United Kingdom
Tel +44 161 973 9856
Fax +44 161 905 3498
stjerome@compuserve.com
http://www.stjerome.co.uk

ISBN 1-900650-32-0 (hbk)
ISBN 1-900650-33-9 (pbk)

Printed and bound in Great Britain by
T. J. International Ltd., Cornwall, UK

Cover design by
Steve Fieldhouse, Oldham, UK (+44 161 620 2263)

Typeset by
Delta Typesetters, Cairo, Egypt
Email: delttyp@starnet.com.eg

British Library Cataloguing in Publication Data
A catalogue record of this book is available from the British Library

Library of Congress Catalging-in-Publication Data
Kiraly, Donald C., 1953-
  A social constructivist approach to translator education : empowerment
from theory to practice / Don Kiraly.
        p. cm.
Includes bibliographical references (p.   ) and index.
  ISBN 1-900650-32-0 (alk. paper) -- ISBN 1-900650-33-9 (pbk. : alk. paper)
  1. Translators , Training of. 2. Translating and interpreting--Study
and teaching. I. Title.
  P306.5 .K574 2000
  418'.02'071--dc21
                                00-010133

Contents

Acknowledgements

I could not have written this book without the help of my sponsors, my family, my colleagues, my students, and my own teachers. First, the University of Mainz and the Deutsche Forschungsgesellschaft provided me with grants to carry out the classroom research. Professor Renate von Bardeleben, my department head at the School of Applied Linguistics of the University of Mainz, provided me with generous counsel, encouragement and freedom to pursue a line of research that is often at odds with standard pedagogical practice. The greatest debt I owe is to my wife Christa and my children Yann and Jessica, who gave me so much time to work on this project - time we would otherwise have enjoyed together. My sister Anne read and critiqued large portions of the manuscript, and my brother Bill provided his graphic design acumen to help me create the charts. So many colleagues have contributed their perspectives and encouragement to the dialogue that has resulted in this book that I could not possibly name them all. I owe special thanks to Anthony Pym for his invaluable comments on the first draft, to Laura Russell, who read and critiqued every page, to Paul Kussmaul and Hans Hönig for their collegial support and encouragement. David Sawyer, Judith Leng Lawrence and Diane deTerra made it possible for me to spend the most prolific months of this project at the Monterey Institute of International Studies. Their enthusiasm for my approach and their incisive constructive criticism helped me draw together many loose threads and finally finish the book. The many students who have attended my classes over the years at the University of Mainz have also been key partners in the dialogue that has culminated in this volume. And finally, I would like to thank Sandra Savignon, who is the epitome of a constructivist, empowering teacher, and who has been my role model in the classroom for the past 20 years. This monograph is dedicated to her.

I of course assume full responsibility for all deficiencies, inadequacies and omissions.

Don Kiraly
March 2000

List of Figures

1. Translation and Translator Education Fields in Flux

Introduction

In recent years, it has become a commonplace in educational psychology that knowledge is constructed by learners, rather than being simply transmitted to them by their teachers. The implications of this viewpoint for the educational process are revolutionary, because it shifts the traditional focus of authority, responsibility and control in the educational process away from the teacher and towards the learner. Attaining competence in a professional domain means acquiring the expertise and thus the authority to make professional decisions; assuming responsibility for one's actions; and achieving autonomy to follow a path of lifelong learning. This is empowerment.

Many different ways of looking at the knowledge-construction process have been proposed, some of them more cognitive, focusing on what goes on in one person's mind, and others more social, seeing knowledge construction as a collaborative, interpersonal activity. From an information-processing perspective, for example, knowledge construction is viewed essentially as an individual, cognitive process:

> What is needed to comprehend a text is not solely contained in the linguistic and logical information coded in that text. Rather, comprehension involves the construction of meaning: The text is a preliminary blueprint for constructing an understanding. The information contained in the text must be combined with information outside of the text, including most prominently the prior knowledge of the learner, to form a complete and adequate representation of the text's meaning. (Spiro *et al.* 1992:64)

This cognitive psychology approach, focused on what is allegedly going on in the individual's mind, has been the focus of a considerable amount of attention in translation studies over the past ten years, particularly in work based on think-aloud experimental methods, as in Krings (1986, 1992), Lörscher (1991), Hönig (1990), Jääskeläinen and Tirkkonen-Condit (1991) and Kiraly (1995). While working on the research that culminated in *Pathways to Translation*, I was drawn, at least partially, into the mindset of the cognitivist approach to translation studies that was emerging in the mid-1980s. Then, as now, I depicted translation in terms of a double bind: as an internal, cognitive process and as an external, social phenomenon. Yet, in analysing the think-aloud protocols produced by novice and expert translators while they performed translation tasks, I was working under the implicit assumption that by having subjects verbalize what they were thinking while translating, it would be possible to identify cognitive strategies as if they were fixed routines, artefacts of the mind that could be extracted, dissected and perhaps even distributed to translators-in-training.

Since completing that earlier work, my understanding has evolved to a point where I see this cognitive science approach to translation processes as epistemologically incompatible with a social process perspective. The former rests on the assumption that meaning and knowledge are products of the individual mind – replicable, transferable, independent of social interaction and essentially static – while the latter assumes that they are dynamic intersubjective processes.

A critique of my own earlier depiction of mental translation processes (see

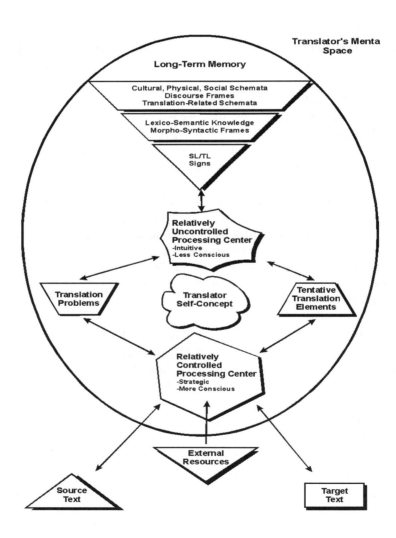

Figure 1: A cognitive processing model of translation

figure 1) will perhaps best explain my shift in perspective away from a cognitivist view and toward a social constructivist one.

Underlying this model is essentially an information-processing view of the mind. Information of different types is seen to be 'stored' in long-term memory and outside resources. The translator is depicted as an independent cognizing agent who 'retrieves' data from various sources as needed and as a function of his or her translation strategies, which are conceived as blueprints or plans for cognitive action to solve problems. The black boxes inside the translator's mind – both of which are depicted as receptacles – are respectively portrayed as the conscious and unconscious sites of information processing. The uncontrolled processing centre is an essentially unconscious workplace in the mind where intuitions bounce through the receptacle containing retrieved information; it intuitively produces tentative translation elements and identifies translation problems that are then processed strategically and more consciously in the controlled processing centre. The translator's self-concept is shown as a cloud hovering in the background of intuitive and cognitive activity. This self-concept is the psychological identity that the translator creates through learning and experience with translation activities, the individual's understanding of him- or herself as a translational information processor.

From such a perspective, the translator's knowledge and strategies could be seen as existing apart from actual translational interaction. Moving logically from this image of the underlying cognitive processes involved in translation, it is but a small and tempting step to use this concept to justify a transmissionist approach to the teaching of knowledge and skills. In addition to teaching comparative syntax and encouraging rote memorisation of pairs of bilingual lexical items and idiomatic expressions, we could also justify the teaching of the 'right' strategies. Teachers could retain their traditional function of transferring knowledge, expanded to include the procedural knowledge of how to produce correct translations. From this perspective, it should be unnecessary to implicate learners in the actual give-and-take of multi-faceted negotiation that characterizes translation as a social process. There is nothing in the model that reflects my current belief that the development of true expertise can only be developed on the basis of authentic situated action, the collaborative construction of knowledge, and personal experience.

I first became uncomfortable with the cognitivist approach when I confronted my finding in *Pathways to Translation* that intuitions (which I defined as non-strategic, relatively uncontrolled, and virtually untraceable mental processes) appeared to be deeply and inextricably involved in the mental processes I was trying to observe. Intuitions do not fit neatly into a 'scientific' cognitivist perspective precisely because, buried as they seem to be in the dark recesses of the mind's black box, they leave nothing but the most ephemeral traces of their links to more conscious, strategic processes. We cannot readily identify their origins, we cannot predict under what circumstances they will emerge, and we cannot 'teach' them.

From a social constructivist perspective, intuitions are dynamically constructed impressions distilled from countless occurrences of action and interaction with the world and from the myriad dialogues that we engage in as we go about life in the various communities of which we are members. By communicating and negotiating with peers and more experienced (and thus more knowledgeable) others, we acquire a feel for correctness, appropriateness and accuracy, a feel that is grounded in our social experiences, and bound up in the language we use and share with other people. This is the place where the present volume departs from the path I took in *Pathways to Translation*. Rather than taking a new fork in the road, I have retraced my steps, moving back to the position derived from my early experiences with language teaching (to be discussed in Chapter 9), and the acknowledgement that, as knowledge is intersubjectively constructed, learning must be socially situated.

A constructivism for translation studies

From a social constructivist perspective, individuals have no choice but to create or construct meanings and knowledge through participation in the interpersonal, inter-subjective interaction that the philosopher Richard Rorty has called the "conversation of mankind" (Rorty 1979). While our personal meanings and understandings of the world can never be identical to those of any other individual due to the idiosyncratic nature of experience, language serves as a common denominator of interpretation that makes it possible for communication to take place at all. As children become acculturated, they acquire and use language to make sense of the world through the sociolinguistic glasses of the communities they are in the process of joining. Subsequent learning can thus be seen as a type of re-acculturation, as a process of becoming increasingly proficient at thinking, acting and communicating in ways that are shared by the particular knowledge communities of which we are striving to become members.

The implications of these epistemological premises for the translator education classroom are far-reaching. They include the need for a radical re-assessment of teachers' and students' roles in the classroom, a new perspective on the function and nature of testing, and a reorientation of the very goals and techniques of the educational programme. It is important to note that *constructivism* is not directly related to the school of literary theory called *deconstruction*, although I am sure that parallels could be drawn. In fact, in another publication (Kiraly 1998), I identified an affinity between the pedagogical implications of constructivism and those of deconstruction drawn by Arrojo (1994) concerning the learning of translation skills through collaboration in an authentic setting. Arrojo is one of the few contemporary translation studies scholars to promote the reorganization of the conventional, teacher-centred classroom into a forum for authentic and interactive learning. I have chosen not to draw deconstruction further into the discussion at this point, but the investigation of the links between these approaches would, however, be an interesting topic for further research.

This book is not intended as a didactic cookbook with ready-made lesson plans and off-the-shelf classroom procedures that can be applied directly to other translation studies classrooms. From a constructivist viewpoint, the ideas presented here, as in all acts of communication, cannot be 'objective' in the conventional sense, corresponding to reality or truth. They are ineluctably coloured by each individual's personal and idiosyncratic interpretations of the principles, events and examples portrayed. While I am describing a teaching method here, it is my own personal method, which will, by necessity and by design, differ in its applications from programme to programme and from teacher to teacher.

Towards a comprehensive teaching method: approach, design and procedures

I would like to clarify my understanding of the concept of teaching 'method' right from the start, by drawing on the framework proposed by Richards and Rodgers (1986) for analyzing instructional systems in the field of foreign language teaching. Their depiction of a teaching method as comprising the three elements of **approach**, **design** and **procedures** seems particularly well suited to understanding the educational framework to be discussed here.

An approach comprises a theory of language and a theory of language learning that serve as the foundation for the principles and practices implemented in a method. From this perspective, the approach is clearly the most fundamental level of a method. It relates to a view of the world and of learning, teaching and language use that can transcend individual teaching and learning environments and the limits of individual institutions. At the other end of the spectrum we find procedures, which include "classroom techniques, practices and behaviour observed when the method is used" (Richards and Rodgers 1986:20).

It is at the procedural end of the spectrum that we find the greatest degree of diversity and variability, at the level where teachers, working collaboratively and individually, implement a theoretical approach in actual pedagogical practice. Design is the link between an approach and pedagogical procedures. In Richards and Rodger's words:

> Design is the level of method analysis in which we consider (a) what the objectives of a method are; (b) how language content is selected and organized within the method, that is, the syllabus model the method incorporates; (c) the types of learning tasks and teaching activities the method advocates; (d) the roles of learners; (e) the roles of teachers; (f) the role of instructional materials. (ibid.:20)

My task here is to outline a theoretical **approach** that I hope many teachers can share; to show how I have interpreted the implications of the approach for the **design** of the key features of classroom interaction; and to provide some examples and suggestions focused on the **procedures** I have developed for my own classroom practice. My overriding goal in dealing with all three aspects is to provide an impetus for further interpretation, elaboration and experimentation, which I hope will initiate a dialogue toward innovation for the empowerment of students of translation.

Sources of inspiration

The ideas presented in these pages are derived from my 15 years of experience as a translator educator at the School of Applied Linguistics and Cultural Studies of the University of Mainz in Germersheim, Germany. The initial experiences I had during my first few semesters, when I tried to appropriate the instructional performance techniques used by other teachers, made me decide either to work toward developing a systematic and humanistic approach to the training of translators, or to leave the institution.

Like most other translator educators, I had also received no special training in translation teaching methods prior to assuming my duties in Germersheim. I was encouraged to sit in on classes run by my colleagues and to pick up ideas on how to teach from them. This very practice, in lieu of any methods or programmes for the training of translator educators, is clearly a major reason why the instructional performance model is perpetuated from one generation of teachers to the next. There has been no forum for investigating the assumptions underlying this approach or possible alternatives to it.

There is a desperate need for comprehensive degree programmes for the training of translator trainers. This, I contend, could be a major first step out of the rut that our profession is in, a step toward the professionalization of translator education. We can start to educate generations of educators who know how to do classroom research, how to recognize and focus on the ever-evolving skills and knowledge that our graduates will need, and how to design classroom environments that lead to professional competence. If pursued with enthusiasm, creativity and the best interests of our students, of the profession, and of society as a whole in mind, these measures cannot help but radically improve the value and efficacy of our programmes as well as the status of the graduate translator.

Classroom research

My initial efforts to break out of the traditional, teacher-centred mould in my own classes culminated in my doctoral dissertation research, completed in 1990 at the University of Illinois, and published in 1995 under the title *Pathways to Translation*. One part of the study was a think-aloud-protocol investigation of the cognitive translation processes of novice and professional translators. The other part involved

the development of initial steps toward a systematic approach to translator education. *Pathways to Translation* was an exploratory study that was meant more to
raise questions than to answer them. Here, some tentative answers to those and
other related questions will be presented. These are answers that have worked for
my students, and that I hope will serve as examples for others. As I stated at the
beginning of this chapter, my assumptions have evolved considerably since *Pathways* was completed, in particular due to my having become acquainted with the
field of constructivist education that has been emerging for the past few decades,
particularly in Anglo-Saxon countries. I was first introduced to constructivism
through the excellent, collaboratively written volume *Constructivism and the Technology of Instruction: a Conversation*, edited by Thomas Duffy and David Jonassen
(1992). I then went on to read scholars including von Glasersfeld (1988), Dewey
(1938), Rorty (1979), Brown *et al.* (1989) and Vygotsky (1994). The more I read,
the more I realized that my personal theories of foreign language learning and translator education can best be articulated from a social constructivist perspective. The
approach to translator education outlined here owes a particular debt to *Collaborative Learning* by Kenneth Bruffee (1995), which convinced me of the viability of a
consistently non-foundational, social constructivist perspective. Bruffee says that
learning, "is not 'a shift inside the person which now suits him to enter ... new
relationships' with reality and with other people. It is a shift in a person's relations
with others, period" (Bruffee 1995:74).

Quintessentially, this view holds that meaning, knowledge, and the mind itself
are inextricably embedded in our personal interactions with other people. This helps
explain and justify the move in this book away from the dual cognitive-social perspective to translator competence and translator education I adopted in *Pathways
to Translation*. As I will explain further in Chapter 2, I now believe that the social,
inter-subjective nature of meaning, thought and mind provide a much more coherent framework for the elaboration of an approach to translator education than a
two-track, cognitive/social approach. I have come to reject the dualistic distinction
of the internal workings of the mind as being something essentially different from
the social interaction between individuals in a community. From the Vygotskyian
perspective that will emerge, I hope it will become apparent that an individual's
thought processes are so intricately intertwined with that person's social history and
interpersonal interactions that it is unnecessary and pointless to try to dissect them
and focus on them as distinct entities.

Several research projects in which I have been involved at the School of Applied Linguistics and Cultural Studies of the University of Mainz (FASK) have
contributed significantly to the agenda of this volume. The first was a school-wide
study on computer-assisted translation skills instruction, which I helped co-ordinate
from 1992-1994. The second project was a two-year (1995-1997) study of classroom instruction based on classroom research methods applied in an action research
framework. The purpose of that research was to identify the roots of the problems

with traditional teaching approaches, and to identify and test alternative approaches to translation skills instruction in various types of translation studies classes. A thesis completed by one of the student researchers on this project, Uta Graceffo (1996) elaborates the outcome of this study. Her findings have contributed significantly to this book, and particularly to Chapter VI, which outlines the genesis of my method for teaching translation-practice classes.

A third related study was another master's thesis done by Claudia Gelies (1997) on the effects of communicative language instruction for translation students; this thesis was submitted to the English and American Studies Department of the FASK during the winter term of 1997-98. The curricula of translator education programmes generally include considerable instruction in foreign languages. While there has been a great deal of debate in the literature as to whether or not instruction in translation skills per se should accompany or instead only follow foreign language instruction, little research to date has been devoted to the kind of foreign language instruction that will best prepare translation students for their future profession. In Chapter IX, I will present an argument for incorporating communicative approaches for classroom language acquisition to replace or at least complement traditional foreign language teaching in translator education programmes.

Freelance translation work

My own activities as a freelance translator over the past ten years have made a very significant contribution to this book. It has been by translating professionally that I myself have learned (and continue to learn) how to translate. Several factors have been most important for the development of my own translator competence. First, feedback from clients, authors, and readers, both positive and negative, has helped me to develop my own personal approach toward translation and my own strategies for dealing with translation problems. Second, advice from and collaboration with more experienced translators has been a key factor that has helped me understand the norms and conventions that apply to the translator's work. And finally, the fact that all of my translation work has been embedded in a real social matrix has been a constant reminder of the myriad real-world constraints on the translator's work. These three factors will also be seen to play an important role in the socially situated approach to translator education I am proposing here.

From my early experiences with English language teaching using second-generation Structuro-Global Audio-Visual methods in France in the late 1970s, I acquired basic underlying principles of foreign language teaching based on co-operative learning, and a view of the educational setting as a microcosm of a natural communicative environment. This basic training set the stage for my personal beliefs in how language learning can best take place. My graduate training in foreign language teaching and teacher education under the guidance of Sandra Savignon at the University of Illinois solidified these views and helped strengthen my conviction that a humanistic, communication-based approach was indeed appropriate for the translation education classroom.

Collaboration

This book is of course not by any means the result of my efforts alone. Collaboration is proposed throughout this book as the primary cornerstone of learning and professional development. Likewise, the book itself is the result of collaborative efforts, in which I was involved to some extent, either as an initiator, advisor or participant. In every translation exercise class I have taught at the FASK in Germersheim, students have contributed to my understanding of what and how to teach within the field of translation studies. In a series of twenty semester-long seminars for undergraduate and graduate students, my students and I have shared our experiences from the two traditional sides of the desk, and numerous groups of students have graciously played along in my sometimes successful, sometimes less successful pursuit of a better learning environment and teaching method. My classroom research project was also a collaborative undertaking involving a number of student data collectors who served as classroom observers and co-analysts of the data.

Targeted readership

This book has been written particularly with current and prospective translator educators and programme administrators in mind. It is intended for those who are currently dissatisfied with the predominant models for teaching practice, and who are seeking an alternative perspective that can serve as a solid foundation for effective and rewarding personal and institutional approaches to translator education. It is also intended for students of translation, who, I hope, will find in it a new perspective on their roles and responsibilities as lifelong learners. For programme administrators, this book is intended to encourage thinking about innovation in the design of educational experiences and programmes. Similarly, administrators need to rethink the qualifications and attitudes that are desirable in prospective teachers; and the kind of teacher training that should be provided to them to ensure that the educational system is founded on a solid pedagogical framework that is implemented consistently from one classroom to the next.

Empowering students as active, collaborative agents of their own learning can lead to an enhanced belief in the benevolence and coherence of the system. Students who are seen by instructors and the institution as the primary agents of their own success are more likely to feel they have a stake in the institution. They are also more likely to assume responsibility for their own learning and to be well on the road to becoming experts and responsible professionals by the time they graduate. They will be more motivated to learn and will contribute more to the development of the institution. Teachers and students should see themselves as instruments of perpetual innovation.

Since I see this book as a contribution to a conversation about how translator education can better help students join the community of professional translators, I will start with a brief account of my own experiences as a translator over the past decade. I believe that the kinds of changes I have experienced in my translation work reflect a pattern of change for translators in different countries working with many different languages. It is these changes that justify, if not demand, that we rethink the ways in which translators are being educated at university-level professional schools today.

From translation competence to translator competence

In 1988, when I began working part-time as a freelance translator in Germany, the source text for my first translation (the manuscript for a wine journal) was announced several weeks in advance and came on paper through the post. I was expected to translate the various articles using a typewriter, and send them back piecemeal as they were finished. The text was typeset at the publishing house and returned to me for proofreading. I marked my corrections and suggested improvements in the printed text and returned it, again through the post, to the publishing house, where the changes were made to the proofs. The resources at my disposal were books on wine in German and English that I managed to find in the university library or purchase through bookstores, along with some documentation and glossaries that I obtained from the German Wine Institute.

The pace of the translation and correction process on those initial and subsequent translations was leisurely by today's standards. I often had days or even weeks of advance warning, days to search for terminology or background information in the library while I waited for source texts to arrive, days allotted for translating and typing up the translations, days for the postal workers to get the translations back to the publisher – all in all, plenty of time to prepare for and complete the job.

Back then, there was no Internet and no electronic mail readily available, and I, like the majority of freelance translators I knew, owned neither a fax machine, nor a modem, nor even a computer. Most of the skills, knowledge and abilities I needed then to fulfil the tasks expected of me as a professional translator could be subsumed under the label of 'translation competence', essentially the ability to comprehend a text written in one language and produce an 'adequate' target text for speakers of a different language on the basis of that original text. By an 'adequate' text I mean one that could be accepted by the text recipient and the commissioner of the job as an adequate translingual rendering of the source text message. Even in those days, translation competence did of course require resourcefulness in finding relevant background information, an awareness of text types, and a practical ability to create a text for a specialized wine-marketing readership in my native tongue. But there were very few technical aids to assist me in my work, and thus my task was essentially limited to the actual craft of translation. Those were the good old days.

Now, just over a decade after tackling my first real translation job for pay, things have changed dramatically. The pace of my work and my job profile as a freelance translator look very different indeed. Today, most source texts reach me almost instantly via fax or e-mail, often with no more than hours or minutes of advance warning, if any at all. Since my translations must almost always be returned via e-mail, my turnaround time for any given job is now drastically reduced. My clients allow virtually no time for the transmission of texts in either direction, and as word processing – thanks to the ease of correction and text manipulation – is quicker than typing, I am given much less time within which to complete my translations. In many cases, time is so short for the completion of large projects that I must share the work with one or more colleagues, sometimes even located on different continents. One of us serves as the project co-ordinator and we work together as a team to produce the translation. Thanks to electronic mail, it is now feasible and convenient to contact colleagues or 'subject matter' experts in other cities or even countries to share responsibility for a translation job. Team members must interact with one another to ensure consistency of formatting, terminology and style, and we can also conveniently proofread each other's work. Collaboration has become a critical tool that not only can make the translator's job easier, but can also help ensure better quality.

The advent of modern electronic media has not only significantly stepped up the pace of the translation process; it has also greatly widened the range of tasks that the translator can be expected to fulfil. The range of tools that are available to me and that my clients generally expect me to own and master has multiplied over the years. Every client and potential client assumes that I have the latest PC hardware as well as a panoply of software at my disposal and that I can use it all proficiently. Not only must my word processor be compatible with the latest versions of the standard programmes used in commerce and industry, but I must also be capable of using spreadsheets, databases, graphics programmes and presentation software for translation purposes. More than once over the past few years, my chances of landing lucrative freelance contracts have hinged on my being ready and willing to purchase and install a graphics or spreadsheet programme I had never worked with before, and my ability to learn how to use it well enough overnight to produce a camera-ready over-write translation.

Today, there are also numerous inexpensive tools available to the translator that were simply not on the mass market a decade ago. Many dictionaries in a wide variety of fields and languages can now be purchased at moderate cost on CD-ROM. Internet access is also economical and readily available, and my clients expect me to search the Internet for background and terminological information if necessary, to ensure that I always produce an accurate, polished, high-quality translation.

While in the past translators may have relied on printed dictionaries, glossaries, and in-house word lists to solve lexical problems, terminology management has now become a complex, interactive enterprise involving the gathering and organizing of linguistic, contextual and even graphic data on special subjects. Numerous computer programmes for terminology management are now available. This makes it convenient for translators to work together with 'subject matter' experts to collect terminological and contextual data in a common database that can be used for various purposes by personnel with different tasks within a company, or by a set of freelancers working on projects in a team. The translator can be expected to know what software is available, how to use it and how to best exploit its advantages to serve the terminology and knowledge management needs of the firm or client.

Technological advances have contributed to the crumbling of barriers in international communication and the global market. This in turn has led to an increased awareness of cultural and textual differences as well as the implications of these advances for the translator's work. A decade ago, software was simply translated; now it is also 'localized,' or adapted to the textual and cultural conventions of the target markets. Multi-cultural technical writing, involving the production of parallel texts in different languages, has become a more cost-efficient alternative to simply 'translating' a culturally embedded technical text from one language to another. Whereas in earlier days, translators might have been expected to "just translate what's on the paper", today there is a much greater awareness of the importance of creating an appropriate effect on a reader, particularly within the translation profession itself. Translation studies as an academic field has matured greatly over the past fifty years, and has gradually liberated itself from the domination of contrastive structural linguistics; most contemporary perspectives in the field view the translator's professional activities essentially in terms of social and cognitive processes and intercultural communication, rather than primarily as a process of linguistic transfer.

When it comes to subject matter knowledge, it is now less a matter of mastering one specialized field prior to beginning work as a translator. Rather, it is one of having the ability to acquire adequate knowledge in new areas as needed, and of developing a finely tuned sensitivity to norms and text types in preparation for tackling a variety of new language-related tasks and challenges. It is impossible to predict years in advance what particular topics one will work on after graduation or over the course of one's career. A well-developed ability to adapt to ever-changing market demands is crucial. Thus, knowing how and where to research new topics adequately and efficiently is an essential skill for translators to acquire.

Translators today cannot afford to be linguistic hermits, sitting alone behind a typewriter and surrounded only by dusty tomes. Translators are embedded in a complex network of social and professional activity. They should not be considered anonymous language lackeys, passively transferring a message from one language to another. Translators are professional text interpreters and communicators. They do not transfer meaning; they *make* meaning as they work. They must have a professional 'self-concept', a profound awareness of their responsibility as active participants in a complex communicative process where they serve a key role that can significantly affect the degree of success of commercial contacts, legal interaction, medical treatment, and technical operations.

It is clear that today, high levels of translation competence, foreign language competence and native tongue competence are in themselves insufficient, albeit essential, features of the translator's overall professional profile. But the translator's marketability also depends on his or her ability to use the modern tools of the trade in a professional manner, to research new topics quickly and efficiently, to justify one's work when necessary, to negotiate and collaborate with other translators and subject matter experts to accomplish tasks at hand. What is essential for graduates is that they be competent enough to tackle a wide variety of assignments and that they be confident enough to undertake new language-related tasks that may not have even existed when they were studying.

Becoming a professional translator clearly entails more than learning specific skills that allow one to produce an acceptable target text in one language on the basis of a text written in another. That is what I would call '**translation** competence'. Acquiring '**translator** competence', on the other hand, in addition involves joining a number of new communities such as the group of educated users of several languages, those conversant in specialized technical fields, and proficient users of traditional tools and new technologies for professional interlingual communication purposes. Acquiring the abilities to comprehend texts written for specialized readers and to produce texts to be used by such readers means, in a very real sense, joining the communities to which those experts belong. One might say that successful translators are able to act (communicate) successfully within parallel expert communities in different linguistic-cultural communities.

Seen this way, the skills, knowledge and strategies that translators should have acquired by the time they complete their studies and enter professional life will be determined by the respective knowledge and cultural communities themselves. Translation norms do differ from culture to culture and they do evolve over time, so we as teachers cannot identify and teach norms as if they were static and immutable, or as if our personal norms were authentic mirrors of some sort of universal norms. Translator competence includes being able to identify and appropriate norms in new communities to which we seek access (as well as to break norms where necessary; Toury (1992), Chesterman (1993)).

The professional translator's job description also varies from country to country, and depends on whether he or she is a freelancer, a secretary, or a translator in a company or in public service. Students may pick one special area of expertise during their studies and yet be drawn by circumstances into radically different areas of translation work over the course of their careers.

Translator competence does not primarily refer to knowing *the* correct translations for words, sentences or even texts. It does entail being able to use tools and information to create communicatively successful texts that are accepted as good translations within the community concerned. Perhaps most importantly, it means knowing how to work co-operatively within the various overlapping communities of translators and subject matter experts to accomplish work collaboratively; to appropriate knowledge, norms and conventions; and to contribute to the evolving conversation that constitutes those communities. With the changes in the translation profession in mind, it is time to reconsider the viability of conventional approaches for educating translators, which date back almost half a century, when the translation profession was something altogether different from what it is today.

2. Rethinking Approaches to Translator Education

> The unheralded importance of activity and enculturation to learning suggests that much common educational practice is the victim of an inadequate epistemology. A new epistemology might hold the key to a dramatic improvement in learning and a completely new perspective on education.
>
> (Garrison 1995:717)

Since I began teaching translation skills some fifteen years ago, I have become increasingly convinced that the conventional, teacher-centred translation exercise class – the primary didactic event in numerous programmes for the training of professional translators – is hardly an ideal venue for the development of a professional self-concept, the conceptualization of oneself as a professional translator. Nor is it well-suited for acquiring the ability to work collaboratively with other professionals, or for learning how to learn autonomously (i.e. independently of a teacher) after graduation. It is my contention that this traditional 'instructional performance' derives from what Bereiter and Scardamalia (1993:188) have called a "common-sense epistemology". This still ubiquitous technique is a procedure that seems very consistent with a positivist or objectivist pedagogical epistemology, which sees the teacher as the possessor and distributor of knowledge – in fact, of truth.

Some critics of the objectivist tradition insist that this educational epistemology is actually implicit. For example, Bereiter and Scardamalia (ibid.) note that "no such theory is propounded anywhere in educational circles, and anyone found espousing it would be mercilessly ridiculed". Nevertheless, if one looks at what goes on in many translation exercise classes, one is likely to admit that "there is some truth behind the caricature" (ibid.). Other critics are more outspoken. Rorty (1979), for example, claims that the foundational assumptions underlying the 'mirrored' view of knowledge have been a fundamental belief in western philosophy since Kant, and Bruffee (1995:95) notes that "They prevail with few exceptions today the world over, from the two Cambridges to Tokyo, from the first grade to PhD. They are so familiar that we take them for granted".

Despite the debate concerning whether the positivist epistemology is implicit or explicit, I would like to contrast my view of it here with the social constructivist viewpoint I am proposing as a viable philosophical basis for an alternative pedagogy of translation. First of all, let us take a look at the epistemology that might be seen as the basis for conventional approaches to instruction, not only in translation studies, but in most other areas as well, from elementary school through the university level:

> Objectivism is a view of the nature of knowledge and what it means to know something. In this view, the mind is an instantiation of a computer manipulating symbols in the same way (or analogously, at least) as a computer.

> Knowledge, therefore, is some entity existing independently of the mind which is transferred "inside the mind." Cognition is the rule-based manipulation of the symbols via processes that will be ultimately describable through the language of mathematics and/or logic. Thus, this school of thought believes that the external world is mind independent (i.e., the same for everyone). (Lakoff 1987:20)

This computer-like, rule-based view of knowledge and perception suggests that an individual's social experiences are incidental to coming to know reality:

> Experience plays an insignificant role in the structuring of the world; meaning is something that exists in the world quite aside from experience. Hence, the goal of understanding is coming to know the entities, attributes, and relations that exist. (Duffy and Jonassen 1992:2)

And consequently:

> Consistent with this view of knowledge, the goal of instruction, from both the behavioural and cognitive information-processing perspective, is to communicate or transfer knowledge to learners in the most efficient, effective manner possible. (Bednar *et al.* 1992:21)

Diametrically opposed to objectivist epistemology are the constructivist views of meaning, which, in their most radical forms, claim that while there is indeed a real world, each individual mind is a self-creating and self-regulating system that perpetually reconstructs itself by producing and modifying its own meanings, or models of that real world.

> Constructivism, like objectivism, holds that there is a real world that we experience. However, the argument is that meaning is imposed on the world by us, rather than existing in the world independently of us. There are many ways to structure the world, and there are many meanings or perspectives for any event or concept. Thus there is not a correct meaning that we are striving for. (Duffy and Jonassen 1992:3)

From such a perspective, learning occurs when we become aware that some part of the mental models we have created of our world does not correspond to some new phenomenon that we perceive. We thus learn through experience, adapting and adjusting our mental models as they prove incompatible with information with which we come into contact in our environment. The implications of this are fundamental, both for the development of the emerging translator's image of the goals of the translation process and their personal experience of the translator education situation:

> In this view, learning is a constructive process in which the learner is building an internal representation of knowledge, a personal interpretation of experience. This representation is constantly open to change, its structure

and linkages forming the foundation to which other knowledge structures are appended. Learning is an active process in which meaning is developed on the basis of experience. ... Conceptual growth comes from the sharing of multiple perspectives and the simultaneous changing of our internal representations in response to those perspectives as well as through cumulative experience. (Bednar *et al.* 1992:21)

It may be that an objectivist epistemology, applied either explicitly or in a "common sense" manner to education, simplifies the teaching process by reducing it metaphorically to the simple transfer of knowledge from teachers to students. Seen from such a perspective, the teacher has a clear mandate: to distribute the relevant truth efficiently and make sure that students have absorbed it. Thanks to this pervasive understanding of teaching and learning (whether implicit or explicit), generations of translation teachers have not needed to be trained at all. Newly hired teachers generally just perpetuate the traditional process, passing on the knowledge that was handed down to them, teaching as they were taught.

It is no wonder that there are extremely few programmes for the training of translator educators; from a positivist, foundational perspective, the teacher's task is as simple and limited in scope as the translator's task once was. Just as the translator's job used to be understood in terms of transferring a text from one language to another, the translator trainer's job has primarily been seen as one of transferring knowledge to the students. The seminars on translator education I have offered at the University of Mainz and the workshops I have run at a number of universities over the past several years have made it clear to me, however, that students and many teachers themselves perceive a great need for change in the translation classroom.

As in many fields and at educational institutions in many countries, the translator's skills have been seen from an institutional perspective as essentially pre-definable, virtually identical for all students, and measurable (in terms of objective assessment of learning progress and the quality of academic performance). In critiquing the predominant pedagogical paradigm of his age, John Dewey (1938:19) said:

> That which is taught is thought of as essentially static. It is taught as a finished product, with little regard either to the ways in which it was originally built up or to changes that will surely occur in the future. ... it is used as educational food in a society where change is the rule, not the exception.

I wish to challenge the common sense view that knowledge is static, and to propose an alternative one that sees the task of the translation student and the teacher in a radically different light. Rather than entailing a set of finite skills and knowledge to be ingested passively, memorized and regurgitated, I propose that translator education be seen as a dynamic, interactive process based on learner empowerment; on

the emancipation of students from the domination of the teacher and from the institution as the designated distributors and arbiters of truth; on a change in focus from
the tyranny of teaching, to learning as a collaborative, acculturative, and quintessentially social activity. In my view, it is the task of the institution and of every
instructor to facilitate the transfer of responsibility for learning to the learners, individually and collectively. Instead of filling them with knowledge, teachers should
serve as guides, consultants and assistants who can help set the stage for learning
events in which students will evolve into professional translators by experiencing
real or at least simulated translation activities in all their complexity. If they can
learn to walk, talk, act and think like translators – then they will be translators.

From constructivism to empowerment

There is no single theory of constructivism. In fact, there are many shades and varieties of constructivism spanning a range of perspectives. There is also no single
individual who can be identified as the founder of constructivism. In fact, rather
than tracing a linear development along one line of philosophical thought, constructivism seems to circumscribe a set of thinkers, theories and approaches that
spring from a plethora of historical and cultural origins.

For example, Garrison (1995), among others, has demonstrated the striking
parallels between the social behaviourism of John Dewey and Lev Vygotsky's
socio-historical theory of psychological development – both of which are considered to represent a social constructivist epistemology. The fact that Vygotsky's theory
emerged against the backdrop of the pervasive Marxist ideology of the early Soviet
Union whereas Dewey's work was grounded in the democratic ideals prevalent in
the US at the same time supports my contention that constructivism has a wide-
spread foundation in intellectual thought across cultural, national and historical
boundaries.

Along with the work of Dewey and Vygotsky, the generative psychology of
Jean Piaget is also generally considered a third major pillar of constructivist thought.
Both the Piagetian and Vygotskian approaches originally emerged from developmental psychology. Both Piaget and Vygotsky saw the development of mental
structures (and by analogy, of all learning) in terms of construction rather than rep-
lication. However, Piaget saw development essentially as an inevitable, biologically
determined, individual process, while the Vygotskian view sees cognitive change
primarily as the internalization of social processes and cultural knowledge.

While the social constructivist ideas of Vygotsky, Bruffee, Rorty and Piaget
have all informed my pedagogical approach, I hope that no rigid, dogmatic reading
of constructivism will emerge to fossilize the method. The empowerment method
should not be seen as a fixed stage in the evolution of translator education methods
that will have come and gone on the threshold of the new millennium. To remain

viable, the method must be seen as a process more than as a product – a never-ending collaborative process of experience, interpretation and re-evaluation. The key, perhaps, to avoiding epistemological dogmatism is to focus more on empowerment, the goal of the method, than on the theories upon which the method is based. Social constructivist thought at present may well appear to be a viable theoretical justification for the approach adopted, but all those who participate in the dialogue of innovation that I envisage will inevitably bring different perspectives to bear on the method, including changing views of the very assumptions upon which it has been initiated. I hope, however, that the goal of empowerment will always remain a cornerstone of the method, guiding approach and design as well as procedures.

Today's students will be tomorrow's professionals, and it is within the institution itself that empowerment needs to take place. By attempting to control the learning process through teacher-centred instruction, we stifle our students' creativity, their sense of responsibility toward their own learning and their future profession, and the development of that professional and expert self-concept that they must acquire in order to function adequately within the community of professional translators. The teacher-centred classroom needs to be re-centred, not so much on the learner as on the process of learning itself. Effective teaching and constructive learning result in empowerment.

I contend that the major change that is needed to break out of the gridlock of the foundational bias in education is a willingness to make explicit the tacit "common sense epistemology" upon which much of translator education is based. We need to take a stand on our deepest beliefs about teaching and learning, and to apply those beliefs explicitly and consistently to the development of teaching methods. Of course, the constructed nature of knowledge is not something that we will be able to prove; it is, and will always remain, a matter of belief. Conventional teaching approaches are also based on belief – belief in the unproved and unprovable transferability of knowledge and skills from teacher to learner. The validity of any pedagogical approach depends on our ability to identify and defend the belief system upon which our educational decisions are based, ranging from curriculum development to the design of classroom activities down to the assessment of learning.

It is certain that some of the ideas presented in this book will stand in stark contrast to educational practices in numerous countries and educational institutions but they may be seen to be very similar to those employed elsewhere; for example, Vienne (1993), Mackenzie and Nieminen (1997). The persistence of the 'instructional performance', despite the fundamental changes in the nature of translator competence and the viewpoints adopted within translation studies in recent decades, suggests that there will be considerable reluctance on the part of teachers and programme administrators to re-assess their educational practice in the direction I suggest. This, I believe, will be particularly true for experienced translator educators whom I ask to call into question their most basic assumptions and beliefs about learning and teaching assumptions and beliefs that may have served as the basis for years of classroom experience. The longer we hold views that define the principles of our teaching practice, the harder it is to reassess those views, to reconsider our basic working principles and to draw implications from that assessment. Translator education cannot, however, wait for some future generation of translator educators to breathe new life and innovation into the classroom. The whirlwind of change in the language market and in the demands placed on graduates of translator training programmes requires a change in educational practice now.

This approach to translator education does not make teachers obsolete. Instead, it redefines their roles and responsibilities as guides, assistants, and catalysts for learning for incipient, and then emerging, professional translators. Nor am I aiming at what has sometimes been described as 'autonomous learning', where each individual would essentially be an autodidact within the institutional framework. Clearly the development of autonomous learning skills in the sense of independence from the teacher as the source of truth is essential for ensuring that translators can continue learning once the programme of studies is over. However, I believe that such skills must be grounded in collaborative social experiences in the construction of meaning. I thus place considerable emphasis on group learning, on shifting the focus of attention in the classroom away from the one-way distribution of knowledge in the traditional classroom, toward multi-faceted, multi-directional interaction between the various participants in the classroom situation. Autonomy from this viewpoint is thus both a group phenomenon as well as an individual one.

Educational dilemmas: from transmission to transformation

Models of curriculum development in education are a good starting point for clarifying and distinguishing the educational implications of objectivist and constructivist views. Miller and Seller (1985), for example, have described the relationship between educational approaches and the philosophical, psychological, and social assumptions upon which they are based in terms of 'dilemmas' with which not only teachers and programme administrators, but also students, are faced. These dilemmas reflect some of the epistemological questions that teachers must answer for themselves in order to fulfil their classroom function. Here I paraphrase Miller and Seller's dilemmas:

Learner seen as a student and client versus learner seen as a whole person
Should the educational process deal with the learner in the classroom more as a consumer of knowledge or as a three-dimensional person with an emotional and physical as well as a cognitive side?

Teacher control versus student control
Who should control the learning process, the teacher or the student? Aspects of the

learning process include the content and goals of instruction, learning procedures, and interpersonal communication in the classroom.

Public knowledge versus private knowledge
Is the knowledge to be learned by the students the same for all of them, or is there a significant personal or idiosyncratic quality to that which is to be learned?

Extrinsic versus intrinsic motivation
Should students be motivated essentially by outside forces, like the teacher or the learning activities, or should their motivation to learn primarily come from within themselves?

Molecular learning versus holistic learning
Should knowledge and skills be divided up into discrete chunks for ease of learning, or should learners be confronted with complex slices of reality within which they will find their own sub-divisions and order?

People share characteristics versus every learner is unique
Can all students learn the same thing at the same speed and in the same way, or does each learner approach a learning task in an essentially personal, idiosyncratic manner?

Individual learning vs. social learning
Is learning something that each individual must do on their own, or should it be a collaborative process?

Knowledge seen as content versus knowledge seen as process
Does learning basically entail acquiring fixed facts or rather creating personal (and interpersonal) meanings?

The poles of these dilemmas can be seen to form matrices of pedagogical beliefs underlying educational practice. Miller and Seller have called the two extremes the "transmission" and "transformation" positions:

The dichotomous parameters of these situations are clearly extremes and most teachers will find their beliefs concerning any particular point somewhere in between. In any event, teachers' beliefs will be apparent in the roles they adopt in the classroom, in the types of learning activities they organize, as well as what and how they expect students to learn.

John Dewey, whom Richard Rorty has described as one of the three most influential Western philosophers of the 20th century, took a stronger stance. He saw the epistemology underlying transmissionist education as the primary ill of American education in his day. From his viewpoint, the learner is an actor, rather than a spectator. He strongly advocated that classrooms be venues for hands-on experience. While noting that classrooms tended to be places where students were expected to be passive recipients of knowledge, he recommended that they be allowed and encouraged to move, experiment, debate, work on projects, carry out research outdoors, in the library and the laboratory. In 1899, Dewey depicted the learning situation in an average US classroom, surely not imagining that he was also describing the typical translation exercise classroom in Europe one hundred years later:

> If we put before the mind's eye the ordinary schoolroom, with its rows of ugly desks placed in geometrical order, crowded together so that there shall be as little moving room as possible ... and add a table, some chairs, the bare walls, and possibly a few pictures, we can reconstruct the only educational activity that can possibly go on in such a place. It is all made 'for listening'. (Dewey, quoted in Phillips 1995:11)

Transmission Perspective	**Transformation Perspective**
Knowledge is transferred	Knowledge is constructed
Learner is a student and client	Learner is a whole person
Teacher should be in control	Student should be in control
Knowledge is public	Knowledge is private
Motivation is extrinsic	Motivation is intrinsic
Learning is molecular	Learning is holistic
Learning characteristics are shared	Every learner is unique
Learning is individual	Learning is social
Knowledge is content	Knowledge is a process

From a transmissionist perspective, the learner comes to the classroom as a passive listener, a consumer of knowledge. And if knowledge can be packaged for distribution, then it can be conveniently dissected into digestible chunks for transmission. If it is transferable, it is natural to also assume that knowledge corresponds to some objective reality and that it is therefore essentially the same for different people. As the teacher is considered the fountain of knowledge, then naturally it is the teacher who should have control of the knowledge distribution process in the classroom. In my view, the structure of contemporary educational systems for the training of translators rests, at the most basic, fundamental level, on the acceptance of this viewpoint. While the history of educational practice may well explain why this epistemological view is a commonly held belief, the wealth of research on alternative pedagogical approaches suggest that the transmission metaphor is not the only and not the most viable one today for the education of professional translators.

From a transformationist position, we would see learning essentially as a personal, holistic, intrinsically motivating and socially effectuated construction process. Given such a perspective, knowledge cannot be transferred from one person (or one text) to another; instead it is transformed or constructed by the individual who makes his or her own meanings through dialogue with other people in a linguistic community. In a classroom based on transformational beliefs, the teacher will assume roles such as guide, assistant, mentor and facilitator and will see his or her job primarily in terms of helping create complex, naturalistic learning environments in the classroom, and providing support for collaborative learning processes. In such a classroom, learning activities will be marked by proactive students working in collaboration with each other and the teacher, and a focus on situationally embedded real-life or realistic projects rather than on the memorization of discrete pieces of knowledge. Rather than a place where students are isolated from the real world after graduation while being prepared to face it, the transformationist classroom is seen as being inextricably embedded within authentic, real-world activity. Thus, learning becomes a forum for guided social and cultural experience. The individualized nature of the learning process will be respected and, rather than distributing knowledge, the facilitator will guide learners in the construction of their own meanings.

Conventional translation skills instruction: the logical consequence of transmissionist educational views

Traditionally, much institutionalised education in Western industrialized societies has been based on a 'transmissionist' view, where teaching and learning are understood respectively as the transmission and reception of knowledge (truth) about the world, contributing to the building up of an increasingly accurate picture of the world as it is. Alternatives to this traditional viewpoint have been proposed for and implemented in a wide range of fields, from science education to creative writing and medicine. But as I discussed in *Pathways to Translation,* even today much of translator education is deeply embedded in the transmissionist tradition, exemplified by the pervasive use of what Jean-René Ladmiral called the *performance magistrale* (instructional performance), and that Christiane Nord has recently called the "traditional technique" (in Nord 1996).

The instructional performance exemplifies the key instructional activity through which the teacher, believing that he or she has the knowledge needed to produce the 'correct' translation, goes about identifying and then filling in the gaps in students' knowledge so that they too can come up with 'correct' translations, meaning the same ones that the omniscient teacher would have come up with him- or herself. In such a classroom it is clearly the teacher's job to 'instruct', i.e. to pass on knowledge, and the student's task to commit the teacher's knowledge to memory. The instructor's teaching role includes the following basic functions:

1. Selecting texts or language samples for students to translate in order to identify holes in their knowledge of how to translate correctly.
2. Having the students translate the texts alone at home.
3. Eliciting translated segments from the presumably faulty translations of the students for off-the-cuff correction in front of the class.
4. Assessing the students' increase in knowledge as the result of instruction over the course of the semester by having students translate a text under traditional exam conditions and then assessing the quality of the translation on the basis of the number of errors compared to the class average.

The students' learning role primarily entails:

1. Working alone outside of class preparing rough translations of the texts chosen by the instructor.
2. Reading off individual sentences or paragraphs in front of the rest of the class for correction by the instructor.
3. Modifying their knowledge to reflect the instructor's corrections.
4. Demonstrating reception of the knowledge communicated by the teacher by completing a translation under exam conditions to be evaluated by the instructor on the basis of the teacher's criteria of accuracy and adequacy.

Figure 2 below illustrates my view of the basic flow of interaction in a traditional classroom environment, set apart from the real world and revolving around the instructional performance. The instructor can be seen as a repository of translation equivalents and strategies that are to be made available to the entire class when one student displays a gap in his or her knowledge by suggesting a faulty translation. Students display their knowledge or lack thereof by reading off segments of their necessarily imperfect translations. The instructor identifies the errors and then parcels out knowledge of the 'correct' equivalents for memorization by the students. The learning that goes on in this type of classroom is not expected to parallel the real work of professional translators. Rather than experiencing real-life constraints for themselves, the students are expected to appropriate the teacher's knowledge and experience, sliced and packaged for didactic distribution.

   Major innovations in any domain of human endeavour can come about when the viability of dominant paradigms is successfully challenged and potentially more viable alternatives are proposed. Educational institutions are, however, particularly conservative – one of their most important functions being to ensure that learners in a particular domain acquire behavioural patterns that fall within existing social and cultural norms. Alternative educational approaches can be difficult to introduce, or even experiment with, because of the inertia that is inherent in formal education as a social process. Since beliefs about what it means to know, to comprehend and to learn are fundamental to the educational process, the implications of an epistemological paradigm shift can be expected to affect what goes on in the classroom radically, from the roles assumed by teachers and students in pedagogical interaction, to the design of the learning activities, right down to the procedures employed to assess learning.

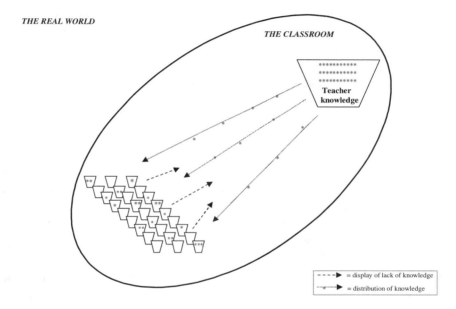

Figure 2. Typical interaction in a translation exercise classroom

Translator education, perhaps even more than other domains, is particularly sensitive to the epistemology upon which it is based because the concept of 'meaning' is so central to the translator's activity. Early models of translation often portrayed the translator's job as one of transferring meaning from a text in one language to a text in another. The words and metaphors that are still used extensively in the field of translation studies to describe this process reflect the assumption that a text can have 'a' meaning in the first place, that this one meaning can be more or less objectively grasped by some agent (the translator), and that it can then be moved to or reproduced in the target-language text. Even the commonly accepted terms 'source text' and 'target text' used in numerous descriptions of the translator's task reflect the transfer view of translation processes dominant in translation studies in general and in the area of translation teaching in particular. In recent years, more and more scholars have suggested a rather different way of looking at the meaning of a text.

Snell-Hornby (1988), for example, speaks of Fillmore's scenes and frames, Chau (1984) depicts text comprehension as a hermeneutic process, and Neubert and Shreve (1992) view translation as a textual process.

From all of these perspectives, texts are no longer seen as having a meaning inextricably embedded in contexts of situation (as I elaborated on the basis of Firthian linguistics in *Pathways to Translation*), and textual meaning is seen as being created as much by the reader (and translator) as it is by the author, through the merging of experience-based background knowledge and clues to the author's meaning derived from the text itself. The meaning-creation view of text reception has become so prevalent in translation theory that it might well be considered the dominant paradigm. However, the implications of these views have yet to be drawn for and applied to the teaching of translation skills. The outdated 'transfer' view of the translation process is a reflection of what has been called the 'conduit' view of communication, exemplified by the one-way transmission of a static message that is sent by one person and received by another. Meanings are thus understood to be first injected into, and then extracted from the words through which they are transmitted. The conduit model "assumes that the sender encodes, or packages, a single meaning and transmits it to the receiver, who passively decodes or fails to decode it. The 'it' remains the same throughout" (Wertsch 1991:73). Wertsch, supporting the viewpoint of Bakhtin, accepts the transmission of meaning as one function of communication, while identifying the equally important function of *making* meaning through communicative interaction. This second, 'dialogic' function of language, as Wertsch describes it, emphasizes the active participation of interlocutors in the communication process. Through this function, the two voices come together in a communicative situation, negotiating and creating new meaning through dialogue. These two functions of communication can also be seen in the educational process. Garrison (1995:729), referring to Engström's neo-Vygotskian definition of the Zone of Proximal Development (to be introduced in Chapter 3), describes the parallel functions of education as a 'double bind', which he says "regards the tension between the need of the students to appropriate historically entrenched tools that empower them as social actors and the simultaneous need of the culture to retool and recreate itself".

While there is a need to pass on the fruits of tradition and past experience through the educational process, there is also increasingly a need to prepare future professionals for lifelong learning; empower them to adapt existing tools to meet new demands; and construct new tools as novel challenges arise in the future.

Professional competence: expertise and professionalism

There may well be skills and types of knowledge that can be acquired effectively in a transmissionist fashion, in particular in domains where knowledge is well structured and orderly. Conventional distributive teaching may be efficient and adequate in areas of activity where there is only one right way to accomplish something, where the learner is not called upon to make choices, to use personal judgement or to weigh conflicting social, cultural, or cognitive constraints against one another. But as Donald Schön (1987:4), writing about the training of professionals, including lawyers, doctors and architects, stated in *Educating the Reflective Practitioner*:

> As we have come to see with increasing clarity over the last 20 or so years, the problems of real-world practice do not present themselves to practitioners as well-formed structures. Indeed, they tend not to present themselves as problems at all, but as messy, indeterminate situations.

In this ground-breaking work, Schön promotes an alternative epistemology of practice in professional education that coincides with constructivist views. The starting point of his argument is his rejection of the conventional educational approach, based on "technical rationality" – his term for the educational epistemology of objectivism, which:

> ... holds that practitioners are instrumental problem solvers who select the technical means best suited to particular purposes. Rigorous professional practitioners solve well-formed problems by applying theory and technique derived from systematic, preferably scientific knowledge. (Schön 1987:3-4)

Over the past ten years, the significant attention that researchers interested in translator training have given to translation 'strategies' attests to the coming of age of this instructional domain, as attempts are made to identify and categorize translation strategies for pedagogical purposes (House 1988, Kussmaul 1995, Kupsch-Losereit 1996, Nord 1996, Chesterman 1997). It is certainly a worthwhile undertaking to investigate cognitive strategies (in our field most often described as plans for solving translation problems) since such investigations can provide us with valuable insights, for example, into the tendential differences in the ways that novices and professionals deal with translation problems. Such knowledge can help raise students' awareness of how to go about solving translation problems effectively. But a conventional transmissionist approach to the teaching of what researchers find to be effective strategies fails to take into account that the identification and resolution of translation problems are greatly dependent on countless independent but mutually influencing factors that impinge on each translator in a unique manner in each given translation situation. In fact, translation can be seen as what various constructivist authors have called an "ill-structured knowledge domain" *par excellence:*

> An ill-structured knowledge domain is one in which the following two properties hold: (a) each case or example of knowledge application typically

involves the simultaneous interactive involvement of multiple, wide-application conceptual structures (multiple schemas, perspectives, organizational principles and so on), each of which is individually complex ... and (b) the pattern of conceptual evidence and interaction varies substantially across cases nominally of the same type ... (Spiro *et al.* 1992 :64)

These two features clearly apply to translators' tasks if we consider that translators are often faced with a multitude of competing schemas on different planes, including the linguistic, social, cognitive and cultural. Each client will have an idiosyncratic set of expectations concerning the design and quality of translations he or she commissions. Some will prefer a more word-to-word rendering of an original text, while others will expect the text to be translated as freely as possible. Terminology is not consistent even within a particular industry like computer hardware or software design, automotive engineering, or banking, for example. In many fields, individual companies have their own specialized jargon or internal corporate language, which clearly poses difficulties for and constraints on the translator. Does the translator have access to all of the company's jargon? And if so, are word lists sufficient or does a given company also use, for example, stylistic features in its technical or marketing texts that set it apart from its competitors? Texts written by experts in a variety of fields in this day of instant text production and dissemination via electronic media are often faulty, severely lacking in coherence, cohesion or even technical accuracy. The translator may or may not have a great deal of knowledge about a particular subject matter, and each one will have different types and amounts of knowledge that will support his or her translational decision-making processes.

No two translation situations can be the same, whether two translators are attempting to complete the same translation or whether one translator is working on different parts of the same translation at different moments in time. Each translator, at each moment, is a unique and never a generic problem-solver because the resources at his or her disposal are in a constant and multifarious state of flux. This places the individual translator, facing a given text with a particular client and readership on a given day, in an utterly unique situation. In Schön's words:

> Often, a problematic situation presents itself as a unique case. ... Because the unique case falls outside categories of existing theory and technique, the practitioner cannot treat it as an instrumental problem to be solved by applying one of the rules in her store of professional knowledge. The case is not "in the book." If she is to deal with it competently, she must do so by a kind of improvisation, inventing and testing in the situation strategies of her own devising. (1987:5)

In translation work, the problematic situations involve not only the macro-situation characterized by the author-translator – text-client-reader relationship, but also include the micro-situations, the myriad of unforeseen moments while working on a translation where the translator has no simple solution to recall from memory and insert mechanically into the text.

When a practitioner recognizes the situation as unique, he or she cannot handle it solely by applying theories or techniques derived from their store of professional knowledge. And in situations of value conflict, there are no clear and self-consistent ends to guide the technical selection of means:

> It is just these indeterminate zones of practice ... that practitioners and critical observers of the professions have come to see with increasing clarity over the past two decades as central to professional practice. (ibid.:8)

This essentially improvisational nature of experts' problem-solving strategies has been the focus of researchers who have applied a constructivist perspective to cognitive processing. For example, Spiro *et al.* (1992:63) state:

> Instead of retrieving from memory a previously packaged 'prescription' for how to think and act, one must bring together, from various knowledge sources, an appropriate ensemble of information suited to the particular understanding or problem-solving needs of the situation at hand.

While this information processing view is limited by its failure to consider the role of intuition in the problem-solving process, it does reflect an awareness that strategies cannot be applied rigidly, in splendid isolation from the unique complexity of each specific problem-solving situation. I suggest that this heuristic process of drawing upon and selecting from widely disparate information (and intuitions) is much more characteristic of the translator's work than is the simple, mechanistic application of boilerplate strategies. As Schön (1987:4) has aptly phrased the situation:

> When a practitioner sets problems, he chooses and names the things he will notice. ... Through complementary acts of meaning and framing, the practitioner selects things for attention and organizes them, guided by an appreciation of the situation that gives it coherence and sets a direction for action. So problem solving is an ontological process – in Nelson Goodman's (1978) memorable word, a form of "worldmaking".

Schön goes on to examine the role of 'artistry' in professional performance, which he defines as "the ways in which competent professionals actually handle indeterminate zones of practice". (ibid.:13) From his perspective, the professional's ability to deal with unforeseen, unpredictable and highly complex situations is like that of masters of the fine arts. It is not purely, nor even primarily, a rational, rule-bound set of strategies that the professional applies in a logical sequence in ill-defined

situations, but essentially intuition and even wisdom that is exhibited in the professional action itself, and not necessarily in the description of such action.

Bereiter and Scardamalia (1993), two other prominent scholars in the area of
expertise studies, speak of the key importance of non-strategic types of knowledge
used in expert behaviour, and which they classify accordingly as: informal, impressionistic and self-regulatory knowledge. Informal knowledge refers to what we know
from our experiences with the physical world; impressionistic knowledge is related
to our intuitions, which are distilled from experience and that can generally not be
explained rationally or systematically; and self-regulatory knowledge is the knowledge of how to manage oneself so as to get a job done. What is particularly notable
about these types of knowledge is that they are all based on experience. They can
only be acquired through action and not through passive absorption.

Quoting John Dewey (in Archaubault 1974:151), Schön admonishes:

> The student cannot be *taught* what he needs to know, but he can be *coached*:
> "he has to see on his own behalf and in his own way the relations between
> means and methods employed and results achieved. Nobody else can see for
> him, and he can't see just by being "told," although the right kind of telling
> may guide his seeing and thus help him see what he needs to see.

Thus, in Schön's (1987:17) words:

> Perhaps, then, learning *all* forms of professional artistry depends, at least in
> part, on conditions similar to those created in the studios and conservatories:
> freedom to learn by doing in a setting relatively low in risk, with access to
> coaches who initiate students into the "traditions of the calling" and help
> them, by "the right kind of telling," to see on their own behalf and in their
> own way what they need most to see.

We do not need to 'teach' strategies; we need to model strategy use (and creation)
for our students; we need to help them and let them create and work with their own
dynamic strategies in authentic translation situations which are rich in the complexity of real-life language mediation tasks.

When applied to the translator's work, Schön's concept of 'professional competence' can perhaps be seen as two separate but interrelated sub-competencies:
expertise and **professionalism**. Expertise I would describe as the competence to
accomplish translation tasks to the satisfaction of clients and in accordance with the
norms and conventions of the profession with respect to producing a translated text
per se. Expertise would include not only the effective utilisation and creation of
strategies for dealing with specific translation problems as discussed above, but
also the ability to use appropriate computer-based tools, to format text appropriately,
to do terminological research in a manner that meets clients' needs for consistency

and accuracy, as well as, for example, the ability to research a new subject matter adequately in order to translate a text in a manner acceptable to the client.

Professionalism, on the other hand, would characterize the translator's ability to work within the social and ethical constraints of translation situations in a manner that is consistent with the norms of the profession. This would involve aspects like the commitment to meet deadlines and to inform a client in due time if a translation will be late, to charge appropriate fees for translational services without either gouging a customer or dumping one's services on the market to undercut the competition. The expert translator would be capable of sizing up a translation commission and determining whether or not he or she can complete the work to the client's specification and within the time allotted; the professional will decline the job if he or she were to determine that they could not do it adequately or meet the deadline.

Conventional translator training has focused almost exclusively on the transmission of translational expertise, and until recently, even the translator education literature paid little attention to the student's need to be initiated into translation as a 'professional' enterprise. As will be demonstrated in Chapters 6 and 7, project-based, collaborative workshop classes lend themselves to such an initiation. By having the students undertake authentic translation work collaboratively in the classroom, they will automatically be confronted with problems concerning how to act in a professional manner, and they will learn together how to resolve those problems. The emerging translator will find no hard-and-fast rules for how to behave professionally. Just as when discussing and assessing different ways of solving translation problems in an expert manner, the identification and discussion of professional questions can also be accomplished best in a collaborative setting in which students work together, and along with instructors and professionals from the translating community, to construct consensual patterns of professional behaviour.

Chesterman (1997) makes a valuable contribution to the study of translator expertise. He takes the five stages of expertise outlined by Dreyfus and Dreyfus (1986), who were among the pioneers in the field of expertise studies, and applies them to the acquisition of translation skills. He then presents a variety of instructional activities and techniques that can be used to lead students toward mastery. Chesterman places particular emphasis in these activities on consciousness-raising and reflection in the acquisition of translation norms, as he follows Dreyfus and Dreyfus (1986) in seeing learning for expertise as movement from conscious awareness of problems and rules to the automatic, intuitive action of experts. Many of the teaching techniques Chesterman discusses are similar to ones proposed by Nord (1997), which I will discuss at length in Chapter 6.

Unfortunately, both of these translation studies scholars fail to acknowledge the need to radically revamp the conventional structures of authority, control and responsibility in the classroom if translator education is to become a venue for developing expertise. They still seem to see the learning process as going on primarily within the head of each individual learner. In the final section of this chapter, I

will briefly outline a heretofore neglected, yet critical implication of expertise studies for translator education: the need for collaborative knowledge building within a
community of learners and teachers.

Implications for teaching: reflective action in a community of knowledge builders

Two key concepts have emerged from the literature on expertise to characterize the
method that I am proposing here for translator education. These concepts are **reflective action,** as developed by Schön (1987); and the **community of knowledge
builders**, which is Bereiter and Scardamalia's (1993) term for the overall framework of an educational setting focused on the development of expertise.

Reflective action: a personal and collaborative key to expertise

The importance of reflection in learning has a long history and there is probably
no single definition upon which its proponents would agree. Law *et al.* (1998:6),
however, list four primary characteristics that can be ascribed to the various depic-
tions of reflection as a tool for learning: consciousness, contextualized problem,
relevant experience, and action. In addition to the informal, impressionistic and
self-regulatory types of knowledge that experts use to undertake professional tasks,
learners must also reflect on what they are doing as they acquire expertise. There
must be an awareness of problematic features of the task at hand; tasks must be
contextualized rather than amputated from genuine experience; the experiences in
which learning activities are embedded must be relevant to the learner's past, present
and future scope of interests and knowledge; and learning tasks must entail active
personal involvement. From this perspective, then, having learners engage in learning activities goes far beyond rote exercises, drills and even lectures, which imply
the committing to memory of pre-determined rules, patterns and facts.

   Reflective action is thinking coupled with authentic tasks in a learning domain.
It can serve a variety of functions in the performance of tasks, including the planning, implementation, and revision of actions taken. Reflection can lead to learning
by providing a virtual mental space in which the means, goals and implications of
intelligent action can be consciously contemplated, revised and integrated into prior
knowledge, potentially resulting in increased expertise. From a social constructivist
perspective, there is also a social aspect of reflective action, which is vital not only
because it enhances collaboration and communication, but because it is collective
reflective action that characterizes a professional community.

A community of knowledge builders

Bereiter and Scardamalia (1993:210-11) developed a collaborative framework for the development of educational systems based on the systematic application of reflective action. They call this framework a "community of knowledge builders". While the primary focus of their writing is on schooling, their approach in my view is equally applicable to a university setting and corresponds in every respect to the method I have been developing independently for translator education.

As Pym (1992) and Chesterman (1997) acknowledge, the norms of professional translation behaviour are held by the community of translators themselves. Of course, when individual translation decisions are to be made,

It is up to the translator to decide what kind of [translation] relation is appropriate in any given case, according to the text-type, the wishes of the commissioner, the intentions of the original writer, and the assumed needs of the prospective readers. (Chesterman 1997:68)

But there is no authoritative body that imposes some set of rules that translators must apply; they find the authority for their decisions by participating actively in the collectively created values, norms and conventions of the translation community. This is, in fact, the basis of the social constructivist approach. From this perspective, the most effective way to lead novices toward expertise is to provide them with opportunities for interacting with peers and experts to collectively – as well as individually – construct the knowledge of the domain. In a community of knowledge builders, everyone is a learner. The knowledge building environment is marked by authentic reflective action, distributed knowledge and authority, ever-increasing levels of autonomy on the part of the learners, and an absence of a single designated authority to judge right and wrong. In such a community, it is by jointly undertaking authentic work, and by collaboratively planning, executing and revising that work, that knowledge is created within the group and internalized by the individual group members.

Summary

Objectivism can be seen as the (implicit or explicit) foundation for traditional educational practice, including translator education. An objectivist perspective leads to transmissionist approaches to education, based primarily on the transfer of knowledge; while a constructivist epistemology leads to transformation, with the goal of empowering the learner to act responsibly, autonomously and competently. Studies on expertise suggest that reflective action within a community of knowledge builders can provide a solid basis for educational design.

Social constructivism provides not only an epistemological basis for the development of knowledge-building communities, but also a variety of tools that can be used to promote and pursue learning in such communities. In Chapter 3, I will present some of the principal tools that I have adopted for applying a social constructivist approach to translator education.

3. Key Principles of Social-constructivist Education

The list of social-constructivist principles that follows results from my personal interpretation of the literature in the light of my own teaching history. These concepts, which I have found particularly meaningful and coherent, have served as dynamic guidelines for my own teaching practice. My understanding of these concepts evolves continuously as I delve into the constructivist conversation and grapple with its implications for my teaching approach.

In this chapter I have outlined my basic constructivist principles in order to first present the underpinnings of my proposed educational approach independently of the specific subject matter of translator education. In Chapter 4 I will demonstrate how I have used these principles as the basis for my translator education approach.

Multiple realities and multiple perspectives

While allowing for the existence of a real, external world, constructivism emphasizes that individuals can only perceive and understand that world from their own, personal perspective. We cannot know the world objectively, but only from our own privileged position as unique experiencers of the world:

> We are not outside of reality. We are part of it, *in* it. What is needed is not an externalist perspective, but an internalist perspective. It is a perspective that acknowledges that we are organisms functioning as part of reality and that it is impossible for us to ever stand outside it and take the stance of an observer with perfect knowledge, an observer with a God's eye point of view. (Lakoff 1987:261)

From a social constructivist perspective, the individual is never alone. We learn to communicate, and then to think, by sharing and contrasting perspectives with other members of the communities to which we belong. Thought, from a Vygotskian perspective, is internalized conversation. Rather than seeing this as a dilemma, social-constructivist approaches to education see it as a challenge – the interchange between multiple realities in a social environment naturally leads to debate, negotiation and thus to change and growth in each individual perspective. The upshot is that learning must be an essentially active and interactive, inter-psychological process. It cannot take place in a social vacuum; we must be confronted with alternative perspectives if we are to increase our understanding of our own perceived world. This also holds true if we are to join new communities of which we wish to be members – for example the community of professional translators.

One of the most powerful qualities of constructivist thought is that it recognizes that cultural and social change are natural products of the interaction of multiple perspectives. It is not only the individual who learns through dialogue by appropriating cultural meanings in what Vygotsky called 'zones of proximal development'; the culture itself also evolves in response to dialogue among its constituent individuals. The reciprocal appropriation of interpretations of reality that is embodied in a constructivist classroom exemplifies the communicative process itself as a tool for maintaining and modifying society:

> Learning is a process that takes place in a participation framework, not in an individual mind. This means, among other things, that it is mediated by the differences in perspective among the co-participants. It is the community, or at least those participating in the learning context, who "learn" under this definition. Learning is, as it were, distributed among co-participants, not a one-person act. While the apprentice may be the one transformed most dramatically by increased participation in a productive process it is the wider process that is the crucial locus and precondition for this transformation. ... The larger community of practitioners reproduces itself through the formation of apprentices, yet it would presumably be transformed as well. (Lave and Wenger, quoted in Bredo 1994:32)

The implications for the training of translators are clear. If the goal of translator education is defined as facilitating the process through which translators join the profession, then the profession itself can be expected to change through the pedagogical dialogue. If translation teachers are themselves practising translators and if they encourage the exchange of perspectives between students, colleagues and working professionals that can be brought into the educational setting, the profession as a whole can be expected to benefit and evolve as a result. The act of teaching/learning will thus not be a one-way transmission process; instead it will be a mutually beneficial process of sharing perspectives:

> A central strategy for achieving these perspectives is to create a collaborative learning environment. ... It is from the views of other group members that alternative perspectives most often are to be realized. Thus, sharing a workload or coming to a consensus is not the goal of collaboration; rather, it is to develop, compare, and understand multiple perspectives on an issue. This is not meant to be simply a "sharing" experience, though respect for other views is important. Rather, the goal is to search for and evaluate the evidence for the viewpoint. (Bednar *et al.* 1992:28)

This brings us to the second major social constructivist concept that will play a major role in the approach to translator education I am proposing: the 'collaborative' learning experience.

Collaborative/co-operative learning

There is, of course, an individual side to cognitive change or learning. Even in interaction and dialogue with others, the individual must appropriate or internalize information and perspectives from the culture and society. This does not, however, mean that learning is essentially or even predominantly a process that the individual must go through alone:

> Internalization, by definition, is an individual process. It is also a construc-
> tive process rather than an automatic reflection of the external events. But
> the child does not have to leave the zone [of proximal development] and then
> work on internalizing in splendid isolation. The internal and external con-
> structive processes are occurring simultaneously. (Newman *et al.* 1989:68)

Peers and teachers working together collaboratively are thus simultaneously creat-ing meanings among themselves and are also internalizing meanings individually. The value of collaborative group work in a wide range of areas of education has been supported by a Piagetian as well as a Vygotskian approach:

> Over the last 15 years scholars working within the Piagetian framework have
> developed a model relating collaboration to cognitive development, in which
> the mechanism promoting development is "cognitive conflict" or "socio-
> cognitive conflict." ... Research based on this model has indicated that social
> interaction between peers who bring different perspectives to bear upon a
> problem is a highly effective means of inducing cognitive development.
> (Tudge 1990:159)

Dunlap and Grabinger (1996:68) succinctly sum up the significant pedagogical ad-vantages resulting from a collaborative learning environment:

> Working in peer groups helps students refine their knowledge through argu-
> mentation, structured controversy, and reciprocal teaching. In addition,
> students are more willing to take on the additional risk required to tackle
> complex, ill-structured, authentic problems when they have the support of
> others in the cooperative group. ... students are more likely to achieve goals
> they may not have been able to meet on their own.

True collaborative learning does not mean simply dividing up the work on a task, a mere division of labour. It is instead the joint accomplishment of a task with the dual learning goals of meaning-making on the part of the group as well as the ap-propriation of cultural and professional knowledge on the part of each individual group member. Difficulties can of course arise in the creation of groups. There can be an unfair division of labour or there may be freeloaders who allow the other group members to do most of the work. Teachers in collaborative classrooms must be skilled at managing groups and projects so as to minimize these problems and to maximize the tremendous benefit to be gained through group interaction.

One great advantage of collaborative group work is that it allows learning activities to revolve around projects that reflect the complexity of real-life situations. Students can work collaboratively to find their own sub-tasks in these complex situations, and can learn to make their own meanings. This is the process of 'learning how to learn', resulting in lifelong learning skills that can serve them in an infinite and unpredictable variety of situations once they leave the institution.

One of the most widely diffused and influential systematic approaches for the use of collaborative learning techniques has been devised by David and Roger Johnson (1991). Their approach, called 'co-operative learning', is based on the social interdependence theory of the American psychologist Martin Deutsch. Deutsch's underlying premise was that human beings are more productive in their social activities when they work co-operatively with others, rather than in competition. The Johnsons see the following five factors as the essential components of co-operative learning: 1) positive interdependence, 2) face-to-face interaction, 3) individual accountability and personal responsibility, 4) interpersonal and small-group skills, and 5) group processing – or reflection on what the group has accomplished and still needs to learn. They feel that positive interdependence among the members of the group, that is, making the success of each individual dependent on that of each other individual, is the most important of the five factors; and the main focus in their extensive array of practical, accessible publications is on ensuring this positive interdependence among the members of a group. As the Johnsons state:

> There is a great deal of research indicating that, if student-student interdependence is structured carefully and appropriately, students will achieve a higher level, use higher level reasoning strategies more frequently, have higher levels of achievement motivation, be more intrinsically motivated, develop more positive interpersonal relationships with each other, value the subject area being studied more, have higher self-esteem, and be more skilled interpersonally. (Johnson and Johnson 1991:17)

Johnson & Johnson's meta-study of over 500 research projects investigating the relative success of collaborative, competitive and individualized approaches to learning found that the co-operative approaches tend to be more effective at promoting learner achievement than either of the other approaches. In general terms, the Johnsons classify the findings of their meta-analysis into three main categories where co-operative learning surpasses both competitive and individualized learning, including 1) greater motivation to achieve and higher actual achievement and productivity by high-, medium- and low-achieving students, 2) more positive relationships among students, and 3) greater psychological health, including greater self-esteem and the ability to handle adversity and stress.

The highly structured nature of co-operative learning and the Johnsons' practical, very accessible publications make this approach easy to adapt to virtually all types of students of all ages and a wide range of domains. Their approach diverges significantly, however, from the one proposed here, because it leaves virtually complete control of class content and organization with the teacher. Rather than empowering students to assume responsibility for their own learning, co-operative education complements and supports the conventional distribution of power between teachers and students. In the words of James Flannery (1992:17):

> One can in fact define cooperative learning (as opposed to collaborative learning) as the use of student learning groups to support an instructional system that maintains the traditional lines of classroom knowledge and authority. If cooperative learning techniques are conceptualized in this way, we see that they tend to help students learn discrete pieces of information that the instructor has already identified. As such, they are simply one more tool that can help the teacher to transmit curricular content to students.

Such an approach is completely at odds with the constructivist approach that I am proposing. While co-operative education as designed by Johnson & Johnson might well be a viable approach upon which other translation teachers may choose to build an alternative method for translator education, the result would resemble only superficially the empowerment method. It would share neither the social constructivist underpinnings at the *approach* level, nor the equitable, empowering distribution of power and role relationships at the *design* level, nor the extensive use of teacher facilitation and collaborative student inquiry at the *procedure* level.

Appropriation

The concept of appropriation was introduced by Vygotsky's colleague Leont'ev as a socio-cultural alternative to Piaget's biological metaphor of assimilation (Leont'ev 1981). The idea behind appropriation is that learning entails the internalization of socio-cultural knowledge. This is the process by which interpersonal knowledge becomes intra-personal knowledge:

> This is more than a complicated way of saying that children do not need to reinvent the wheel. At the simplest level, it is arguing that because humans are essentially cultural beings, even children's initial encounters with objects may be cultural experiences, and so their initial understandings may be culturally defined. In this sense, appropriation is concerned with what children may take from encounters with objects in cultural context. (Mercer 1992:36)

Newman *et al.* (1989) emphasize that appropriation is a reciprocal process. It is thus not only those designated as students or learners in a classroom who appropriate knowledge, but the teacher as well. From this viewpoint it can be helpful for the teacher to appropriate the learners' viewpoints in order to promote the teaching-learning dialogue. It is more an interactive process than a one-way movement from teacher to learner. By picking up learners' ideas, re-contextualizing them, and reinserting them into the classroom discourse, teachers can provide students with valuable alternative perspectives on knowledge they already had. Rather than working solely with concepts that are new and foreign, existing structures can thus be expanded, modified and recast:

> The child's appropriation of culturally devised "tools" comes about through involvement in culturally organized activities in which the tool plays a role. ... The child has only to come to an understanding that is adequate for using the culturally elaborated object in the novel life circumstances he encounters. The appropriation process is always a two-way one. The tool may also be transformed, as it is used by a new member of the culture; some of these changes may be encoded in the culturally elaborated tool, as the current sociohistorical developments allow. (Newman *et al.* 1989:63)

This viewpoint is supported by John Dewey's conceptualization of educational processes in terms of transactions between an individual and the environment of which he or she is a part. For Dewey, action is perhaps best understood in terms of interplay or a dialogue between an individual and the social and physical environment. Bredo (1994:28) gives an example that is particularly applicable to the translator's task:

> Writing can ... be seen as a mutual matter of composition rather than simply the transfer of ideas from brain to paper. One writes, responds to what one has written, and so on, altering interpretation and aim in the process. The same may be said for conversing or for thinking itself. Each is the result of a dialogue, a way of relating or mutually modulating activity, in which person and environment (ideally) modify each other so as to create an integral performance. Seen in this way, a successful person acts with the environment, shaping it to modify himself or herself, in turn, and then to shape the environment, and so on, until some end is achieved.

Appropriation, then, is a mutually constructive process involving a dialogue between an individual and his social, cultural and physical environment. The term suggests that learning is an (inter)active constructive process and not a transfer of knowledge. It also suggests that learning is a function of the situation in which it occurs. Appropriation can never be isolated from a particular learning environment; learning only 'makes sense' when it is couched in its sense-giving situation.

The zone of proximal development

Lev Vygotsky's socio-historical theory of developmental psychology revolves around his concept of the *zone of proximal development* (ZPD), which is the situation-bound 'virtual domain' in which appropriation, and consequently development, occur. As Vygotsky summarizes:

> We propose that an essential feature of learning is that it creates the zone of proximal development; that is, learning awakens a variety of internal developmental processes that are able to operate only when the child is interacting with people in his environment and in cooperation with his peers. Once these processes are internalized, they become part of the child's independent developmental achievement. From this point of view, learning is not development; however, properly organized learning results in mental development and sets in motion a variety of developmental processes that would be impossible apart from learning. Thus, learning is a necessary and universal aspect of the process of developing culturally organized, specifically human, psychological functions. To summarize, the most essential feature of our hypothesis is the notion that developmental processes do not coincide with learning processes. Rather, the developmental process lags behind the learning process; this sequence then results in zones of proximal development. (Vygotsky 1994:57)

Unlike the intelligence quotient, the ZPD should not be seen as a relatively permanent characteristic of an individual. Instead, it is more of a fleeting 'virtual space' of potential growth, a window of opportunity that is created within a specific learning situation and that can lead to learning and thus socio-cognitive development. Vygotsky clearly emphasizes the socio-cultural environment in which learning takes place as a crucial factor in the learning process. Thus the designation 'social constructivism', which has been applied particularly to the neo-Vygotskian form of constructivism.

In an educational setting, a distinction is made between the ZPD and any other type of instructional moment in which a teacher provides learning assistance:

> It is the job of the constructivist teacher (or interactive technology) to hold learners in their 'zone of proximal development' by providing just enough help and guidance, but not too much. Exactly this happens in many naturalistic learning situations such as mother-child relationships and apprenticeship settings. (a 1992a:163)

The concept of guidance is fundamental here. From this perspective, the early stages in the learning of skills in any domain involve assisted performance, with the amount of assistance needed by the individual declining as competence in the task increases.

Eventually, the learner is capable of self-directed assistance without outside inter-vention, and when a skill has been mastered, it is executed in a highly automatic manner without control from the outside and with little internal control.

> The concept [ZPD] embodies two key features of human learning and devel-opment. The first is that learning with assistance or instruction is a normal, common and important feature of human mental development. The second is that the limits of a person's learning or problem-solving ability can be ex-panded by providing the right kind of cognitive support. (Mercer 1994:102)

Ochs (quoted in Gallimore and Tharpe 1990:197) points out that research on edu-cated parents and other caregivers in middle-class US homes has shown that assisted performance within zones of proximal development is a standard feature of parent-child interaction:

> Long before the child has actually produced its first word, it is treated as if it in fact does have something to say. ... When young children actually begin producing words, this set of assumptions by the caregiver continues. The caregiver, typically the mother, considers the young child to be expressing somewhat imperfectly a communicative intention.

Gallimore and Tharpe (1990) lament that this type of 'instruction', which is so suc-cessful in child rearing, rarely carries over into classroom discourse: "This is very unlike the verbal exchanges students experience in their school lives. The teachers generally ignore children, talk over them, and dominate the proceedings (ibid.).

Social constructivism places crucial importance on the type and quality of the socio-cultural interaction within a particular learning environment because it sees the situation itself as a major factor determining the boundaries, focus and impact of any given learning opportunity. From this perspective, then, the learning of a particular skill or the acquisition of any piece of knowledge cannot be dissociated from the setting in which that learning occurs:

> The limits of the ZPD for any particular child on any particular task will be established in the course of an activity, and one key factor in establishing those limits will be the quality of the supporting interventions of a teacher. That is, the ZPD is not an attribute of a child (in the sense that, say, IQ is considered to be) but rather the attribute of an *event*. It is the product of a particular, situated, pedagogical relationship. (Mercer 1994:102)

A number of social constructivist authors take pains to point out the difference be-tween constructivist learning and 'discovery' learning, the latter suggesting that students can work essentially without a teacher's assistance to discover what the teacher wants them to know (Bednar *et al.* 1992; Savery and Duffy 1995). From a social constructivist perspective, the ZPD requires the presence of others, whether they be peers, teachers, parents, or a master in a master-apprentice relationship, to help lead the individual learners (and the group as a whole) toward the construction of new knowledge that is not pre-defined by the teacher. As Fosnot (1992:169) notes, constructivist learning is thus more like 'invention' than 'discovery':

> Many of the concepts we teach in the schools require construction involving reordering and invention. I use the word "invent" here on purpose so as to differentiate it from discovery learning. Discovery is a more passive process of uncovering to get at the truth (an objective truth which the teacher holds). The process of construction is more like the process of inventing, or at least re-inventing, in that it is akin to the creative process. It requires the reorganization of old "data" and the building of new models for that learner.

An interesting perspective, which Garrison (1995) describes as the best definition yet of the ZPD, is that of Engström (1987), who puts forth the concept of the double bind between the transmission and generation functions of language discussed in Chapter II. Engström describes the zone of proximal development as the "distance between the everyday actions of individuals and the historically new form of the societal activity that can be collectively generated as a solution to the double bind potentially embedded in ... everyday actions". (Engström, quoted in Garrison 1995:729)

This conceptualization of the ZPD provides a useful metaphor for the type of interaction that is appropriate in a constructivist classroom. It emphasizes the key role of the teacher as that of a guide rather than a distributor of knowledge, the close relationship between socio-cultural interaction and learning, and movement from assisted performance to independent competence. The ZPD provides the cornerstone for an alternative pedagogy in which teachers see themselves as catalysts for learners' interpersonal and intra-personal construction of knowledge. It paves the way for true dialogue in the classroom, recognizing the pedagogical workspace as a locus for acculturation, socialization and knowledge construction.

Situating learning: active involvement in authentic, experiential learning

The concept of learning through authentic action is fundamental to the constructivist view:

> The activities of a domain are framed by its culture. Their meaning and purpose are socially constructed through negotiations among present and past members. Activities thus cohere in a way that is, in theory, if not always in practice, accessible to members who move within the social framework. These

> coherent, meaningful, and purposeful activities are *authentic*, according to
> the definition of the term we use here. Authentic activities then, are most
> simply defined as the ordinary practices of the culture. (Brown *et al.* 1989:34)

Situating learning means leaving the event that is to be studied within an authentic situational environment. In the case of translation, for example, the learning of professional translation skills would best be achieved through the collaborative undertaking of professional translation tasks, in all of their complexity, under the guidance of a professional translator. Rather than dissecting skills, knowledge, or instructional content for easy digestion, the constructivist perspective holds that for learning to be authentic and productive, learning tasks need to remain embedded in their larger, natural complex of human activity. As learning, from a constructivist perspective, is always directly related to the situation in which that learning occurs, we must retain the complexity of the situation – of course taking into consideration the learners' current level of knowledge and skill development. Authenticity will thus always be seen as relative with respect to this level. The learning of content must be embedded within the natural use of that content. The authenticity of learning tasks relates as well to the understanding of learning as an active process rather than a state, an outcome of a process:

> Many methods of didactic education assume a separation between knowing
> and doing, treating knowledge as an integral, self-sufficient substance, theo-
> retically independent of the situations in which it is learned and used. The
> primary concern of schools often seems to be the transfer of this substance,
> which comprises abstract, decontextualized formal concepts. The activity and
> context in which learning takes place are thus regarded as merely ancillary to
> learning – pedagogically useful, of course, but fundamentally distinct and
> even neutral with respect to what is learned. Recent investigations of learn-
> ing, however, challenge this separating of what is learned from how it is learned
> and used. The activity in which knowledge is developed and deployed, it is
> now argued, is not separable from or ancillary to learning and cognition.
> (Brown *et al.* 1989:32)

Knowledge or truth, from this perspective, is not and cannot be extracted from the teachers' own learning experiences to be passed on to students: "Knowledge is thus (in a situated interpretation) inseparable from the occasions and activities of which it is the product" (Bredo 1994:29).

There is no knowledge, then, that needs to be acquired definitively and perfectly by learners as the result of a conventional instruction/reception process. The constructivist view sees learning much more as ongoing evolution that cannot end with mere instruction. In this view, knowing is an inherently dynamic process of meaning making:

> All knowledge is, we believe, like language. Its constituent parts index the world and so are inextricably a product of the activity and situations in which they are produced. A concept, for example, will continually evolve with each new occasion of use, because new situations, negotiations, and activities inevitably recast it in a new, more densely textured form. So a new concept, like the meaning of a word, is always under construction. (Brown *et al.* 1989:33)

The benefits of the adoption of this viewpoint for the individual learner are dramatic:

> People who use tools actively rather than just acquire them ... build an increasingly rich implicit understanding of the world in which they use the tools and of the tools themselves. The understanding, both of the world and of the tool, continually changes as a result of their interaction. Learning and acting are interestingly indistinct, learning being a continuous, life-long process resulting from acting in situations. (ibid.)

Viability

The term 'viability' comes from the pragmatic philosophy of Richard Rorty (1979), and has been emphasized by the self-professed 'radical constructivist' Ernst von Glasersfeld to characterize the goal we set for our mental models within a constructivist perspective. The concept suggests that the constructions of reality we create in our minds are maintained as long as they work for us. Perturbations in our perceptions of the environment can cause us to modify our constructions, thus leading to appropriation. The process of seeking viability rather than truth can be seen in all areas of scientific thought through the ages as our collective understandings of the world have changed, from the classic example of the Copernican revolution when suddenly the sun stopped revolving around the earth to the proper treatment for heart disease:

> Philosophers of science (e.g., Kuhn 1970) have, for many years, stressed the process of social negotiation within scientific communities which have brought forth these 'standard objective views'. And it is truly amazing how quickly these views change. Up until a few years ago, by-pass operations were considered benign and routine; now, I understand, the conventional wisdom is to use non-surgical methods to clear the blockage, if at all possible. If the 'standard objective view' changes so often, what is 'objective' about it? (Cunningham 1992:159)

From a constructivist perspective, intellectual history has not been a process of getting closer to the 'truth' about how the universe functions; instead it illustrates our natural drive to create viable mental models and plans of action, adapting them to our understandings of the world, which continue to evolve as we continue to experience. Viability, then, is the test of functionality for the mental models we hold at any given moment:

> One of the revolutionary aspects of the constructivist approach to communication, then, is that it drastically changes the concept of 'understanding'. There can no longer be the claim that the meanings of words must be *shared* by the users of the language because these meanings are derived from fixed, external entities. Instead, here once more, there is at best a relation of *fit*. That is to say, we tend to conclude that what we have said is understood by the listener if the way he or she reacts to our utterance seems compatible with our expectations. However, as we discover only too often, what seemed understanding at first, disintegrates when a seemingly unproblematic utterance leads to quite unexpected reactions in a new situation. (von Glasersfeld 1988:89)

Viability is a crucially important concept in my approach to constructivist education because it embodies the key understanding that learning is not an attempt to get closer to the truth, but to create tools that enable us to function efficiently with respect to the physical reality and the socio-cultural environment of which we are a part. Viability also suggests that learning is a dynamic, rather than a finite process. We don't acquire knowledge and skills once and for all; we gradually and continuously refine and shape our understandings as we go about the business of living. This puts the concept of 'lifelong learning' in a new light, as it suggests that learning is co-extensive with living. Above all it is thus authentic life that must go on in a learning environment, situated against the background of the learner and embedded in real social relationships.

Scaffolding

Scaffolding refers to the support offered by the teacher to assist learners in the collaborative construction of their mental models. It is a central concept in social constructivist thinking because it emphasizes the understanding that the constructivist teacher does not simply give students an activity to complete on their own, at least not as long as support is needed for the students to complete the task competently:

> Some influential perspectives on education and learning would suggest that if a problem solving activity or learning task is well-designed, then pupils should be able to pursue it independently and teacher interventions should be minimal. ... However, the neo-Vygotskian perspective does not necessarily support that view. Instead, the necessity of some kinds of teacher support in an activity may be regarded as a virtue, because it is only when 'scaffolding' of some kind is required that we can infer that a child is working in a ZPD.

> ... We can therefore conclude that a task which is designed so that children
> are able to accomplish it without any assistance whatsoever is unlikely to
> stretch their intellectual capabilities. (Mercer 1994:103)

The scaffolding metaphor could suggest a rigid, pre-determined support for a learning architecture proposed by the teacher. The reciprocal nature of appropriation
from a neo-Vygotskian viewpoint, however, allows us to see the scaffold as a flexible structure that emerges within the ZPD as a function of ongoing negotiations
between the teacher and the learners:

> Scaffolding is not just any assistance which helps a learner accomplish a task.
> It is help which will enable a learner to accomplish a task which they would
> not have been quite able to manage on their own and it is help which is in-
> tended to bring the learner closer to a state of competence which will enable
> them eventually to complete such a task on their own. (Maybin *et al.*, quoted
> in Mercer 1994:97)

Scaffolding can take a variety of forms, from the providing of hints to the exemplary completion of an entire task. As the scaffolds become dispensable, they are
gradually withdrawn, so that the student can complete tasks without outside assistance, either individually, or in collaboration with peers. Even without scaffolding,
it is clear that skills and knowledge can continue to evolve and mature. If scaffolding is provided appropriately and judiciously, it will lead students to autonomous
action and thus learning. This allows a teacher to work with a number of groups in
the classroom at the same time. The teacher can move from group to group as requested, providing scaffolds to help the group get over particular problems, and
then moving on to the next group in need of assistance.

Clearly, scaffolding does not mean handing students ready-made solutions or
even pre-forged tools for solving problems they encounter in learning situations,
nor does it suggest paving the road for students to follow toward the attainment of
the teacher's meaning. Instead, it is more like the placing of helpful signposts on
the path as the learners create it – helping them not to travel the teacher's path, but
to build viable roads of their own. It is up to the teacher to recognize a path that is
forming well and to spontaneously provide scaffolds that will help the knowledge
and skill constructors in their work:

> Instruction occurs in the interaction between novice and expert, who together
> structure their communication so that the novice is brought into the expert's
> more mature understanding of the problem. ... The expert modifies the scaf-
> fold as the novice's capabilities develop, adjusting support to a level just
> beyond that which the novice could independently manage. (Rogoff and
> Gardner, quoted in Choi and Hannafin 1995:61)

Scaffolding represents a type of teacher-student interaction that varies radically from traditional classroom discourse:

> In the traditional approach there is a tendency to break the work down into pieces that can be learned without reference to the forward direction of the sequence. There is no need or opportunity to understand the goal of the sequence while learning the components. Thus, there is a tendency to emphasize rote learning of lower level components. (Newman *et al.* 1989:153)

Scaffolding, on the other hand, does not break down a complex task into easily grasped chunks because that would prevent learners from finding their own meanings in the whole event. It is instead a form of coaching toward the construction of the students' own viable interpretations of an event. Scaffolding has been likened to the type of assistance provided by masters in traditional master-apprentice relationships: "A key aspect of coaching is the provision of scaffolding, which is the support, in the form of reminders and help, that the apprentice requires to approximate the execution of the entire composite of skills" (Collins *et al.* 1989:456).

Staying with the apprenticeship metaphor, scaffolding is actually the second stage in the progression from novice to expert behaviour. The first is observation of behaviour as performed by an expert. Just as the apprentice will usually watch the expert at work before beginning to perform a task himself, in the learning of complex intellectual skills, the same progression can be followed:

> The interplay between observation, scaffolding, and increasingly independent practice aids apprentices both in developing self-monitoring and -correction skills and in integrating the skills and conceptual knowledge needed to advance toward expertise. Observation plays a surprisingly key role; Lave hypothesizes that it aids learners in developing a conceptual model of the target task or process prior to attempting to execute it. (ibid.)

Socio-cognitive apprenticeship

The concept of scaffolding epitomizes the key instructional role of the teacher; it is supportive behaviour characterized by guidance, interaction, empathy and spontaneity. The concept of scaffolding has led to the technique of 'cognitive apprenticeship', a useful metaphor to describe pedagogical interaction in intellectual domains. Cognitive apprenticeship is a process in which students are acculturated into authentic practices through activity and social interaction much as craft apprentices are trained:

> Cognitive apprenticeship supports "learning in domain" by enabling students to acquire, develop, and use cognitive tools in authentic domain activity.

Similarly, craft apprenticeship enables apprentices to acquire and develop the tools and skills of their craft through authentic work at and membership in their trade. Through this process, apprentices enter the culture of practice. So the term *apprenticeship* helps to emphasise the centrality of activity in learning and knowledge and highlights the inherently context-dependent, situated, and enculturating nature of learning. And *apprenticeship* also suggests the paradigm of situated modelling, coaching, and fading ... whereby teachers or coaches promote learning, first by making explicit their tacit knowledge or by modelling their strategies for students in authentic activity. Then, teachers and colleagues support students' attempts at doing the task. And finally they empower the students to continue independently. (Brown *et al.* 1989:39)

This learning autonomy is dependent on the development of the ability to reflect on one's own work and compare it to the performance of professionals. The success of socio-cognitive apprenticeship relies on this ability to monitor one's own progress toward mastery and to make necessary changes without guidance. The need for this reflective capacity will be particularly important after graduation, of course, when potential employers will expect the translator to work independently, solve new translation problems as they arise, and be a productive team member capable of continuing to learn collaboratively within the specific environment of the firm itself.

Collins *et al.* (1989:455) specify the multi-stage nature of the cognitive apprenticeship process:

First and foremost, apprenticeship focuses closely on the specific methods for carrying out tasks in a domain. Apprentices learn these methods through a combination of what Lave calls observation, coaching, and practice, or what we, from the teacher's point of view, call modelling, coaching, and fading. In this sequence of activities, the apprentice repeatedly observes the master executing (or modelling) the target process, which usually involves some different but interrelated subskills. The apprentice then attempts to execute the process with guidance and help from the master (i.e., coaching). ... Once the learner has a grasp of the target skill, the master reduces (or fades) his participation, providing only limited hints, refinements, and feedback to the learner, who practices by successively approximating smooth execution of the whole skill.

This conceptualization needs, in my view, the added refinement of the collaborative perspective – which sees the interactive group of apprentices as the locus of learning or meaning-making. I thus prefer to call the process *socio-cognitive apprenticeship*, through which a group being initiated into a professional community represented by the teacher appropriates the knowledge of the language of that community through the guidance of the teacher, but always situated in conversation among the group of peers.

I agree with Collins *et al.*, who, while clearly supporting the cognitive apprenticeship approach as a highly viable component in the learning of complex cognitive skills, do not believe it is the only way to learn:

> Reading a book or listening to a lecture are important ways to learn, particularly in domains where conceptual and factual knowledge are central. Active listeners or readers, who test their understanding and pursue the issues that are raised in their minds, learn things that apprenticeship can never teach. To the degree that readers or listeners are passive, however, they will not learn as much as they would by apprenticeship, because apprenticeship forces them to use their knowledge. (ibid.:459)

Nevertheless, constructivists posit that, regardless of the learning situation, students will be involved first in interpreting phenomena, events and ideas that they perceive in their environment and then in building or constructing their own understandings on the basis of these interpretations. Candy (1989:108) has formulated this dual nature of constructivist learning processes as follows:

> Thus, constructivism in education is concerned with two things: how learners *construe* (or interpret) events and ideas, and how they *construct* (build and assemble) structures of meaning. The constant dialectical interplay between construing and constructing is at the heart of a constructivist approach to education, whether it be listening to a lecture, undertaking a laboratory session, attending a workshop, reading a text, or any other learning activity.

Transformation and the acquisition of translator competence

The contemporary view of translator competence I presented in Chapter 1 is that of a complex, highly individualized and social-context dependent interplay of cultural, cognitive and intuitive processes. It is apparent that intuitions, based on personal experience with language and the real world, play a major role in the translation processes of each individual. This suggests that the value of a teaching approach in which the parcelling out of translation equivalents to an entire group of translation students at the same time (when one of them has produced what to the instructor appears to be an incorrect translation solution) is inappropriate, if not counter-productive. If we see translator competence as a creative, largely intuitive, socially-constructed, and multi-faceted complex of skills and abilities, then the primary goals of translator education will include raising students' awareness of the factors involved in translation, helping them develop their own translator's self-concept, and assisting in the collaborative construction of individually tailored tools that will allow every student to function within the language mediation community upon graduation.

To sum up, from this perspective, there is rarely a single, 'correct' translation, and certainly no single, correct process, strategy or technique for coming up with an adequate solution. In contemporary theories of translation, language use is seen as a form of interpersonal communication, which by its very nature implies the necessity of interpretation and negotiation of meaning. Rather than it being the instructor's job to 'teach' correct translation equivalents or even the right strategies for finding those equivalents, it is my belief that instructors can and should try to guide students toward the awareness of pertinent factors that may be involved in the translation of a wide variety of texts embedded in specific communicative situations, create with them authentic, scaffolded learning activities in which the students can experience the work of professionals first hand, and to help them construct appropriate, individually adapted tools and cognitive skills for solving the myriad new translation problems that they can expect to encounter when they leave the institution and no longer have the instructor to provide *the* correct response.

I hope that chapters 2 and 3 have clarified the underlying non-foundational, social constructivist views upon which my approach to translator education is based. In the next chapter, I will try to situate my interpretation of these theoretical constructs by depicting the instructional design I have developed for my own translator education classes.

4.   On Instruction and Construction in the Classroom

> ... the pedagogically most suitable key-concepts are those associated with **experiencing**, **exploration**, and **discovery** ...
>
> Toury (1992:69)

Traditional course types: in the service of transmissionist design

As discussed in Chapter 1, pedagogical **design**, seen as the implementation of an underlying pedagogical approach, is manifested in the course types that are used to accomplish educational goals within a programme of studies. In German university programmes for the training of translators, three basic course types have been used traditionally as the instructional settings for almost all of the classes offered in the curriculum. The first type is the lecture (*Vorlesung*), primarily used for survey courses in cultural studies and history, applied linguistics and the subject areas that students choose for their translation concentration (medicine, economics, law, and engineering). The lecture is designed to expedite the transmission of knowledge to large numbers of students sitting in rows facing the teacher, who speaks or reads to them on a topic for one 45- or 90-minute session per week. Then there is the exercise class (*Übung*), which is generally seen as a type of modified lecture where students are expected to acquire knowledge and skills from the teacher and practise using them in controlled exercises. This type of course is used for translation practice, for basic and remedial foreign language classes, and for teaching students how to use computer-based tools. The third type of course is the *Seminar*, which is offered at the undergraduate and graduate levels primarily to teach special topics in literature, cultural studies and translation studies. The seminar involves independent research work that is carried out by individual students and presented orally before the teacher and the other class members as well as being submitted in written form. In an educational setting based on objectivist views of learning and teaching, seminars tend to parallel the lecture/practice class arrangement with regard to the type of interaction permitted or encouraged. Usually following several introductory lectures by the teacher on given topics, individual students take turns functioning as teacher-proxies, reading off their own lectures to the other students. The teacher is always present, in charge and in control, filling in knowledge not covered by the presenters and answering any questions that the otherwise silent and generally passive lecture recipients might ask.

In our programme, there are virtually no overt institutional constraints governing the instructional procedures that are to be used in the different class types, but there is an implicit consensus on what is appropriate for each type of class. In fact, classes of all three basic types and in all language departments tend to share certain objectivist characteristics. First, the teacher is likely to consider him- or herself (and be seen by the learners) as the principle fountain of knowledge, regardless of the class type. It is not only in lecture courses that teachers will stand in front of a group of learners and talk, with the students sitting mutely and passively, listening and perhaps taking notes. Even in so-called 'practice' classes, the teacher almost universally takes his or her place in the front of the room, facing rows of amassed students, distributing knowledge and eliciting displays of knowledge and knowledge gaps from the students. The students attempt to discover and reproduce the correct solutions as defined by the teacher. Most of the practice work is done by students alone at home in an attempt to take knowledge passed on to them in class and apply it correctly to sample problems to be checked against the teacher's knowledge of the correct answers at the next session. The teacher is always present in class to provide input and feedback, to organize student practice, which entails memorizing and manipulating that input, and to test whether it has been adequately ingested or not.

The chief concern that a constructivist view would have about 'classical' translation exercise classes, in which learning activities are essentially reduced to the transcoding of sentences amputated from real translation situations (Nord 1996), is that they tend to be patently inauthentic, inactive and disempowering. Professional translators generally do not transcode phrases and sentences in a contextual void. As a rule, genuine translation tasks are embedded in a multifaceted communicative situation with an identifiable user and readership, and they are accompanied by task specifications from the translator's employer or client (*Auftraggeber*). Authentic translation practice, by analogy, would thus entail active participation in situated, context-bound translation activity that provides translation students with opportunities for learning how to weigh situational factors and how to acquire enough background information about a topic and a text in order to interpret it adequately with the goal of meeting the respective task specifications. As noted by Brown *et al.* (1989), conventional classroom activity tends to be 'hybrid' in the sense that it is attributed to one community (that of professional translators for example), but is actually implemented in that of another (the academic community). In a translator-education setting, this means that while students may think that they are performing the same work as full-fledged translators, they are actually engaged in only a weak, de-situated facsimile of that authentic activity – a facsimile which may be very far removed from the actual work carried out by the professional community. As Brown *et al.* (1989:34) state:

> Many of the activities students undertake are simply not the activities of practitioners and would not make sense or be endorsed by the cultures to which they are attributed. This hybrid activity, furthermore, limits students' access to the important structuring and supporting cues that arise from the context. What students do tends to be ersatz activity.

In a transmissionist translation exercise class, for example, students will generally grapple with what the teacher identifies as translation problems. They do not interact in any meaningful way with the author of the original texts they work with; there is no client involved who has requested a translation; nor are the students translating for any real target readership. After all, the teacher can presumably understand the original text adequately and has probably already produced an excellent model translation, so there is no real 'need' for students to undertake the translation in the first place – except as a pedagogical exercise. In a teacher-centred class, students will not discuss problems with their peers in the quest for better solutions, as that would be considered dishonest or disruptive from an objectivist perspective, so they must individually seek translation solutions that will be acceptable to the relevant authority (the grade giver). The learner does not need to weigh the requirements and expectations of the client against those of the final text user. In fact, they are involved in no more than a contrived pedagogical situation, not an authentic communicative situation; the conventional teacher-centred translation practice exercise is a purely contrived situation that is far removed from the complex social interaction and cognitive-problem solving of the translator's actual activities. In such classes, translational activity is reduced to a mechanical search-and-replace game, where students try to guess what the teacher wants and then copy down the 'right' equivalents provided by the teacher for later retrieval.

There are, of course, numerous teachers who invite and encourage extensive student participation in the classroom. These teachers, I would suggest, know, at least intuitively, that education is a constructive acculturation and empowerment process more than it is a process of mirroring reality and truth. What is needed is overt recognition of the viability of these beliefs and their systematic and consistent application to teaching.

In each of the three class types discussed above, the lecture, the exercise class and the seminar, objectivist assumptions prevail, with the basis of the educational process being understood as the transmission of knowledge from those who know more to those who know less. Despite often being immersed in a crowd of students in class, each individual is in fact an isolated cognitive processor. The teacher directs knowledge at each student individually, transmitting information for passive, private, cognitive consumption and storage. Communication among the students themselves is usually considered unnecessary, if not undesirable. Testing serves the purpose of identifying and quantifying learning (understood as cognitive retention of knowledge) by each isolated individual on appropriate occasions each semester and at key junctures in the programme of studies.

Livening up classroom activities and making them appear more practice-relevant while leaving the structures of authority and pedagogical belief untouched will not, I fear, go far enough toward perpetuating real innovation in translation classrooms. The inherent inertia in the imbalance of power within the educational institution will work to ensure that superficial didactic change will be short-lived and that the effect of the programme will continue to be **disempowerment** rather than **empowerment.** Students, as well as teachers, naturally contribute to the perpetuation of the status quo. As Gideon Toury has said (1992:68):

> Obviously, the fact that teachers have the power to enforce norms on their students often results in an irresistible temptation to exert this power. On the other hand, many students themselves prefer to have an authority dictate narrowly-defined modes of behaviour to them and train them in the application of rigid principles.

Both this "irresistible temptation" on the part of the teacher to enforce norms and the students' preference to be dictated to derive not from natural laws of learning but from deeply ingrained habits acquired during schooling. There is no doubt that a great effort is needed to break this deadlock.

Nord's practice-oriented method

In my review of the literature on translator education, I have found no published works that explicitly attempt to apply constructivist principles in the development of a method for the education of professional translators. Nevertheless, a few translation teaching scholars have made recommendations for alternative instructional procedures that reflect a concern for having learning experiences reflect authentic professional practice, and that could thus be consistent with the constructivist approach I am proposing. One of the most extensive and detailed discussions on pedagogical practice in translator education that I have come across is the article by Christiane Nord (1996) entitled *Wer nimmt mal den ersten Satz?* (Who will take the first sentence?). Many of the instructional techniques Nord describes are potentially compatible with my constructivist approach, and I would like to present her method in some detail here because of its exemplary status and because her article is not accessible to those who do not read German.

Nord proposes two different class types for the development of translator competence in an institutional setting. The first is a propaedeutic, or introduction to translation studies, where students would acquire basic competence in translation-related skills, and the other is the translation exercise class, which she says represents about 50% of the courses offered at German translator education institutions. Nord notes that while the translation exercise class is an extremely important part of the curriculum, it is also sharply criticized by both teachers and students. The latter, Nord says, complain because they fail to experience success in such classes and find themselves at the mercy of the "all-knowing teacher"; and teachers complain about the discrepancy between the amount of effort they put into preparing for such courses and the learning or teaching effects achieved, and also about the deficiencies in the competence and knowledge exhibited by their students.

In developing a rationale for the adoption of alternatives to the traditional teacher-dominated instructional performance, Nord discusses the goal of the educational programme: the development of translator competence, which she sub-divides into abilities (*Fähigkeiten*), knowledge (*Wissen*), and skills (*Fertigkeiten*). The abilities that she sees as being vital for the development of translator competence are: analytical ability for comparing the translation assignment and the source text; the ability to select appropriate strategies; linguistic creativity for the implementation of decisions; and judgmental ability for quality assurance (Nord 1996:316). In her view, these abilities should be well developed at the beginning of the programme of studies and can even serve as the basis for an aptitude test determining acceptance into translator training programmes.

Nord's translation-relevant knowledge includes practical and subject-matter knowledge, linguistic and cultural knowledge, theoretical and methodological knowledge and a sensitivity to cultural differences. This knowledge, Nord says, can be acquired in special content courses as well as during on-the-job training and stays abroad.

Translation skills would include: translation assignment interpretation, text analysis, translation research, and strategy development. These skills, she says, can be developed in the propaedeutic and practice classes without being embedded in a genuine translation situation. While Nord proposes having teachers give students a realistic translation assignment whenever possible, her method still focuses on the central role of the teacher as the designer, organizer and judge of the success of student learning.

After sketching an approach and design where she emphasizes the importance of having pedagogical activities embedded in realistic translation situations with clearly defined task specifications, Nord goes on to outline no fewer than 17 instructional scenarios with a number of variants that can be used to complement or supplant the monotonous and inauthentic teacher-centred instructional performance I discussed in Chapter 2. Some form of all of these techniques can be adapted for use in the constructivist approach to translator education I am proposing. The list below includes all of her suggested alternative techniques, which she categorized with respect to their appropriateness for **(a)** beginning, **(b)** intermediate, and **(c)** advanced students.

Translation revision (a) – students are given a source text and a faulty translation, which they must improve upon.

Translation with a parallel text (a) – In addition to the source language text, students are given a target language text that will provide them with support for producing a translation more easily.

Interpreting (a) – Students simulate interpreting for each other in everyday situations.

Summary translation (a) – A source text is read aloud; individual students summarize it in written form. These versions are then compared in small groups.

Multiple choice translation (a) – Students receive a source language text and a selection of different versions of text chunks to be used as modules to compose a translation.

Paraphrase translation (a+b) – Students write up an abbreviated version of a source text and turn it into a complete translated text at home for discussion in class.

Guided translation (a+b) – Students are given a source text in which the teacher has marked (and perhaps named) problematic points in advance.

Small-group translation (a+b) – A text read and prepared in advance by the students at home is divided into independent units, which are then translated within a limited time. The completed translation solutions are presented to the group on overhead slides, 'defended', and discussed.

Parallel translation (b+c) – A source text is given to students to translate for different purposes in response to significantly different translation assignments.

Summary translation (b+c) – Students receive a written text which they summarize verbally.

Team translation (b+c) – A team of 3-4 students prepares a rough translation that is copied and handed out to the other course participants, who have also translated the text themselves. The team explains its decision-making processes and 'defends' its translation in front of the rest of the group.

Sight translation (b+c) – One learner skims a relatively long text and then translates it orally, emphasizing coherence and fluency.

Test translation (b+c) – Written translation of a text of a specified length within a time limit under 'examination conditions', which entails using no supporting tools or only those allowed by the examination regulations. The teacher corrects the translations and the texts are discussed in class. A variant of this would be a commented test, in which students would be instructed to write notes in the margins explaining deletions and additions, showing missing references, etc. Another variant would involve having the students correct each other's work.

Partial translation (b+c) – Characteristic or important sections of a relatively long text are translated (for example the beginning, the conclusion or selected segments) using one of the procedures listed above. The rest of the text is translated by the students individually or in small groups in specially reserved class sessions. Problems that arise can be presented and discussed at a later joint session.

Sight translation of meaningful units (c) – Together, the students analyze the contents of the source text and divide it into units of meaning which are then sight translated.

Project translation (c) – Different tasks (research, partial translation, final editing, checking terminology for consistency, etc.) are assigned to individual students. A deadline is set for completion of the job, after which the group can discuss problems that arose, proposed solutions, etc. Beforehand, the teacher is available to the students to give advice; there are no joint class sessions.

Translation without a brief (c) – Students come up with their own appropriate translation assignment for the text the teacher gives them, and they then translate the text accordingly.

Publishable translation (c) – Students translate a text at home and submit it in publishable and printable form (perhaps saving it on disk, using a specified programme, etc.)

It should be noted that the progression of activities from level (a) through level (c) is based on the complexity of the task as determined by the teacher. Nord is particularly concerned that students may be overwhelmed by the complexity of genuine translation situations. In her view, one of the teacher's key roles is to reduce this complexity in order to make sure that learners can comfortably handle the tasks given them. There is a crucial difference between this type of complexity reduction, which is typical of objectivist approaches to education, and the concept of scaffolding. From a constructivist perspective, being able to come to terms with the many facets of authentic situations is one of the most vital abilities that the student can develop. Here, it is essential to bring real-world tasks into the classroom precisely to provide learners with their own experience in dealing with the natural complexity of genuine professional work. Rather than restricting their intervention whenever possible to "moderating and if necessary arbitrating" (Nord 1996:326), it is the teacher's task to provide the necessary dynamic support (scaffolding) within these authentic situations to ensure that students actually do learn and progress toward greater competence – and full membership in the translating community. Rather than leaving advanced students on their own to discover solutions for themselves, teachers need to monitor continuously the progress of the students within the learning environment, to provide support where necessary, and to ensure that students' knowledge continues to develop within their evolving zones of proximal development (ZPDs).

A constructivist critique of Nord's method

While Nord's extensive list of alternative pedagogical procedures clearly represents a significant contribution to the improvement of teaching in translator education, I suggest that her method could be significantly enhanced by linking her ideas, which seem to focus primarily on syllabus **design** and pedagogical **procedures**, to a constructivist **approach.**

Figure 3 is an alternative way of looking at the development of translator competence. Rather than seeing competence as being synonymous with expertise, which can be built up atomistically through progressively providing increasingly complex pedagogical activities contrived by the teacher, I would like to look at translator competence at the completion of the programme of studies as a function of both learners' **expertise** and **autonomy** within a scaffolded framework of **authentic** practice.

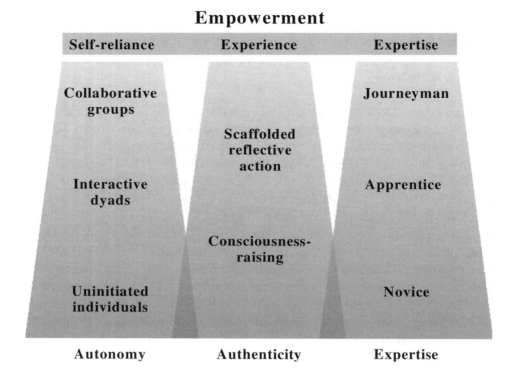

Figure 3: Dimensions of development toward translator competence

The expertise dimension, outlined in Chapter 3, corresponds approximately to Nord's ability, knowledge, and skills triad. Autonomy, as discussed at length in earlier chapters, is the ability of learners to function competently and professionally, independently of the teacher. It includes the ability to work competently on their own and as collaborative members of a team. Authenticity is the degree to which the activities undertaken in the classroom are representative of the nature and complexity of activities performed by professional translators in the course of their work. On the basis of the arguments presented in this volume up to this point, I hypothesize that expertise can be expected to evolve from novice to journeyman within an institutional setting in direct relationship to progression along the continuum of autonomy, from non-membership in the community of translators, through dyad and small-group interdependence, to teacher-independence (empowerment) as an individual and a team member. I have borrowed Hoffmann's (1998) tentative definitions of the various stages of expertise:

- Novice: "a probationary member" of a knowledge community with minimal exposure to the domain.

- Initiate: a novice who has commenced introductory instruction.
- Apprentice: a student undergoing a programme of instruction beyond the introductory level.
- Journeyman: an experienced and reliable worker, or one who has achieved a level of competence.
- Expert: "The distinguished or brilliant journeyman, highly regarded by peers, whose judgements are uncommonly accurate and reliable, whose performance shows consummate skills and economy of effort, and who can deal effectively with certain types of rare or "tough" cases. Also, an expert is one who has special skills or knowledge derived from extensive experience with sub-domains" (Hoffmann 1998:85).

From this perspective, the students who enter our programmes of study are usually novices. We initiate them into the domain through introductory courses, they go on to learn as apprentices and are expected to reach the stage of journeyman by the time they complete their programme of studies. True expertise can develop only after many years of real-world experience after completion of the programme of studies.

Progression on the dimensions of expertise and autonomy will be embedded in authentic reflective action from the beginning, focusing primarily on two stages: 1) consciousness-raising about the nature of the translator's work, and 2) scaffolded authentic projects, which will be genuine whenever possible and otherwise simulated.

For Nord, the establishment of authenticity is restricted at all but the highest levels of instruction to providing students with a realistic translation assignment for every exercise (situated exercises). Near the completion of their studies, she feels that students should be given opportunities to undertake group translation projects and the submission of publishable translations, the two of her seventeen procedures that approximate global tasks in the everyday work of a professional translator. The rest of Nord's list of techniques are either sub-tasks that translators might have to perform within the context of their work or purely contrived exercises that would be used by a teacher to help students develop particular sub-skills.

As presented by Nord, most of the individual techniques proposed would not necessarily entail a significant change in the structure of authority and responsibility in the classroom, a change that is indispensable for turning the traditional educational setting into a venue for empowerment. An authoritarian, transmissionist teacher could employ most of these techniques in a completely conventional manner, reserving control, power and responsibility for him or herself, and thus perpetuating the disempowerment of students. It is by making explicit underlying assumptions and linking them to pedagogical goals through pedagogical design that will determine what transpires in the classroom – the passive mirroring of teachers' distributed knowledge with an essentially passive group of voiceless students, or an active, collaborative community of knowledge builders.

From a constructivist perspective, gaining access to a new community is the learner's overriding task, which is accomplished by moving to the boundary of that community and gradually being drawn into its discourse and action. From this perspective, all learning must be 'situated', that is, placed in relation to the learners' previous accumulated experience (knowledge) as well as to the target professional behaviour. Learning is best accomplished through meaningful interaction with peers as well as full-fledged members of the community to which learners are seeking entry. I suggest integrating these techniques into a constructivist framework embodying the dimensions of expertise, autonomy and authenticity in a first step toward the development of methods for educating translators that can represent significant and systematic alternatives to the ubiquitous instructional performance.

My proposal is to focus on the publishable translation project as the key learning event for translation practice starting immediately after an introduction to translation studies in which students would be involved in consciousness raising about the nature of translator competence. Rather than attempting to build up students' translation-related skills and knowledge atomistically in simulated exercises prior to translation practice, it would be much more constructive to start each pedagogical event with a highly realistic, and if possible genuine, translation project. Project-related sub-tasks will emerge naturally from the students' work on each joint project. Rather than it being the teacher's task to contrive activities to simulate translation sub-tasks, it would be their job to assist students in identifying those aspects of their expertise that are not yet well enough developed to complete the translation job at hand, and to provide scaffolding for acquiring the necessary skills and knowledge. Figure 4 illustrates my conceptualization of pedagogical activities focused on authentic projects.

Here, an authentic whole-group collaborative translation project would serve as the primary pedagogical activity for a course or course module. Ideally, a project would be a real translation job commissioned by a client and thus embedded in a full complement of situational features, including, for example: a strict deadline, a real reader or readership, the availability or lack of terminological and subject-matter support from the client, formatting constraints and specific quality demands. An entire class could undertake the project together, with, for example, the teacher serving as the project co-ordinator, expert advisor, technical assistant and mediator between the translators and the client. The group as a whole would be faced with the complexity of the overall project from the beginning and would use the situational features of the project as points of reference as they plan, complete and revise their work. The teacher, students and client can first negotiate the conditions under which the project will be undertaken, and the students, with the assistance of the teacher, can then identify and plan the steps that they will go through to submit a competent, publishable translation as well as how to distribute the work among themselves. As the project and classroom manager, it will be the teacher's job to help organize, moderate and expedite the group's efforts. The teacher can suggest that students work collaboratively in small learning groups of three to four students to accomplish parts of the project. He or she may also suggest different stages for completing the project, including, for example, the search for parallel texts, library and Internet research, peer proof-reading and editing.

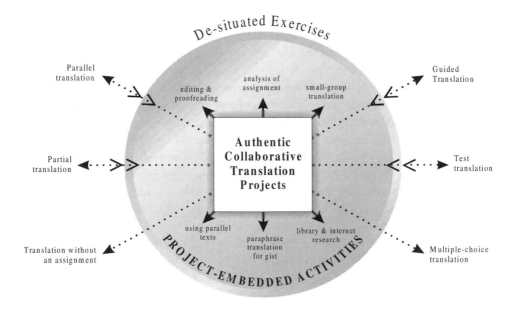

Figure 4: Maximizing authenticity in the translation exercise class

Many of these activities will resemble pedagogical procedures that Nord (1996) recommends. But in my pedagogical model, they are intricately interwoven with the authentic collaborative translation projects themselves. To the extent that procedures Nord suggests do not emerge naturally from actual projects, I suggest that they are less appropriate for promoting learning from a constructivist approach. The procedures that appear to be the least authentic include partial translation, multiple-choice translation, guided translation, parallel translation, translation without an assignment and test translation. However, the double arrows on dotted lines linking these activities to the authentic projects in my model are intended to suggest that many of them can acquire a significant level of authenticity if they are integrated into an actual project at hand.

In my experience, a wide range of sub-tasks emerges naturally within the scope of each project. As these sub-tasks are dealt with in small groups on the basis of specific difficulties that arise, the teacher can help scaffold learning far better than would be the case in a large-group frontal instruction situation.

I would definitely agree with Nord that students need to become familiar with the various aspects of translator competence prior to beginning translation practice, for example in an introduction to translation class, but I do not see the appropriate function of such a class as providing students with ready-made skills and knowledge that they will need in order to translate later on. From a social constructivist perspective, the introduction to translation studies class might best be seen as the site of an initial encounter between a group at the boundary between the community of non-translators and that of professional translators. Here, the group begins to generate its own viable cognitive tools, appropriating them through interaction with the knowledge community and with their peers. It is important to remember that the construction of viable tools is a dynamic, perpetual process. Each new genuine experience throughout our period of training and our professional lives is an opportunity to hone our professional skills. Rather than mastering the correct use of dictionaries and other reference materials during their introduction to translation studies, for example, we can see learners' initial work with such materials as the beginning of an apprenticeship in using them as valuable, but less than infallible, tools. Until it helps accomplish authentic tasks, a reference work is no more than a virtual or potential tool. It acquires its function and its utility through personal experience in using it.

While the 'translation exercise class', with its typically objectivist features, may be the norm in a particular educational institution, it is up to teachers and students to develop and share alternative, more viable instructional types – to actively promote change within the institution toward the adoption of more suitable settings, approaches, and techniques for accomplishing its evolving goals. Given that the exercise class is specified in our curricula as the appropriate classroom structure for acquiring translator competence, and as teachers' conceptions of the exercise class are tightly interwoven with objectivist assumptions about learning and teaching, it is difficult to break away from a didactic performance, even if we try to apply the kinds of alternative exercises that Nord suggests. The distribution of authority and responsibility is likely to remain unchanged as long as the assumption that knowledge is distributed remains intact.

The constructivist workshop: a forum for learner empowerment

In an article aptly entitled 'Everything has its price', Gideon Toury summed up concisely the constructivist alternative to the ingestion of teacher norms by students. "What a trainee really needs is the opportunity to abstract **his own** guiding principles and routines from actual instances of behaviour, with the help of responses to his or her performance which are as variegated as possible" (Toury 1992:69). What are needed, then, in addition to empowering principles, goals and instructional techniques are class formats that permit and foster this construction process.

I propose the concept of the 'workshop' to describe a generic alternative class-room format that serves as the fundamental procedural format for my courses, regardless of the topic or the official course type indicated in the curriculum. Gentzler (1993) attributes the invention of the workshop classroom format and its applica-tion to language-related learning to I.A. Richards' (1929) *Practical Criticism* reading workshop approach, which served as the model for both the creative writing and the literary translation workshops that emerged at universities in the US during the late 1960s and 1970s.

My understanding of an appropriate function for the workshop differs radically from Richards'. In my view, the workshop can be a venue where authentic practice can occur among peers learning *with* (not *from*) a facilitator to construct their own understandings of social phenomena. Richards' pedagogical goal, as Gentzler (1993:13) makes clear, was quite different:

> In his actual workshop, Richards did not seek variable responses, but rather unified solutions to communication problems, generating rules and prin-ciples by which individual interpretations could be made and properly judged ...
>
> Such a model presumed a primary poetic experience that can be exactly and completely communicated to another person, if one were properly educated.

This view is radically different from the social constructivist view of knowledge, learning and communication that serves as the basis for the method outlined here. From my perspective, there can be no single, correct reading of a text. Just as it cannot be the goal of translation to uncover the true meaning of a text, it also cannot be the goal of translator education to replicate a teacher's principles and strategies in students.

In a social constructivist workshop, there is no all-knowing authority; the facilitator instead performs tasks like initiating discussion, managing interaction among the group members, summarizing and rephrasing arguments, etc. The facilitator, being a member of the community that the learners wish to join, will also contribute his or her perspective to group discussions and try to channel the discourse in ways that would be acceptable to full-fledged members of the target community. I have found that the 'workshop' can be adapted easily to all of the courses I have had to teach. Regardless of the subject matter or level, it is always designed to provide a forum for conversation – for the situated, interactive and empowering construction of meaning by the participants – including myself as the facilitator.

Through conversational activities involving the presentation of multiple perspec-tives, negotiation, debate, and constructive criticism, learners can collaboratively construct – develop, modify and expand – their own knowledge about the topic at hand, whether it be the basic features of medical, engineering, legal or economic language, the discourse of literary analysis, a deeper understanding of the foreign culture, or the professional norms and conventions of the translator's craft. In all of my classes, students work collaboratively with their peers, with me as the facilitator, and with language and subject-matter professionals from outside the institution; their goal is to learn how to act, think and work like expert translators, gradually moving as a group and as individuals into the professional community of professional translators.

The workshop format can be applied to any type of skill or subject domain offered in the translator education programme. From a constructivist perspective, students would participate in courses on literary and cultural topics as a means of joining the community of educated speakers of the languages they are studying. Similarly, the workshop format can provide an excellent forum in which to appropriate basic concepts, the specialized language use and the world view of at least one technical community, as they will have to understand and produce texts in the respective language variety as if they themselves were doctors, lawyers, business consultants, etc. Today, translators must also be proficient users of computer-based translation tools, from word processors to terminology databases to the Internet. Working toward this special technical competence can also be seen as collaborating to gradually enter the discourse community of computer-based tool users. In fact, virtually every class session in the educational programme can be seen as an opportunity for students to interact at the boundaries of one or more communities. In every course, negotiation, collaboration and conversation will be key ingredients in situations that will allow students to gradually construct the knowledge they need to become full-fledged members of the target groups.

Students need to become actively involved in the appropriation of knowledge in all of the sub-domains of translator education, and not just in translation skills classes. Sitting passively while listening to a lecture on economics, law, engineering or medicine, for example, is insufficient preparation for future specialized translators who will have to work within the respective field competently and with the confidence that they know what they are talking about and how to talk about it – clearly prerequisites for producing professional-quality texts in that field. If lectures are to be useful from a constructivist perspective, they need to be complemented or punctuated by pair and small-group discussion sessions in which students grapple actively to make sense of the subject domain. Learning is not a spectator sport; the appropriation of knowledge always occurs through work, not osmosis. This work of necessity entails the active negotiation of meaning with members of the knowledgeable community and with peers at the periphery who also wish to join that community.

From a social constructivist perspective, seminars need not simply be ersatz lectures, where students take on the role of knowledge disseminators as proxies for the teacher. Instead, the seminar can take the form of a research-workshop where students and the teacher together can create learning experiences around a project through which they define the boundaries of the domain they want to explore as well as the sub-domains within it. A workshop-based seminar is replete with opportunities to collaborate. Topics do not have to be presented as lectures by individual students, but instead can be introduced for example through interactive mini-workshops designed by students working in small groups. Students can draw on primary and secondary readings from a field and work them into their discourse, not simply reporting on standard wisdom, but synthesizing the views of experts with their own multiple perspectives, integrating it all into their own new perspective which can then also be negotiated with the teacher and their classroom peers in spirited and mutually respectful dialogue. Clearly, students must first be introduced to collaborative group work through introductory activities co-ordinated by the teacher. Students in fact have to learn how to learn, to break out of their ingrained habits of sitting passively, trying to absorb information from the teacher. They must first learn to see the advantages of collaborative learning and to respect their own and each other's opinions and views. Without preparatory work, student-led 'workshops' tend to take on the transmissionist characteristics of conventional seminars, with the presenting group taking on the role of knowledge distributors for the other class participants. In Chapter 5, some techniques will be presented that I use to help students learn how to design and run interactive mini-workshops.

Students who are participants in workshops organized by other students must understand that not only do they have the right to question, critique and add to what is presented, but that they also have a responsibility to make contributions and provide their own perspectives. They must see themselves as active builders of their own knowledge, and see their task in the seeking out of multiple perspectives for synthesis with their peers – not of mastering the wisdom offered by the teacher or a teacher proxy.

On the basis of the constructivist principles I discussed in Chapters 2 and 3, I have adopted the following set of social constructivist principles to guide me through the instructional design of all of my workshops.

1. As the most valuable learning experiences are authentic experiences, it is essential to situate learning

Several translation scholars (Nord 1988, 1996; Kussmaul 1995; Hönig 1995; Mackenzie and Nieminen 1997) have recommended the use of a realistic translation assignment in course work to help students situate the text they are supposed to translate and see it in a broader scenario of language use in context. Simply providing an imaginary assignment will surely have some, albeit very limited, impact on the authenticity of the situation. If used in a conventional, teacher-oriented class, the didactic assignment would be invented by the teacher, and the students' translations would still be judged for accuracy and acceptability against the arbitrary yardstick of each teacher's idiosyncratic criteria. There will still be no real translation situation and no feedback from the real world outside of the classroom. And it is precisely this link to the real world that I feel is the key to an adequately authentic translation situation.

With the ordinary practices of the translation community in mind, I try to situate learning for my students by securing real translation projects for them or helping them find their own. Often I have been able to share with students jobs that have been commissioned to me. While clients naturally insist that I personally assume full responsibility for the quality of the translation, I find they are often willing to have students participate in the project. In order to create an authentic learning situation, I in turn transfer responsibility for an excellent job to the students themselves. If I find myself lacking a real, paid assignment to share with students, I will often give them the task of finding a text in need of translation or re-translation, for example tourist brochures, technical instructions accompanying home appliances, or web sites. In this way the students learn to identify factors that are of importance to the translator's decision-making processes and how to work together with peers and the teacher to solve real translation problems. As the facilitator, I often assume the job of project co-ordinator myself. I then have the task of making sure the work is done in a timely and professional manner to the satisfaction of the client. This change in the habitual authority structure of the classroom allows and empowers students to think, solve problems and learn for themselves.

2. The most valuable learning experiences are imbued with multiple perspectives – not the transmission of a single truth

Rather than working toward one final translation, I encourage students to come up with parallel translations, that is, a set of viable translations, all of which can be expected to fulfil the functions of an acceptable translation for the client and the final readership. The presentation of my own perspective to the students could too easily be taken for the 'correct' or authorized version. Therefore, I try to get students to come up with their own answers. While I will often offer my own suggestions, I make sure that these are not to be mistaken for the final word. It is particularly rewarding for learners when their teachers point out and discuss student solutions that are better than their own. This shows the students that their own insights can be at least as creative and viable as the teacher's. From a social constructivist viewpoint, the potential for learning emerges from the interaction of different perspectives; having the students work in groups rather than alone allows such different perspectives to emerge. When students are confronted with competing perspectives, they learn to weigh the advantages and disadvantages of different points of view and to select the most viable from among them.

3. Truly collaborative work is an essential part of every learning experience

The potential benefits of collaborative work for the translation education classroom are multifaceted. Through collaborative work, students share and exchange ideas on what translation problems there are and how to solve them. Together, they can hone their tools for solving translation problems and together they can join the community of professional translators, having discussed the problems, the conventions and the norms. In some cases they will agree to appropriate existing norms and conventions; in other cases they will come up with new ones. Despite Newmark's claim to the contrary (1973); there is no set of definitive translation rules. There are only norms and conventions, most of them tacit, that have formed and that continue to evolve through the practice of the translating community against a background of joining this conversation, for working much as professionals do, facilitated by the continuous and systematic support of the teacher to help frame, guide and even lead the discussion and accompany the group toward full community membership.

True collaboration in the classroom does not mean having learners do translations individually in the company of peers. It means sharing responsibility for empowering the entire group as emergent professionals. The process of decision-making becomes a second primary focus of attention in the class along with the artefacts of those processes. To ensure true collaboration in the classroom, students must be mutually dependent on each other for accomplishing goals. In their professional lives, as in most human endeavours, translators will have to be able to work co-operatively with each other. Interdependence fosters and teaches responsibility, while individual accountability ensures that each student is contributing to the common goals of the group as well as acquiring the necessary social and translational skills to work professionally upon completing the programme.

4. The goal of each class will be to construct multiple and viable (rather than 'correct') solutions to problems that emerge naturally from authentic projects

The imposition of the teacher's norms (no matter how representative they may be of the norms of the professional community) on students is detrimental to the development of a strong sense of self-confidence and responsibility on the part of students. It reduces the learning task to one of blindly ingesting those norms. Through collaborative work, discussion, experimentation and the confronting of multiple perspectives, students can learn, as Toury (1992) pointed out, that "everything has its price". While being aware of societal norms, they must also understand that each specific translation situation will involve a unique combination of situational factors that will require flexibility and creativity rather than the retrieval and mechanical application of correct solutions. Not only must students be aware of societal norms, but they must also know how and when to break them when necessary (Chester-man 1997).

It is through peer work that this decision-making capability can be developed. This changes the perspective of a solution as being right or wrong to being more or less viable in a given context. The popular idea that something is always lost in translation needs to be replaced in the minds of emerging translators with the concept that translation is always a give-and-take process, something is always lost and also gained. How often do we hear that a translation is better than the original? Translators are not doomed to produce inadequate work. They can work toward the goal of being able to produce consistently viable, acceptable solutions that need not be measured against a yardstick of the ideal solution (teacher norms). This also applies to the construction of strategies. In the end, individuals apply collaboratively constructed strategies in unique ways to the myriad translation problems they encounter. The fact that we are always assimilating, adjusting our knowledge in response to influences in the environment should remind us that every translation situation is unique.

5. Rather than teaching correct answers (truth) to my students, it is my pedagogical task to scaffold learning, provide substantial support for knowledge construction early in the course or programme, and gradually relinquish control over the learning environment to the students themselves

This scaffolding process occurs both over the course of each semester and from the beginning of the programme of studies through the end. Upon entering the academic programme, students have generally just completed secondary school where they have been indoctrinated with foundational learning. They come to the classroom with certain expectations about what learning and teaching entail. For this reason, it is essential for the constructivist teacher to provide an adequately supportive environment from the beginning of the class so that students do not simply drift along in what might appear to be the anarchy of a de-centralized, constructivist classroom. Of course, students will know from other activities they engage in – interaction with family and friends, team sports, musicianship, etc. – how to work collaboratively with others. They are likely not to have experienced much collaborative work as part of their schooling, however, and they are likely to bring with them from school transmissionist expectations regarding their learning responsibilities in the university environment. In early semesters, I therefore provide adequate support at the beginning of a class by framing the situation for the students, by providing them with group-forming and collaborative working tasks, showing them that they can learn inter-dependently and yet effectively within an academic setting.

Once they have acquired adequate experience with collaborative processes in order for positive group dynamics to carry them along, I begin to withdraw control, but always making sure to provide support as needed. Early in the programme, I will often sit in on group work even when students have not requested my assistance in order to help identify zones of proximal development. Until they are familiar with constructivist working methods themselves, it may prove difficult for them to assume responsibility for their own learning. As they progress through the programme, I have found that the vast majority of students adapt readily to a collaborative learning approach and they tend to create their own group dynamics that evolve with minimal guidance but without much interference from me. The scaffolding process is highly dependent on the teacher's sensitivity to the students' willingness and ability to learn collaboratively and to the dynamics of individual groups.

6. My translator education classes are designed as socio-cognitive apprenticeship workshops, where students at the periphery of the translation community are gradually drawn into the community's discourse until they are competent, full-fledged members of the community themselves

On the basis of the educational research on situated action (Resnick 1989), the translator education situation can be seen in terms of **socio-cognitive apprenticeship**, a forum in which a guide or facilitator, who is a member of the target community, interacts with a collaborative working group to help that group move toward full membership in the community itself. This means that as the facilitator of learning, I model expert translation processes for the students and try to raise their awareness of potential translation problems, norms and conventions from the perspective of the community of professional translators. I do illustrate my own problem-solving processes for the students, but only to serve as one source of information for their own constructions of appropriate professional behaviour, strategies and techniques. By moving from group to group, providing assistance, advice and guidance, I constantly serve as a model of thinking and acting that the learners can use as one of many resources to inform their own constructive discussions in the classroom setting.

Constructivist initiation and authentic practice

In Chapters 5 and 6, case studies will demonstrate how I have adapted the conventional (teacher-centred) translation exercise class and the introduction to translation studies course to embody my constructivist pedagogical approach toward student empowerment. In my opinion, these two course types are a readily available institutional framework for the constructed acquisition of translator competence. Before moving on to the case studies, I would like to outline a constructivist interpretation of these classroom formats.

Introductory workshop in translation studies

The introductory course can serve as the institutional gateway to the community of professional translators, as well as a venue for their initial needs assessment as apprentices being introduced to the translator's craft. It is in this forum that the individual students who have come to the institution to become professional translators can meet at the boundary of the new community and begin to enter the conversation that constitutes that group. Rather than encouraging rote learning of the basic skills and knowledge that translators can be expected to possess, I use this introductory workshop as a site of collaborative research to allow students to look at the overall tasks and responsibilities of professional translators and work out for themselves through interdependent work what the sub-domains of those tasks and responsibilities are. Here, learners can be expected to begin to see for themselves the importance of literary and cultural studies, of stays abroad, of creative writing, of computer competence, etc. by considering, observing and discussing what professional translators do, and by dealing with sample translation problems in situation. My experience with this type of class over the past five years has shown that a consensus tends to emerge by the end of a one-semester introductory workshop about the abilities, skills and knowledge that a translator needs to have – a consensus that is very much in line with the profession's consensual image of the competent professional translator.

The translation project workshop

Clearly the most obvious way to situate learning in courses specifically designed to draw students into the community of professional translators is to provide them with authentic, that is real or highly realistic, translation opportunities within the institutional setting. To be able to situate learning for their students, translation teachers must be active professional translators themselves, or at least have extensive professional translation experience. As one of the constructivist teacher's main tasks is to represent the community that the translators-in-training are trying to join, he or she must actually be a member of that community in order to be able to model its ways of thinking, its behaviour and its norms. Professional translators are personally aware of the kinds of constraints actually placed on translators in the marketplace; they are able to use that knowledge to design learning situations in which the students can work within similar constraints themselves and devise viable strategies for dealing with them. Teachers who translate professionally themselves can bring to class translations they have actually done for clients and can even pass on work they themselves receive to their students – of course with the approval of the client – or they can help students seek out real translation jobs for themselves.

The teacher remains available to provide assistance, to identify students' zones of proximal development, and to help manage the classroom situation so that collaboration runs smoothly. The starting point for this type of translation exercise class would be a project – a complete, real translation task embedded in an authentic social matrix. It is not my job as a facilitator of learning to define or specify the sub-tasks that students must accomplish in order to achieve the overall outcome of a professional-quality translation and the multifaceted learning that will naturally occur during its production. Instead, I set the stage for the students themselves to identify the sub-tasks they will have to accomplish to complete the overall job. Translator competence includes being able to determine in advance whether or not one can accomplish the translation task under the actual constraints imposed on the job. Do I have adequate time to complete the job? Do I have sufficient background knowledge of the topic of the text? Do I have access to additional outside information that will be necessary to complete the job? Are there adequate feedback and support channels available, for example to experts in the field, the author of the text, or to the client, in order for me to complete the job adequately and efficiently? These are key questions that a professional translator must resolve on a daily basis. The teacher cannot simply extract rules or principles from personal experience and pass them on to students for memorization. Learners will clearly understand the constraints better and be able to work with them better if they have had to deal with them personally – and viscerally – during training. By discussing and negotiating the answers to these questions concerning a series of situated translation tasks, students will acquire a sense of what is important and how to solve the innumerable new problems that are certain to arise in the future.

By practising translation in this situated fashion, students are actively doing exactly what professional translators do: translating real texts to be used by real clients and read by real text recipients. In this way they will gradually learn the discourse of the translating community, and they will acquire significant personal and interpersonal experience of how to translate. Similarly, they will learn to work collaboratively with others, surely one of the most important skills they are likely to need after graduation. They will learn to compromise, to give and accept criticism, and they will come to understand that there are no 'right' answers, only more or less viable ones. They will acquire not only **translation** competence – but **translator** competence as well. Yet they will not be left alone to 'discover' the process for themselves. They will have the consistent support of the facilitator and the group of peers to provide fresh ideas, feedback, praise and constructive criticism. The translation project workshop as an instructional format could become a standard, yet multifaceted pedagogical framework for providing students with a guided sequence of real, professional translation experiences.

Figure 5 depicts a generic framework for a constructivist workshop-based classroom. The dotted line surrounding the classroom events suggests the permeable nature of the educational setting – the classroom is seen as a dynamic venue for authentic interaction, with students being able to draw on outside resources and interact with clients, potential readers of their translations and perhaps even the author of the original text. Similarly, external resources – whether they be hard copy, computerized or human – are readily available for incorporation into the learning process. The groups are comprised of unique students, each of whom comes to the learning situation with his or her own perspectives and background knowledge. The transmissionist teacher has been replaced by a facilitator whose job it is to promote learning by setting the stage for constructive collaborative inter-action. Not only do the members of each small group collaborate with each other to achieve common goals, but the groups themselves interact with each other as well, thus providing additional perspectives and fomenting interpersonal communication and task management skills.

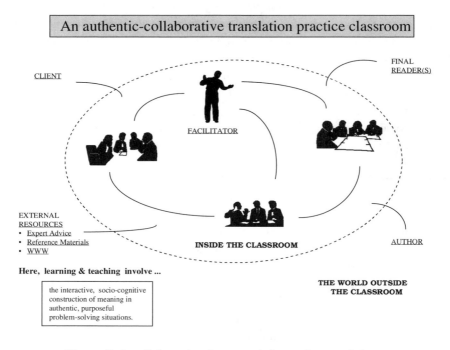

Figure 5: A collaborative framework for project workshops

Summary

A major dilemma built into foundational approaches to professional education is that the learner is expected to be an essentially passive recipient of knowledge dur-ing the programme of studies, but upon graduation must then function as an expert and a professional. What happens is that students tend to leave the institution, not as professionals or even semi-professionals, but as pseudo-translators who have studied and practised and tested their way to a degree, but who have essentially no real, first-hand experience of the pressures and constraints placed on the language professional. They may have achieved some significant mastery of some sub-domains of translator competence through ersatz activity, but they lack full membership in the community of translators, which can only come through collaboration and professional experience.

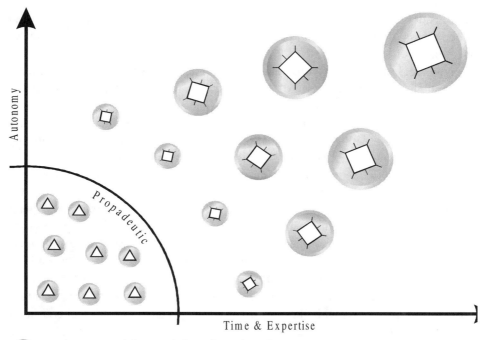

△ consciousness-raising workshops in an introductory course

▢ authentic collaborative translation projects with embedded activities

Figure 6: Progression of expertise and autonomy

Figure 6 portrays a way of looking at the progression of students on the continua of expertise and autonomy within the translator education institution. I envisage the propaedeutic, or introduction to translation studies, at the beginning of the programme of studies as a transition point between the prior learning (and acquisition) of foreign language skills and authentic scaffolded practice in the work of professional translators. It is here that consciousness-raising about the nature of the translation profession, and about the responsibilities of the professional translator, will take place.

The constructivist approach begins with the global goal of the educational process: membership in the community of professional translators, which entails having and using abilities, knowledge and skills that are characteristic of, and appropriate for, members of that group. The principles of authenticity and situated cognition suggest that all educational activities derive from and are directly related to target knowledge and skills. Learners must see the relevance of all classroom activities to their later professional work. Exercises that seem pointless or gratuitous to the students clearly cannot lead to significant learning. Nor are they likely to contribute to students' motivation. Keeping target knowledge and skills in the focus of pedagogical considerations at all times will contribute significantly to the efficiency and effectiveness of the educational programme and to a positive collaborative atmosphere in the classroom as well.

In an ideal translation exercise class, pedagogical interaction will take the form of an interactive workshop, regardless of the traditional course-type it is associated with in the curriculum. A workshop is a meeting of peers who share the goal of joining the community of language professionals, a space where they converse, negotiate and debate with each other and representatives of that community with my help as a facilitator. By learning the language of the community, by learning to think, act and work like its members, they themselves become members of the community. The workshop members work collaboratively, sharing responsibility for learning and for success with each other interdependently. But neither they nor I ever lose sight of their individual accountability. Not only do they come to know the norms and conventions of the community of translators, they also develop their own viable translation strategies; they learn how to use the tools of the trade in context, how and where to obtain information they need in order to translate, how to negotiate with authors, clients, subject matter experts, and how to work constructively and co-operatively with their peers. The principal goal for a translator education programme is to have graduates be capable of moving with professional competence and confidence within the community of professional translators upon graduation.

Surely this goal is widely shared by translation students, programme administrators and educators around the world. I am quite certain that it is only the means for achieving that goal that will be a matter of debate. In Chapter 5 and 6, I will illustrate on the basis of an introductory workshop and team translation projects respectively how I have applied the constructivist principles outlined so far.

5.   Initiation through Dialogue

> From sage on the stage to guide on the side.
>
> (King 1993:1)

In this chapter, I will present a case study of an introduction to translation studies course based on the constructivist framework presented in the first four chapters. This is a prototypical example of the course that I have offered some 20 times over the past five years. In the next chapter, we will look at an example of a project-based translation exercise class. As I have indicated elsewhere, these scenarios should not be taken as blueprints that can be applied directly by other instructors. They are intended, however, to serve as illustrations of my approach and to provide a spring-board to help other teachers develop their own alternative techniques, adapted specifically to their respective teaching environment, language combination and translation direction (into or out of the students' mother tongue). My own approach varies from group to group and evolves from semester to semester as each unique set of students and I acquire new understandings about the translation profession and the collaborative learning process. This view of knowledge as a dynamic process rather than a static set of artefacts ensures that I continue to learn along with my students and that each class is in many ways a new and unique experience for all involved.

Initiation into the professional dialogue

Until a few years ago, there were no courses offered in any language department in the translator and interpreter training school at the University of Mainz to provide students with an overview of the work of the professional translator. In 1994, the English and American Studies Department began to offer a *propaedeutic*, or Intro-duction to Translation Studies, which is now obligatory for all students studying English at the School. This means that well over half of the student body will take part in this course during their first or second semester, including students from a wide variety of foreign countries. On average, about one third of the participants in any section of this class will be non-Germans.

A major source of inspiration for this course was an article by Hönig (1988), entitled *Übersetzen lernt man nicht durch Übersetzen: Ein Plädoyer für eine Propädeutik des Übersetzens* (You don't learn how to translate by translating: A call for an introductory course in translation studies). Hönig proposed this introductory course as a forum for initiating students into translation theory applied to the translator's craft. If we put first semester students into translation exercise classes without ensuring that they have acquired a basic understanding of what translation entails, we can hardly expect them to free themselves from the word-bound type of transcoding that masquerades as translation in secondary school foreign language classes. While all students enrolled in English must attend this course at the beginning of their programme of studies, there is no common curriculum for it. Each teacher is free to design the course as he or she sees fit. I have chosen to apply a constructivist foundation to the two sections of the course I teach each semester. My personal goal for the course is to help the students move along the road toward empowerment, both as participants within the educational programme and as emerging language mediation professionals. I naturally have my own understanding (that is, knowledge) of the profession, which I share with the students over the course of the semester, but I do not try to impose that knowledge on them. In fact, I expect my own understandings of the translator's tasks to evolve as a function of the interaction that takes place within the class. In order to **scaffold** learning, I begin by providing a significant amount of structure and support for students' learning experiences, gradually withdrawing control as the semester progresses. If instructors participate in a dialogue to develop instructional policies and to plan required courses (which may not always be the case), the introduction to translation studies could be an excellent way to establish a common framework for initiating students not only to the profession, but also to a common teaching approach they will encounter throughout their program of studies.

Session 1: Setting the stage for dialogue

As I enter the room, I encounter a sea of expectant, inquisitive faces seated in rows, side by side. There is an undercurrent of animated conversation as the students get to know each other on their very first day as university students. The chatter, infused with first-day excitement, begins to die down as I move to the front of the room. It is clear that I am the one in charge and in control. Most of the students in attendance have their notebooks open to a blank page with an array of pens and pencils lined up, ready to receive wisdom from me. It would be so easy at this point to open my notebook and begin to read. My students would sit silently, obediently scribbling notes for regurgitation on the test at the end of the semester. I could easily avoid the hubbub of small-group work, the questions I cannot answer, the loss of control. But would learning occur? Fortunately for the students, Johnson & Johnson's (1991:171) memorable and scathing criticism of the conventional university lecture that they seem to await rings in my ears, "The information passes from the notes of the professor to the notes of the students without passing through the mind of either one".

While the students' attention is focused on me, I remind them of the prerequisites for the course: essentially that they be enrolled in English as a major or minor language; that they be willing to take responsibility for their own learning; and that they be prepared to work in an immersion English environment throughout the semester. I also tell them that they will be working in a collaborative manner with my assistance to jointly develop an understanding of theoretical and practical aspects of the translator's work. In order to rekindle the group's initial energy before I take the stage, I quickly move on from my introductory comments to our first team-building activity.

The students are asked to introduce themselves to someone sitting nearby whom they have not yet met, and to share with that person one piece of personal information about themselves, for example a special interest or hobby, experiences in foreign countries, or whatever they wish to communicate. Next, they have to get up individually, move to some other part of the room and introduce themselves to several other students, one at a time, again telling each new acquaintance a different bit of information about themselves. After five minutes or so of moving around the classroom, I have all the students sit down again, after which each one presents one of the other students to the rest of the class. During this time, the students share with the rest of the group information they remember about each other. In this way, each student starts to get a personal impression of each of the other members of the group. Affinities and antipathies start to surface, a factor which will be essential for effective group development as the semester progresses. This is the beginning of the formation of a community – a group of people who will be working together with common goals to acquire common as well as individual knowledge about the translator's profession. A major objective of having students share information with each other about themselves is to foster the emergence of a sense of trust emanating from community membership. As Johnson and Johnson (1991:154) have stated:

> Trust is a necessary condition for stable cooperation and effective communication. The higher the trust, the more stable the cooperation and the more effective the communication. Students will more openly express their thoughts, feelings, reactions, opinions, information and ideas, when the trust level is high. When the trust level is low, students will be evasive, dishonest, and inconsiderate in their communications.

The activities that we will be engaged in during the following weeks and that will build upon this introductory session are designed, among other things, to contribute to this sense of trust by requiring students to depend on each other for support in the mutual construction of knowledge. They will work regularly in different groups, repeatedly establishing a rapport with different combinations of students within the context of group activities.

The students entering the programme are generally so used to being treated – and treating each other – like dead bodies and talking heads in secondary school classrooms that they are often surprised and amused by our initial non-academic activity. Nevertheless, almost every one of them quickly adjusts to this way of working in which each student is considered a multifaceted individual and not just an anonymous classmate. In addition to beginning the work of community-forming, getting-to-know-you activities are a good way to emphasize the non-conventional format of the class right from the beginning and to begin changing students' initial expectations about what participation in the course will entail.

Initial attempt to identify goals

The next step is to ask each student to form a pair with one of the remaining students with whom they have not yet spoken, and to write down on a piece of paper one thing that they hope to learn in this class over the course of the semester. They do this individually, and then with their respective partner. Finally, each pair links up with another, and in groups of four, the students then share their answers with each other. We discuss the results as a whole group, with me writing down the consensual list of expectations on the blackboard.

The following list of learning expectations, which one class came up with, is typical of the initial learning expectations that emerge from this activity:

- Acquire knowledge of specific translation techniques
- Improve bilingual vocabulary (German and English)
- Learn how to use dictionaries efficiently
- Learn how to analyze texts
- Learn about the basic structure of translated texts
- Compare and contrast linguistic structures in different languages

These vague expectations seem to reflect the common lay perspective on translation processes that students generally have at the beginning of their programme of studies. They tend to see translation as a mechanical, primarily linguistic process, where social, cognitive and cultural factors play only a modest role, if any at all. In fact, as we shall see in the activities that follow, the students' latent knowledge of the complexity of translation processes is much more sophisticated than it appears at first glance, and it is by using mutual appropriation techniques that a much more extensive consensual view can be reached by the group within a surprisingly brief period of time, and without any lecturing by the instructor.

Negotiating joint goals for learning

Once the class has produced an initial joint list of its expectations for the semester, I have an initial **zone of proximal development** to work with, a virtual learning space hovering just beyond the students' current joint state of knowledge, and through which I can try to get the students to move toward a more complex and viable understanding of the translator's work. Now I ask the students to get together in pairs with someone they have not yet worked with, and to brainstorm again, this time writing down their answers to the following question: *What kinds of knowledge and skills does a professional translator need?* I ask each pair of students to write down as many distinct responses as they can agree on in pairs. This is the next stage in the development of collaborative working habits – they must negotiate with peers to reach a consensus. Each pair is then asked to get together with another pair to compare and merge their lists, again negotiating to come up with one list they can all agree on. The initial discussion is done in pairs because it provides the interacting students with the greatest degree of security. They can brainstorm freely and without embarrassment, and will be able to manage the personality dynamics better than if they were placed in larger groups from the beginning. The larger the group, the more potential there will be for some students to be dominated by others. It is important that they all have an opportunity to assert themselves in a pair situation first.

Appropriation is a key feature of the interaction that follows. At this point, the facilitator assumes the role of appropriating – interpreting and recasting – the students' ideas, listing them for the whole class to consider. As the students propose types of skills and knowledge that they believe are important for the professional translator to acquire, I write them down on the board, grouping them together using categories like social features of translator competence, computer-based skills, real world knowledge, technical knowledge, knowledge of terminology and database management, cognitive strategies, linguistic features, and cultural aspects of translation. If the group fails to mention certain types of skills and knowledge that I think are important, I offer examples of them myself, interspersed in the discussion, but I will not add them to the list unless the students agree that they are relevant and significant. Similarly, as the students at times suggest skills or knowledge types that I believe could be formulated more clearly, I will often re-formulate those ideas myself and ask the students whether they agree with my versions or if they prefer their own original ones. We usually end up negotiating these points of disagreement, but the group has the final say. This is an empowering technique that strengthens the facilitator/learner relationship in the classroom by demonstrating to the students that they are decisive actors in planning our course. The incorporation of my suggestions into their discourse is the reciprocal side of appropriation, through which students change their understandings on the basis of new evidence coming from outside sources. Such merging of new information with preconceived notions is a key feature of true learning from a constructivist perspective.

This is my way of **scaffolding** learning from the beginning, providing significant amounts of assistance when it is called for, but at the same time empowering the students by insisting that they have a voice in the development of our joint course agenda. Students also learn in this way to have confidence in and be prepared to build on their own current knowledge about what translators actually do. Regardless of the level of students' knowledge at the beginning of the course, a key element in my own agenda is to move steadily away from instructor control and toward the students' control over their own learning as the semester progresses. As quickly and smoothly as possible, I relinquish my role as "sage on the stage" to adopt one resembling more a "guide on the side".

After grouping on the board the types of skills and knowledge the students have identified as necessary for the professional translator, I present to the class my own list of topics that I had prepared in advance, not as the definitive syllabus, but to serve as a flexible tool for appropriating and focusing the disparate results of brainstorming.

This list might include the following points, although I may have to make adjustments depending on the results of our discussions up to this point:

- Overview of the translator's tasks
- Translation as a linguistic process
- Translation as a social process
- Translation as a cultural process
- Translation as a textual process
- The translator's tools

These are broad topics that I have found can serve to conveniently segment the complexity of the translation process. My initial plan, which I submit to the students for approval, is to have them work in groups of three to prepare a 90-minute workshop on each of these general topics over the course of the semester. At this point, the class is of course free to modify or even reject any of these topics and replace them with ones that they consider more relevant. Before moving on to our next task, however, we will come to a consensus on the list of topics that will be covered by the workshops.

Elaborating group research questions

Our next task is to negotiate a consensual list of research questions on the basis of the students' initial learning goals, their list of skills and knowledge that they feel professional translators need, and our jointly agreed upon list of topics. This activity will result in a mutually constructed syllabus to structure the course for the remainder of the semester.

The six topics are written on separate sheets of paper, which are then distributed throughout the room. I ask the students to get together in groups of three around a topic at random and to brainstorm to produce a list of questions for which they would like to acquire answers on this topic over the course of the semester. Their task is again to produce a common list, which will require them to negotiate and collaborate with their peers rather than work in the stark isolation of transmissionist interaction. The time allotted for this, and all of the other activities during these initial classes, will vary from group to group. I generally do not specify a time limit, but gently move the group on to the next activity when discussion begins to flag throughout the room. If one group falls silent while the others are still deep in animated discussion, I take this as an opportunity to join that particular group, to identify the reason why the discussion has become bogged down, and to provide hints and suggestions that will help those students move beyond the apparent impasse and reanimate the discussion. As the facilitator, I find that I must constantly be vigilant of such opportunities during small group work, because these are the moments when students are particularly receptive to my input. Just as lecturing is so inefficient because it treats the students as if they were all at the same point in the learning process, mentoring in these small-group discussions is extremely efficient because it can focus in on the specific learning needs of individual students.

This initial brainstorming session is followed by several others, with all of the students moving on to form new groups, each focused on a different topic sheet – where they add to, delete from and modify the questions listed there as necessary. In this way, over the course of the first 90-minute class, students will have the opportunity to work with as many different combinations of students as they feasibly can. I remind them of the importance of group dynamics and co-operation for creating a smoothly functioning group, as they will have to work in interdependent groups to prepare and run workshops later on in the semester and where they will be dependent on their fellow group members for their own success.

Group forming and switching continues until each student has participated in the syllabus construction process for each of the topics I have proposed. The final stage of this process involves reading off the list of questions to be answered for each of the topics at hand. This then is our tentative syllabus for the rest of the course; with one of the students' main objectives being to acquire knowledge related to each of the questions that the group as a whole has formulated. While I have scaffolded the construction of our syllabus myself, I make sure that the students have a clear voice at every stage of the syllabus design process. The primary goal on my personal agenda for the course will be to empower the students to identify their own goals, to ask appropriate questions and to assume responsibility for answering them collaboratively. The following list is typical of what classes come up with at this stage in our preparations:

OVERVIEW OF THE TRANSLATOR'S WORK
- What are the job prospects for graduate translators in Germany and abroad?
- Do translators translate only into their mother tongue?
- Are translators prepared during their academic programme to meet the demands of the marketplace?
- Do translators work out of as well as into their mother tongue?
- What particular constraints affect the freelance translator?
- To what extent do translators specialize in one or more technical fields?

TRANSLATION AS A TEXTUAL PROCESS
- What are the key features of textuality?

- Do professionals tend to produce a linguistically faithful rendering or an adaptation of the original?
- To what extent does the 'text type' influence the way a text is translated?
- What are some of the characteristics of different text types in German and English?
- Do professional translators actually perform text analysis during their day-to-day work? If so, how?

TRANSLATION AS A SOCIAL PROCESS

- Who are the key actors in the translation process?
- Where do the translator's loyalties lie with respect to these actors?
- What are the translator's responsibilities and options when it comes to inaccuracies and ambiguities in a text to be translated?
- What strategies can a freelance translator use to acquire and keep customers?
- How do customers understand the social roles of the participants in the translation process, and how do they understand the translator's task?

TRANSLATION AS A CULTURAL PROCESS

- In what ways do cultural differences play a role in the translator's craft?
- Does a translator have to be bicultural as well as bilingual?
- In what ways are translation rules, norms and conventions different in different cultures?
- How important is an extended stay abroad for future translators?
- In what ways do the university's cultural studies offerings enhance the translator's competence?

TRANSLATION AS A COGNITIVE PROCESS

- Is there any value for the future translator in knowing what goes on in his or her mind when translating?
- What techniques are used to investigate cognitive translation processes?
- Are there universal or culture- and language-specific translation strategies that future translators can (or must) learn?
- What distinguishes the cognitive processes of the professional translator from those of the novice?
- How does the translator's mind store language-specific knowledge?

THE TRANSLATOR'S TOOLS

- What strategies can be discerned for the effective use of different types of dictionaries?
- What other reference materials besides dictionaries are particularly valuable for translators?

- How important are computer-based tools for the professional translator of today?
- What computer-related skills do graduate translators need to have acquired by the time they leave the institution?
- Do automatic and machine-aided translation represent a threat or a useful aide to the professional translator?

As we approach the end of our first 90-minute classroom session, we have clearly made great progress expanding upon the initial list of expectations produced by the students at the beginning of the session. We have a much better differentiated list of learning goals and group research questions, and the stage is set for seeking the answers to these questions over the course of the semester. The students have already begun to understand our class in terms of a collaborative experience, with me acting as the facilitator rather than as a conventional knowledge-transmitting teacher. Over the course of this first session, they have devised their own syllabus, a syllabus that I could have prepared in advance and simply transmitted to the class. But the syllabus we have designed together reflects the prior knowledge of these particular students; it is focused on relevant research questions they have created jointly about the translator's profession; and it reflects the students' own agenda for learning. This approach to syllabus design embodies Brundage and MacKeracher's maxim, "Adults learn best when they are involved in developing learning objectives for themselves which are congruent with their current and idealized self-concept" (Brundage and MacKeracher 1980:21). A syllabus imposed by the teacher disenfranchizes the students; a syllabus they design together empowers them.

Appropriation of the instructor's teaching goals

After the syllabus has been determined, I will outline the workshop framework I have devised as the basic forum in which the students will construct knowledge about the translation profession. I explain the value I see in an interactive and collaborative workshop as an alternative to lectures and individual student presentations, and I provide some guidelines to help the students create constructivist learning experiences. These include encouraging them to integrate interactive exercises and discussions in every workshop. I also recommend that workshop organizers draw on their personal experience, invite expert visitors from the translating community to participate when appropriate, and prepare their respective workshops in a truly collaborative manner, with all of the group members pulling their own weight. I provide each group with a set of readings from the contemporary literature on translation studies, which are to serve as expert perspectives upon which they can draw in preparing their workshops. The students will work together in groups of about three to prepare a workshop on one of the topics and to run it during one class session during the latter part of the semester. Workshops are expected to last a minimum of 60 minutes each, and the groups are permitted to leave part of the time remaining in our 90-minute class period for additional discussion, which can be facilitated by the instructor if they prefer. As a rule, the workshops end up taking almost the full 90 minutes allotted to each group, and I am rarely called upon to facilitate. The final set of questions we have produced, which serves as our syllabus, is typed up and distributed to the students the next session. Within two weeks of this initial session they must decide which workshop they would like to help run. All of the reference articles are placed on reserve in the library and remain there throughout the semester.

Assessing student learning

Assessment procedures and principles are also discussed at the conclusion of this first session. In Chapter 8, I will make a case for a radical reassessment of conventional marking practices. Nevertheless, the university requires me to provide each student with a mark according to the standard scale of 1.0-5.0, with 1.0 being the highest possible mark and 4.0 being the lowest passing mark. The placing of sole responsibility for assessment upon the teacher in a conventional classroom ensures that authority, power and control remain with the instructor, the sole arbiter of the quality and success of students' work. With the overriding goal of empowerment in mind, in this introductory course (as well as in all other courses I teach), I instead share responsibility for the assessment of learning with the students themselves.

I see the course as an organic unit; it needs to come full circle, ending with the questions raised at the beginning of the course. The assessment of learning, then, will logically focus on the research questions that comprise our joint syllabus. To the extent that the students and the facilitator feel they have made significant progress toward answering those questions over the course of the semester, we will all have been successful teachers and learners.

Following each group workshop, an assessment sheet like the one in Figure 7 below will be distributed to each of the students in the class, including those who have just run the workshop.

The final mark for the workshop comprises three equally weighted parts: the self-evaluation of the workshop leaders, the evaluation by the rest of the class members who have participated in the workshop, and my own evaluation as the group facilitator and representative of the translation profession. In each course I have assessed in this way, there has been a remarkably high level of agreement among the three components. One of the immediate benefits of having students assesses themselves and each other is that it shifts the targeted audience of workshops away from the teacher and toward the other students in the class. Instead of trying to produce discourse that will match the comprehension level of the teacher, workshop leaders who are dependent on the self-perceived learning success of the other students in the class tend to scaffold their discourse; they remain one step ahead of the rest of the group as they progress through their workshop, but do not talk over their own heads to impress the instructor.

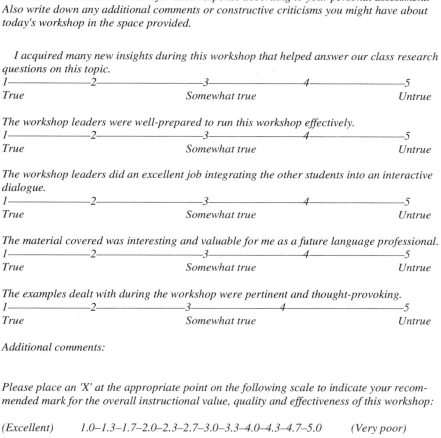

Evaluation Sheet

Date:
Workshop title:

As you know, you will be participating in the evaluation of the quality, effectiveness and instructional value of each of the workshops held in our class this semester. Please read the questions listed below and select the mark for each response according to your personal assessment. Also write down any additional comments or constructive criticisms you might have about today's workshop in the space provided.

I acquired many new insights during this workshop that helped answer our class research questions on this topic.
1————————2—————————————3——————————4————————5
True   Somewhat true   Untrue

The workshop leaders were well-prepared to run this workshop effectively.
1————————2—————————————3——————————4————————5
True   Somewhat true   Untrue

The workshop leaders did an excellent job integrating the other students into an interactive dialogue.
1————————2—————————————3——————————4————————5
True   Somewhat true   Untrue

The material covered was interesting and valuable for me as a future language professional.
1————————2—————————————3——————————4————————5
True   Somewhat true   Untrue

The examples dealt with during the workshop were pertinent and thought-provoking.
1————————2—————————————3——————————4————————5
True   Somewhat true   Untrue

Additional comments:

Please place an 'X' at the appropriate point on the following scale to indicate your recommended mark for the overall instructional value, quality and effectiveness of this workshop:

(Excellent)   1.0–1.3–1.7–2.0–2.3–2.7–3.0–3.3–4.0–4.3–4.7–5.0   (Very poor)

Figure 7: Sample Assessment sheet for student workshops

At this point, the first session of the semester comes to a close. The students can be expected to leave the classroom having a fairly clear concept of our working approach and their own, mutually-designed agenda for this initial step toward joining the community of professional translators. Although one or two students may be put off by this unorthodox approach, those who return to the second session are almost always highly committed to the class, to their workshop group and to our working method.

Session 2 – Initial model workshop

During this second session of the semester, I run the first of two introductory work-shops myself in order to model the workshop management process for the students. My primary goal is to illustrate, through cognitive apprenticeship, some of the in-structional and interactional behaviour that can help turn a workshop into a much more effective learning experience than any lecture or mere presentation could be. Another goal is to raise some of the basic theoretical issues that translation studies have dealt with, issues that I hope will be taken up further in the students' own workshops. One topic that I have chosen a number of times for this introductory workshop is the question: *Where does meaning reside?* The vague term 'meaning' invariably arises several times during the initial brainstorming session in each group, and thus justifies taking up the question of the significance of 'meaning' for the translator. We look for a consensual, albeit tentative, understanding of 'meaning' over the course of this workshop. My specific teaching goals are for the students: (1) to realize the importance of focusing on texts in situation rather than on words in isolation; (2) to be aware of different ways of looking at 'meaning' from the transla-tor's perspective, and (3) to reconsider and revise the notion carried over from foreign language instruction in school that sees meaning essentially as a fixed property of individual words. The texts I choose for this activity are usually tourist texts or advertisements in which visual elements also play a role, so that we can also focus on non-verbal factors involved in meaning-making. In order to get students to see words against the backdrop of textual and situational context, I take an atomistic view for this first activity (in fact the opposite of what one might expect in a constructivist classroom!), asking them to choose the smallest level of meaning that translators normally work with. While the concept of the phoneme or morpheme may come up, we usually focus first on individual words, moving up to the collocational, sentential, and supra-sentential levels. The first task, then, is for stu-dents to take some nouns and verbs from the text and see if we can agree as a group on what they 'mean'. They work in pairs or small groups, and have access to mono- and bilingual dictionaries. For one of the sample texts I have used for this activity, some of the words I have the students define might include:

> *prevail   shady   the blues   shadowy   drenched   laden*

I ask them to write down whatever constitutes the meanings of these words for them. Their associations have included the following:

> *prevail*: win an argument or battle
> *shady*: an unsavoury character, a spot protected from the heat of the sun
> *the blues*: New Orleans, melancholy music, liquor
> *shadowy*: a dark alley, fear, a place where shadows abound

drenched: soaking wet
laden: loaded, weighted down with something to be transported

The students naturally have a variety of associations for each of these words but I find that they are almost always compatible with my intuitions as a native speaker of English. What is important is that the students as a group always come up with a variety of 'potential' meanings for any word I choose, which leads to a discussion of the polysemous nature of words taken out of context. Content words, we will conclude, tend to be polysemous, often conjure up idiosyncratic associations in different individuals, and must be dependent on the environment in which they appear if readers or listeners are to ascribe a relatively unambiguous 'meaning' to them.

We then move up to the collocational level of meaning. I add a word or two from the co-text of my original text to the words I already have on the board and ask the students in what ways the juxtaposition of the words affects the meanings of the individual words that we had discussed before:

blue-and-white houses prevail	*shadowy peace*	*Portuguese blues*	*sun-drenched squares*	*flower-laden windows*

Students begin to think at this point about the influence of co-text on individual words, and this allows them to begin to break away from the naive view that translators translate words in isolation and that lexical meanings are inextricably bound up within individual words regardless of the context in which they appear. This will contribute to the development of a healthy attitude towards dictionary use as well, as dictionaries by nature contain only generic collocations, if any at all. Except by mere chance or the fluke of high frequency, they will not even contain fragments of the co-texts that translators are actually faced with, and they can therefore often only serve as a starting point for the resolution of lexical translation problems. While this may seem simplistic and obvious to the professional translator or translation teacher, I have found through my experience teaching this course to approximately 400 students over the past five years that these realizations generally come as a revelation to them.

We then move up to the sentence level of the text. I give the students a number of individual, disconnected sentences from the text and ask them in what ways the sentences have meaning that the collocations and the individual words do not. At this point, syntactic structure becomes apparent as a factor in meaning-making. By taking any given sentence and re-situating it in a potential context in which it might occur, I can get the students to begin thinking about speech acts and how the 'meaning' of a given sentence can vary depending on who says or writes it, to or for whom, and in what specific social context. At this juncture, I can mention the concepts of 'scenes' and 'frames', suggesting Fillmore's terms as another way of looking at different types of 'meaning'.

Discussing the concept of a syntactic *frame* which helps language users structure the meaning they want to make, and *scenes*, which suggests a movie-like, culture- and experience-based memory for concepts we associate with words, leads us to the highest level of situational meaning within a text, where we focus on it as a coherent and cohesive whole. I distribute the text as a colour photocopy, where the colour blue adorning the houses is particularly striking. The text reads as follows:

Portuguese Blues

The blues that adorn the white houses of Óbidos, 50 miles from Lisbon, are typical examples of local colour. It's a feature beautiful enough to have been the inspiration behind a few songs and not all of them sad. But these blues are only one example of the area's inspirational beauty. Flower-laden windows, narrow cobbled streets, sun-drenched squares and a medieval castle, now a magnificent 'Pousada', add colour, too. In other regions, such as Alentejo, blue-and-white houses prevail in contrast to the wheat-covered plains, the shadowy peace of the Holm oak trees and the cool olive groves. With all this local colour, it would be easy for us to go on singing the praises of Portugal. After a visit, you'll be tempted to write a few verses of your own.

The students read through the text individually so that they can see how the 'meanings' they had discerned for individual words, collocations and sentences would be influenced by the text as a holistic unit. It is also appropriate here to go beyond the individual text level and talk about intertextuality and how that individual text reflects cultural norms for a particular text type.

By this time, the students have definitely begun to appropriate the multiple perspectives on meaning that have emerged during our discussions and to revise their original assumptions about where meaning resides. My interventions throughout the discussion often take the form of questions or assimilations, where I interpret and rephrase comments that students have made. By hearing me constantly ask new questions rather than provide answers, the students quickly adapt to the role of knowledge constructors who are seeking their own answers. Interaction is lively, with students drawing on their own experience and volunteering ideas that other students respond to in turn. It is a good idea at the end of the session to come back to the original question of 'where does meaning reside?' and perhaps to have students in pairs try to answer the question now in no more than three sentences. The answers will of course be different from each other; if I had wanted them to come up with the same answers – my answers – I would have delivered a lecture to them. Throughout the session, I have been working toward the elicitation of **multiple perspectives** on the question, rather than a uniform set of answers.

The discussion process in these sample workshops always focuses on what the students have to say rather than on what I would like them to know, although there is no denying that the latter helps me to scaffold students' learning. I start off with a provocative question to get the discussion started; students run with that question in various directions, and I contribute where I deem it helpful to guide the discussion toward closure, consensus and group learning milestones. The direction the students take need not be that which I originally envisaged, and in fact the discussion often takes a turn for which I am not completely prepared. It is this uncertainty factor which keeps the teaching process from turning into boring, repetitive routine. In fact, I am certain that in every session where I have used this reciprocal appropriation technique, students have contributed knowledge from their own experience that has provided me with a perspective I did not have before. A true dialogue in the classroom also ensures that the students will learn two of the most important lessons of all – that they have valuable contributions to make toward helping others learn, and that they must actively seek knowledge if they expect to acquire it. My main tasks as group facilitator include seizing upon students' insightful contributions during our discussions and appropriating them from and for the students by reformulating them, drawing them into our emerging classroom discourse and thereby contributing to a more fruitful discussion than could possibly have emerged in the form of a lecture on the basis of my own personal experience and knowledge.

The knowledge that we have created during this initial sample workshop can, of course, do no more than scratch the surface. Many of the ideas we have developed can serve as a starting point, for example, for the workshop that will be held on 'translation as a textual process'. At no point in the course will I assume that the learning of a particular concept or skill is complete. There will always be room for looking at concepts already presented from **multiple perspectives**, from different angles and in different contexts. I want the students to see learning as an ongoing, cyclical, and in fact, never-ending process of interaction and appropriation.

Session 3 – Part 1: Second model workshop

During this session, I run a second sample workshop, this time actually involving some translation work, to provide students with another example of an alternative workshop format that may give them additional ideas for running their own workshops. One of the texts I have used for this second workshop is the following tourist item, a brief text that was part of one of my first translation commissions when I began working as a freelance translator in Germany:

Liebeserklärung an ein Stückchen Paradies

Dürkheim – nur Fremde setzen dem Namen 'Bad' voraus – läßt nicht nur die Herzen der Pfälzer ein wenig höher schlagen. Mag es daran liegen, daß viele mit dieser zauberhaften Landschaft vielleicht ihre Vorstellung von einem kleinen Flecken im Paradies verbinden. Fast südlich ist das Klima, das schon im März Mandelblüten in ungeahnter Fülle beschert. Bereits im April öffnen die Magnolienblüten ihre Kelche. Und draußen überwintern die Feigenbäume, deren Früchte selbst Dürkheims Feinschmeckerköche zu immer neuen Ideen inspirieren. Kaum ein Fleckchen Natur in deutschen Landen ist mit solch einer Vielfalt ausgestattet wie gerade die Pfalz. Spargel und Kiwi gedeihen hier in trautem Einklang mit den verschiedenen Traubensorten, die an Millionen Rebstöcken reifen und Dürkheims Wein weit über die Grenzen der Pfalz hinaus bekannt werden ließen.

The text comes from a tourist brochure on the Rhineland-Palatinate, the federal state in southern Germany where the Germersheim campus of the University of Mainz is located. I have the students translate the text in pairs and underline problems that they come across while translating, classifying them according to the following categories: linguistic, cultural, textual, social or other. This advance organizer, which is based on the one used during the final segment of the initial syllabus design session, helps students to relate the problems at hand to previous learning and also to prepare them for learning more about these topics in the upcoming student workshops.

I then get several pairs to volunteer to read off their translations, asking specifically for versions that they think are very different from each other. The students are encouraged to tell the group which version they prefer and why. Thus, rather than transmit to them rules and norms that I may have appropriated for myself through my translation work, I make the students initiate their own learning processes by identifying what they already know about good translation.

It is essential to remember that although students may arrive at the university as uninitiated translators, they nonetheless have a great deal of experience behind them as text users. While we may be able to use the institutional setting to help them refine and expand on their prior knowledge, we must acknowledge that they do not come to us as blank slates. Students' prior knowledge is a gold mine that we can help them tap. Having them identify what they already know, and ask questions about what they do not yet know well, are key steps in facilitating learning.

The students tend to agree intuitively that the more adequate translations are the ones that are not only accurate with respect to detail but that are also stylistically best adapted to the textual and linguistic norms of the recipient culture. There are a number of potential problems in the text, however, which may not be apparent to the majority of students. Most of the problems they identify, for example, are on the word level, such as "how do you say *Kelch,* or *Mandelblüten* in English?". However, a few students usually do identify some problems at the cultural or social level. Someone might notice that the German text contains incomplete sentences, a feature much less common in comparable English texts. And someone else might wonder about whether a phrase like "a little piece of paradise" is idiomatic in English. We discuss the problems that students identify in each other's translations, and then if appropriate I focus on additional problems that I have found. For example, usually no one sees the cultural problems one might have with the sentence: "Dürkheim – nur Fremde setzen dem Namen Bad voraus". At this point in our discussion, there may be a significant zone of proximal development that I can work with to move students a major step further in their understanding of translation processes and potential problems.

The students' first versions look something like: "Only *strangers* or *foreigners* put the word *Bad* in front of the name". First I ask why they think the author has made this statement in the first place. Is the intention to actually inform the reader of what the people of Bad Dürkheim call their town? If so, why is that relevant in the original text, and what role should it play in the translated text? And what about the connotations of the words *Fremde* and *strangers* in these parallel contexts? I ask the students to think about whom the original text was written for and for whom they are translating it. They usually come up with "German tourists who intend to visit Bad Dürkheim", and "Foreign tourists who intend to visit Bad Dürkheim", respectively. Then the question arises as to what *Bad* means to the German reader as opposed to the English-speaking reader.

At this point, we will discuss our (invariably different) interpretations of the author's intent. To me, for example, it seems that the author wants to portray Bad Dürkheim as a friendly little town where everyone, even tourists, can feel at home. But when the German thinks of towns she knows that have *Bad* attached to the proper name, she will know that they are towns built around a natural health spa, that there are lots of affluent guests wandering about, that the mood is sedate and muted, and that the locals, inundated with outsiders, may be distant and stand-offish. So the author tells the reader, who presumably wants to visit the town for other than health reasons, that the locals call their town just plain *Dürkheim*, leaving aside the stuffy independent morpheme *Bad*. Of course, I present this as nothing more than my personal interpretation, and I try to encourage the students to come up with their own, so that we can see that translation must involve an interpretation of the original text and the author's intention – that there can be no one right answer.

Another point that may arise is whether we can expect the foreign visitor to know what *Bad* refers to in German. And even if she reads in a tour guide that it refers to a spa town, will that visitor feel the flavour of the term and imagine the town as potentially cold and distant, needing to be warmed up by the author's comment about leaving off the *Bad*? Then we might discuss possible translations of the

German word *Fremde* in the first line. Most, if not all, of the students' original versions have used either the term *foreigner* or *stranger* to express *Fremde*. This takes us back to my first model workshop where we discussed the polysemous nature of lexical items out of context. While bilingual dictionaries will provide both terms as 'equivalents' of *Fremde*, how can we determine which is appropriate in this context? How far up the 'meaning' scale do we need to move before we find adequate clues to help us make a decision here? In fact, we can see that either *stranger* or *foreigner* collocates perfectly with the other words in the sentence, which is syntactically well formed. In my interpretation, we have to move up to the level of the probable intention of the text as a whole before we can make a decision. I ask the students what associations are invoked when they hear the word *stranger*? Their associations are generally quite negative. Often someone will conjure up the image of the dusty desperado sauntering up to the counter of a saloon in the Wild West when a local cowboy says suspiciously, "You're a stranger in these parts, aren't ya?". On the other hand, why would the author be speaking of 'foreigners' in the original text? Is it not difficult to imagine why only foreigners would put *Bad* in front of *Dürkheim*? With this kind of priming of the pump, someone is likely to come up with the term *outsiders* for *Fremde*. The use of this term allows visitors to eventually think of themselves as 'insiders', as friends of Dürkheim. They are already being let into a little secret about the language that marks Bad Dürkheim's locals. Then another student might ask if it makes any sense to include this bracketed clause at all unless we add a brief explanation of what *Bad* refers to in German. Yet another might say she would have to contact the author to find out why the statement is in the original, or the client to find out whether or not it needs to be expressed in the translation. There need not, and probably cannot be, a definitive solution. I have interpreted the text in my own idiosyncratic way, creating knowledge for myself to help me make the most viable solution, that is, the one that I feel is most adequate in this situation. This does not make it the only, or the right solution. And this is the point to which I wanted to bring the students with this activity; not to teach them tricks and techniques for coming up with the correct solution, but to ask enough questions and draw on enough information to come up with a viable solution. I also wanted them to become aware, on the basis of their initial failure to consider cultural implications of language, that situational factors really do play a major role in the translator's decision-making processes.

Session 3 – Part 2: Selecting workshop groups

Having experienced my two sample workshops, the students are now ready to begin working collaboratively on their own workshop preparation. They have had two weeks to browse through the articles I have placed on the reserve shelf in the library for them. Now, I instruct the students to get into groups of three to begin work on the topic that they are interested in presenting in a workshop. There can be no more than three students per group, and they will have to decide for themselves which alternative group to move to if the topic they were most interested in already has three workshop leaders. Once the groups have formed, they review the questions that have been passed down to them in the form of our jointly designed syllabus. Having brought the articles to the classroom from the library for this session, I distribute them to the respective groups, which are given adequate time to browse through them again, so that each group member can select one that she will be responsible for. By placing full responsibility on each individual for comprehending, interactively interpreting and then communicating to the other students the ideas in the various articles they read, I pave the way for the students to work actively toward deep comprehension of the academic literature dealing with their topics. During these early sessions, I move constantly from group to group contributing my understandings to each group's emerging consensus about the meanings, value and implications of each of the articles read. Many students and even whole groups seek me out during my office hours to pursue discussions started in class, and students regularly report that they meet often outside of class to continue developing and sharing their ideas. An essential goal of this session's activities is to begin establishing what Johnson and Johnson (1991) have called 'positive interdependence'. As the name implies, this is an induced state of constructive mutual interaction among the group members. Johnson and Johnson have identified three types of positive interdependence, all of which have been incorporated into my approach to this class:

- *Goal interdependence*
- *Resource interdependence*
- *Role interdependence*

Goal interdependence exists when the students in a group share common goals and are dependent on the success of the other group members for their own success. The students in a group share the goal of leading a joint workshop, rather than three separate presentations, and they will all receive the same mark for their workshop. Resource interdependence refers to a situation where no one student can succeed at the task at hand without drawing on the resources of each of the other group members. For these workshops, each student within the group is assigned the task of reading and assimilating one text on the workshop topic selected by the instructor and then presenting it to the other members of the workshop group. The group as a whole is responsible for having a grasp of the concepts presented in all of the articles, and they are thus all motivated to work together to explain and understand the concepts from the various articles. Role interdependence reflects the fact that each member of the group has certain roles to manage that complement the roles of the other students in the group. In-class observations of activities in which roles were assigned according to the Johnson & Johnson scheme have shown that students tend to find these assignments too restricting. In fact, there is a natural tendency for roles to be adopted intuitively by students in a well-balanced group (Graceffo 1996) and it may not be necessary to do more than arouse students' awareness of such roles. Role allocation will occur in any event as a natural part of the workshop preparation and running process, so role interdependence will occur spontaneously. Of course, the instructor can step in where personality conflicts inhibit the balanced allocation of roles within the group. (This topic will be dealt with in more detail in Chapter 6, when we deal with collaborative translation exercise classes).

For Session Four, to be held the following week, each student from the group presenting the workshop will be expected to outline the main points of the article she has chosen so that the other group members can understand and react to them, and assimilate the concepts presented in them. The pedagogical objectives here are manifold. First of all, as each student in the group has read a different article representing a unique perspective on the workshop topic, numerous opportunities will arise naturally for comparing and contrasting the experts' and the students' multiple points of view. Second, the students will be working in a small group of peers to try to understand the different author's points of view. Peers can often help each other comprehend a difficult text better than a teacher can. And as considerable research has demonstrated, tutoring or peer teaching is one of the best ways for the tutor herself to learn. Each group will also be exposed to ideas espoused by prominent figures in the field of translation studies. Each small group of students will attempt to distil the essence of those three articles, compare and contrast them and present their consensual view of these disparate viewpoints to the other students with the help of examples activities.

By participating in such collaborative learning activities early in their programme of studies, they will learn the value of doing so later on when they will have to prepare seminar papers or work in teams to produce translations. This will help them learn a key principle that will make their professional lives easier and their work more competent: translators need not work in social isolation; they can and must know how to communicate and negotiate meanings with supervisors, clients, co-translators working on joint projects, authors and subject-matter experts.

Sessions 4 through 6: In-class workshop preparation

During session 4, when the students begin presenting the ideas they have gleaned from their articles to their fellow group members, it will quickly become apparent that the authors of the articles themselves – recognized experts in the field of translation studies – in fact rarely seem to completely agree on much of anything. They do not have *the* correct answers to the students' research questions any more than the teacher does. Granted, they are perhaps better informed by having participated more in the dialogue of the expert community. But now the students themselves are to be drawn into this dialogue with the experts and their peers at the same time. The following is an example of the kind of discussion that is typical of these 'text presentation' sessions. (The original discourse was in German and the translation is my own):

> **Presenter (Student A)**: The author of the text says that he would prefer an approach that is less academic. Then he starts explaining hermeneutics. That's a concept from philosophy that has to do with text comprehension. The idea is that people can only understand a text to the extent that they themselves can associate something with that text. That is, depending on your situation, what you already know, and what associations you might make with the text, you will understand the text in a particular way. Then he goes on to say that you have to understand a text when you try to translate it, and if you don't understand it, you can only translate words, and that is what the author doesn't think translators should do.
> **Student B:** Of course then the sense will be changed.
> **Student A:** But you'll do that anyway.
> **Student B:** Me personally? *[laughs]*
> **Student C:** You as a translator.
> **Presenter:** Oh, yes ... and then he lists in some detail the effects of the hermeneutic principle.

The presenter uses her own words to present the concept of 'hermeneutic translation' to her group mates. She assimilates the author's concepts, rephrases them in her own words, and through conversation works interactively with the group to understand them and weave them into their own understandings of translation theory and practice.

The following excerpt from another text presentation that deals with the pros and cons of literal vs. communicative translation illustrates a mutual construction process where the presenter herself is unsure of the author's intention. The other group members show through their feedback that they have construed an understanding similar to hers by listening to her presentation:

> **Presenter:** ... and then he says something that I didn't really understand (quoting from the text): *"The text they are required to produce must be functional. Both [texts] must seem natural, so natural in fact that translations are indistinguishable from originals"*. So I think ... I don't know if I've understood this right, but I think that they have to be as natural and functional as the original ... that is, they have to sound natural and fulfil the same function ...
> **Student B:** And not sound like a translation.
> **Presenter:** Yes, exactly.
> **Student C:** They still have to sound like an original.
> **Presenter:** Yes, well, that's how I understood it.

At another point in this text presentation, the conflicting viewpoints of the authors as assimilated by the different group members result in the active making of new meaning on the part of the group:

> **Student B**: But when a text is technical in some way, I mean when there are sizes and measures and so on in it, then even though it's not identical for every translator, it's almost the same. But general language texts are interpreted differently by each translator, and are therefore translated differently by them as well.
>
> **Presenter:** Yes, but you can also translate instruction sheets in different ways...
>
> **Student C**: That's right.
>
> **Presenter**: ... depending on whether you are translating it for specialists or for someone who wants to put some IKEA shelves together ...
>
> **Student C:** Exactly.
>
> **Presenter**: ... and doesn't even know how to turn a screw.
>
> **Student B:** That may be true, but let's say you have three translators translating an instruction sheet for specialists, then they can't translate it any way they want; they have to write down what's there.
>
> **Student C:** That's why it always depends on who the client is.

Here the students are clearly constructing valuable knowledge through their conversation with each other. Using published journal articles as a springboard and their own world knowledge as examples, here they are discussing and coming to valuable understandings of the translator's responsibilities and options. Herein lies the key value of small-group work. The students take raw materials and create knowledge that **belongs to them**. The teacher/facilitator may guide them to readings that will spark their conversation, may help them comprehend jargon, and may contribute his or her own insights to enrich the multiple perspectives they need to understand the translator's work – but the students undertake the active creation of knowledge for themselves.

Working in this manner in a small group is much less threatening than discussing one's opinions in front of the whole class. There is little anxiety; students feel free to express what they do not understand and are not afraid of criticism. My function during the first workshop preparation session is to move from group to group, providing guidance, helping students over difficult spots in the articles, and explaining terminology. It is at this point that each individual group must begin to form a close-knit, collaborative team that can work efficiently together. It is also my responsibility now to break up groups that are not working well together, suggesting that students reassign themselves to different groups in which they can work more effectively. It must be clear to the students by the end of this session that they alone will be responsible for scaffolding learning for the other students, and for introducing them to the material and for guiding the construction of knowledge in the group to help answer the research questions we identified during our first session.

Sessions 7 through 15: Student-run workshops

The scaffolding process is now complete. As the 'guide on the side', I have facilitated the formation of a community and of efficient, collaborative working groups; helped them identify valuable and attainable goals for the course; provided them with a comprehensive set of readings to help start their discussions; and assisted them in the preparation of their workshops. From the first session of the semester until the sixth session, I have been modifying my participation, moving from a prominent teaching and guiding role on the first day of class to this point when the first student-led workshop begins, where I can pass control of teaching on to the students themselves. I will of course remain available to assist and facilitate right through the final session, but by Session 8, the students have taken the floor. They have assumed a significant share of responsibility for teaching, learning and assessment.

At this point in the semester, the first workshop is held; the small groups that have been learning and preparing together for weeks now assume the role of (hopefully constructivist) teachers. The workshop leaders are already set up when the rest of us arrive, and they immediately take complete charge of running the workshop. I sit with the rest of the students and participate with them as a peer in all of the workshop activities. The groups almost universally produce interesting and lively workshops, revealing a solid understanding of essential concepts related to their topic. They have interpreted the assigned texts, organized the sub-topics they wish to present, devised interactive activities and prepared a selection of examples upon which to focus the discussion. Rarely does anyone read from a script or try to lecture to the rest of the class. The students have clearly appropriated a constructivist stance toward learning and teaching.

The activities that take place in the workshops are limited only by the students' imagination. They invariably choose texts from a wide variety of sources to use as examples and they devise their own exercises and activities to illustrate the points they want to make. They may have us do brief translations for different readerships, or have us simulate a translator's social interaction, with roles assigned for the client, subject matter experts, readers of the original language, readers of the target language, as well as a team of translators. Some of the most popular workshops are those where an expert is brought in from the community, for example a translator or other language professional working in a company, a translation agency or as a freelancer. The workshop leaders often help the group prepare questions for the experts in order to initiate a dialogue with them. These activities are a self-evident extension of the social constructivist idea that learners are linguistically and socially joining a professional community. By coming into the classroom and sharing their experiences with these students, the experts have a chance to share their real-world, non-ivory tower perspectives that can significantly enrich the viewpoints held and expressed by university instructors. While preparing their workshops, the students will come up with a variety of activities that they will discuss within their small group and with me as I move from group to group assisting them in their work. Having taught this course many times in the past, I can provide the workshop members with feedback on the success of similar activities I have experienced in previous workshops. This allows me to help guide them in their design of useful and effective techniques. Of course, a group may decide to ignore my advice and attempt an activity that I do not believe will work. They must, however, have the freedom to do so. Once I have provided the initial facilitating constraints on the workshops during the first sessions of the course, and have begun to move off the stage and into a guiding role at the periphery of student interaction, I can only provide advice which they may consider and either accept or reject. This is part of the necessary process of transferring responsibility for learning to the learners themselves.

Session 16: Final assessment

The overall assessment of learning in this class can take many forms, focused either on the individual or the group and depending, at least to some extent, on institutional constraints. I feel that it is important, in order to be consistent with the constructivist and collaborative values embodied in my course, to include a group assessment, during which the students can demonstrate (particularly to themselves) that they have started to acquire the essential skills of working effectively as members of a professional team. As part of the final assessment, I often go back to a text that I have used in one of my introductory workshops (for example the text on Bad Dürkheim) and give each student (or small group of students) a translation brief, asking them to produce an annotated, publishable translation of the text into English. The notes should explain decisions they have made, which I encourage them to categorize according to our initial scheme: social, cognitive, cultural, linguistic or textual.

In addition, short answer questions covering the content of the individual workshops can be devised in an empowering manner by having each workshop group submit a number of questions that the other students should be able to answer after participating in that workshop. During this final assessment session, the students can then choose to answer, for example, three out of five questions on each topic. Having the students contribute the questions for the test emphasizes their responsibility for their own learning and reminds them that the teacher considers them to be competent learners, sharing teaching and evaluating roles that are conventionally attributed solely to teachers. I often have a colleague simulate the role of the client and mark the translations on the basis of the translation evaluation system outlined in Chapter 7. Each workshop group can be assigned responsibility for assessing the quality of the answers to questions they have submitted on their own workshop. The evaluations of these final activities can then be combined with the workshop marks to come up with a final global assessment for each student's learning success.

We have now come full circle, returning to the students' initial questions about what translators need to know. I am convinced that most students leave this course with a much better understanding of the work of the professional translator than they had when it began. I know that they have greater confidence in their own learning abilities, that they have learned to work collaboratively, and that they are very willing to assume responsibility for their own learning. They also know how to proceed in their translation-related endeavours with a better foundation than they would have acquired through learning-by-doing alone, and have been exposed to theory that they themselves have rendered accessible and applicable.

Translation studies seminars

Over the past ten years, I have applied these constructivist principles to 20 under-graduate and graduate seminars on various topics of applied linguistics, foreign language teaching and translation studies. Many of the students who attend these seminars have not attended an introduction to translation studies taught in a constructivist manner or any of my project-based translation exercise classes, and I therefore find that it is just as important to proceed slowly through all of the steps toward empowerment that I use in the introductory course. This reduces the chances of alienating the more advanced students who have already sat through hundreds of hours of transmissionist instruction at the university. In translation studies pro-grammes where constructivist instruction is the exception rather than the norm, more advanced students who are already very familiar with a conventional positivist ap-proach can be very reluctant to change their attitudes toward learning. (This is also the case with teachers. Those who have been teaching for a decade or more in a conventional manner are less likely to reconsider their teaching approach than those who are just beginning their teaching career.) If given a choice of which ap-proach to adopt at the beginning of a course, I find that many students would prefer to be subjected to a teacher-dominated transmissionist method rather than try some-thing different.

The only way that I have been able to successfully implement my constructivist approach in an institution steeped in positivist traditions has been to take a strong stance in favour of the approach, develop a strong theoretical framework support-ing it, demonstrate to students, colleagues and supervisors that it can work, and apply it steadfastly to every class I teach. As I have indicated elsewhere in this book, a selection of individual activities thrown into a conventional classroom can-not produce significant change; they will not contribute toward the development of a culture of innovation. Teachers will have to work collaboratively to outline a

constructivist approach, design and procedures, and apply them consistently if they
are to have a chance of success.

Conclusion

The interpretation of constructivism and its application to syllabus design and
pedagogical techniques that have been illustrated here are naturally my own constructions, the products of my own experience and my own teaching environment,
which no other teacher could (or would want to) replicate exactly. It is for this
reason that I have tried to give the reader a glimpse into a prototypical classroom
rather than provide a detailed list of appropriate activities. No such list could do
justice to the myriad teaching situations that are as numerous as translation instructors. Other constructivist-minded instructors can take this approach as but one model
of one teacher's perspective, interpretation and application of constructivist thought
to the translator education profession. It will be up to them to begin searching for
ways to develop their own approach, designs and procedures with their colleagues
and students. Multiple perspectives are as vital for innovative teachers as they are
for learners.

6. Authentic Experience and Learning in a Translation Exercise Class

> Truth that has been personally appropriated and assimilated in experience cannot be directly communicated to another ... As a consequence ... I realise that I have lost interest in being a teacher ... I realise I am only interested in being a learner.
>
> (Carl Rogers 1967:276)

Introduction

In this chapter, I will discuss a case study involving a course type that is widely used in translator education curricula, ostensibly as a forum for involving students in the 'practice' of translation: the translation exercise class. The class portrayed here was the first one I offered that was consistently organized around constructivist principles. It represents the first stage in the participatory action research project I initiated at our institution that was designed to develop practical applications of my emerging constructivist approach toward the empowerment of our translation students. As I will discuss in more detail in the concluding chapter, action research is a multifaceted approach to seeking answers to local problems, and one that I feel can be particularly valuable for perpetuating innovation in the often unreflective practice of translator education. The participatory form of action research, in which teachers typically function as researchers in their own classrooms, is widely used by educators who are interested in investigating their own teaching practice with a view toward improving it. Ideally, they will share their findings with fellow teachers, working collaboratively to effect change on a larger scale within their respective teaching/learning environments. In keeping with this perspective, I am reporting here on my own fledgling attempts to find solutions to the pedagogical problems I had encountered in conventional classroom instruction, which I perceived as emanating from the dominant positivist paradigm that underpins educational practice.

One common and particularly apt depiction of the action research process is that of a spiral or a perpetual cycle comprising the stages of planning, action and observation, and reflection (McTaggart 1991). In keeping with this viewpoint, I will first describe briefly the curricular setting for the class in question, as well as how it was organized. I will then outline the findings of my observations of the class in progress, and will conclude with a discussion of the implications of those findings for the classes I went on to offer the following semester, and thus for the next stage in the development of my personal constructivist method.

Planning and implementing the case study class

Objectives of the study

The goal of my project was to implement an initial, tentative pedagogical design for an alternative, empowering translation exercise class. It would be based on the constructivist approach I had started to develop on the basis of the theory discussed in the first four chapters and on ten years of practical experience in the application of empowering techniques in the translation exercise classroom. As my assumptions about the nature of knowledge, learning, and teaching had already been defined by my social constructivist approach, it was not my goal to test particular hypotheses about the relative value of a constructivist approach compared to a conventional, teacher-centred, transmissionist one. That kind of comparison might have called for a scientific experimental research design. I was personally more interested in finding out how I could best apply this approach in order to have a positive effect on students' translation competence, on their emerging self-concept as translators, and on their attitudes toward the learning process. After observing classroom activity, group formation and changes in students' attitudes over the course of the semester, I wanted to focus on how my initial rough-hewn method could be elaborated and fine-tuned on the basis of those observations. Through a participatory action research design, I hoped to 1) plan and implement my initial pedagogical design, 2) observe how the students handled and reacted to the various elements and stages in the plan, and 3) draw implications from the results and apply those findings to my design of the next class.

The setting

As discussed in Chapter 4, the translation exercise class is the primary venue for the acquisition of professional translation skills in the translator education programme at the University of Mainz, as well as at numerous other translator education institutions. In our programme, these classes are conducted both into and out of the mother tongue for every language offered. Every department offers both general and specialized translation classes, the latter in one or more technical fields (depending on staffing capabilities): science and engineering, business and economics, law, and/or medicine, with computer sciences soon to be added for some departments. During the fourth semester, which culminates in the intermediate exam (*Vorprüfung*), and during the last semester prior to the comprehensive degree examinations (*Diplomprüfung*), teachers usually focus on exam preparation in the practice classes. The teachers who are designated to choose the texts for and evaluate the intermediate and final examinations in a given semester usually teach at least one section of the corresponding course during that same semester.

    Attendance is optional for all of our translation exercise classes. Students may even take the end-of-semester test in a class without having attended the class at all. Marks earned in these classes bear no weight at all in the students' final marks for their degree. Consequently, except in the case of classes designed specifically for students taking their intermediate or final exams at the end of the semester, attrition tends to be high, particularly during the fifth through eighth semesters. At this point in their studies, students have made it past the hurdle of the intermediate exam and have numerous other academic commitments to meet, including, for example, a written and an oral examination covering their special subject field, a number of graduate seminars in literature and linguistics, and the preparation of their masters thesis.

Because of the frequent lack of motivation and enthusiasm that many of my colleagues and I had experienced in classes at this advanced stage, I decided to choose a seventh-semester class in which to implement the initial form of my constructivist method. The course was for German-English translation practice involving general language texts, and was offered during the winter semester of the 1995-1996 academic year. Whereas in this class the students were translating from their mother tongue into a foreign language, my more recent experiences working with native speakers of English from German into English suggest that the basic method would be very similar regardless of the translation direction.

Data collection

As I planned to have the students working extensively in small groups throughout the semester, I enlisted the assistance of several advanced students who were not enrolled in the class to carry out the observations with me. During a series of preparatory sessions, we discussed and practised unobtrusive direct observation and also developed a questionnaire on students' attitudes to be distributed at the end of the semester. Then the three student assistants attended each class session and collected data in the form of taped recordings of small group work (which were later transcribed), direct observations of large-group interaction as well as non-verbal behaviour in the small groups, and survey data from the questionnaires. We based the design and implementation of our observational tools on classroom research literature from the field of foreign language education (Allwright and Bailey 1991, Chaudron 1988, van Lier 1989).

The students

The class comprised 24 students, 4 males and 20 females, and met for ten sessions of three hours each from October 1995 through January 1996. Normally, classes at the School meet for only 90 minutes per week, but because the real translation project we would be working on had to be completed by the beginning of January, the students agreed to meet for twice as long per session, but for fewer weeks. Despite the students' heavy course load, none of them had any reservations about doubling our class time. The students were asked at the first class whether or not they were willing to participate in this action research experiment. I informed them that, if they agreed, we would be working on a joint group project and that we would be experimenting with ways of working collaboratively to accomplish a task that no single student could accomplish on her own. They were informed that most of the classroom discourse would be recorded on tape and later transcribed, and that student observers would be present in the classroom on a regular basis to take notes on classroom events. Of the 24 students who showed up on that day, all agreed enthusiastically to participate, and none expressed any concern about being recorded.

The authentic assignment

As discussed in Chapter 3, a constructivist approach emphasizes maintaining a maximum degree of authentic, real-world complexity in learning situations. It is not up to the curriculum or the teacher to pre-process the skills and knowledge that students are to acquire, or to present material in an atomistic fashion, starting out with 'simple' features and building them into more complex ones, as a positivist approach would dictate. Cognitive apprenticeship presupposes that one always begins with a complex, authentic, real-world task. As the students begin to identify for themselves their own sub-tasks and problem areas, those aspects can be addressed by the teacher and dealt with through scaffolding as the need arises. From the beginning of the course, the emphasis is placed on the plausible final goal of completing an authentic translation to professional standards; this encourages students to keep their personal and group agendas in focus, to reflect on difficulties they may have with any of the myriad aspects of the translator's work, and to create and practise personal strategies to improve their own competence.

The translation task that presented itself just in time for the beginning of the semester consisted of a chapter from an edited volume on various topics related to life in a small region surrounding the administrative district of Hanau, Germany. As a freelance translator, I had been offered the job of translating the entire book comprising seven chapters on various aspects of the district, from history to the arts, and economics to industry. Due to my teaching obligations, I could not do the entire translation on my own, so I assumed responsibility for project management and for the quality of the final product. One chapter was set aside for my translation exercise class, and the other six chapters were subcontracted out to professional translators, all of whom were native speakers of English with whom I had worked on projects before. Each of the sub-contracting translators was given responsibility for completing one entire chapter in order to maximize the consistency of style and terminology within each chapter. Every chapter had been written by a different author whose name was indicated in the book. It was not necessary, therefore, to ensure stylistic consistency throughout the entire book. The chapter that my class did and that will be reported on here dealt with the history of money and banking in Hanau. The fee that we earned for our part of the translation, if divided up among the many students in the class, would have represented a very modest sum per student, and the students and I agreed instead to give the money we would earn to a charity of the students' choosing.

Organizing the project

As I had just begun two years before to teach my Introduction to Translation Studies in a consistently constructivist manner, none of the participants in this experimental translation exercise class had experienced the kind of introduction to collaborative group work outlined in Chapter 5. One of my research concerns was the extent to which preparation for working collaboratively is necessary or useful, but I did not have the students in this class engage in any particular preparatory activities. Instead, I outlined the task at hand, let the students read the text that we would be translating, and discussed with them the working conditions that had been laid out for me by the client; these included the layout, the intended readership, the remuneration, and the deadline for submitting the finished product. I made it clear that the translation would be their own, and that I would serve as the project co-ordinator and as one of various human resources that they could consult, in or outside of class, with any questions that they might not be able to resolve in groups. On the basis of the literature about group formation in collaborative and co-operative education, I recommended that the students work in groups of three or four throughout the semester. There is considerable debate about the value of having students select the group members they wish to work with versus having the teacher form the groups on the basis of personality or learning style. I decided to have the students select their own groups, hoping to find out from observed group interaction whether or not the teacher should consider getting involved in the group-forming process.

The class decided to divide up the work in such a way that each small group would have approximately the same amount of text to translate. Each student was given the entire text as a hard copy. The students were encouraged to seek additional resources, and during the first session we discussed what those resources might include, for example specialized dictionaries on money and banking, encyclopaedias, parallel texts and atlases. To provide the class with additional native speakers as language consultants, I arranged to have two English mother-tongue exchange students attend and participate on a regular basis as native speaker counsellors in our working sessions. University requirements specify that at least one test must be given and marked in each course, and I decided to have the students complete a group translation instead of the usual individual ones in order to observe how the collaborative process affects the test-taking situation. The topic of assessment is dealt with in more detail in the next chapter.

After briefing the students on our basic constraints for completing the project, I opened the floor to discussion concerning efficient modalities for tackling the job. Rather than dictate to the students how to proceed, I made it clear to them that they were free to organize themselves as they chose, and that I would only be offering recommendations based on my own professional experience as a project co-ordinator and team translator. I did insist, however, that together we establish a schedule that would allow us to use our limited time efficiently and meet our sub-mission deadline. We agreed that each small group would produce a draft of its portion of the translation to the best of their abilities, and that each group's joint translation would be passed on to several other groups for feedback. The original translating group would get their text back from each proof reading group, would reconsider its own translation in the light of that feedback, make changes as neces-sary, and pass that revised version on to another group for additional feedback. In some groups, the students decided to divide their portion of the text among the group members, with each one completing a rough draft of that small sub-section alone at home. Other groups decided to translate their portion of the text to-gether in class.

In response to student questions, we discussed such aspects as the background knowledge we could expect our intended readership to have; the extent to which we should try to reflect the author's style and logical progression within the text; what dictionaries and other resources were available in the library to help solve the termi-nological problems they had already encountered; whether or not we needed to adapt our translation to a particular variety of English; and whether or not we would have access to the photographs, which might help us understand parts of the German text better, and also enable us to translate the captions that had been given to us. Ques-tions also arose concerning the appropriate formatting and layout for our translation; how to deal with what the students saw as infelicitous constructions in the German text; and how we could go about efficiently standardizing the terminology among the small groups.

Except for the constraints passed on by the client, I imposed very little structure on class organization and procedures. As the students perceived new needs over the course of the project – including, for example, getting additional background infor-mation from the client, bringing in additional native speaker consultants so that there would be one to assist each group for one entire session, and resolving con-flicts within the small groups – we worked together to meet them, as will be demonstrated in the sections below which deal with specific aspects of the project learning environment.

Planning the classroom sessions

Following the introductory meeting, we allocated six sessions for the individual small groups to 1) complete a rough draft of their section of the text, 2) proof read the drafts of at least three other groups, 3) also obtain feedback from three other groups on their own draft, and 4) incorporate any changes they deemed necessary into their drafts. In order to provide the entire group with the reactions of a potential member of the target readership, I reserved one class session for a native speaker of English to come to class and provide feedback on the translation as an English language text. He would read through the entire draft aloud and make comments on parts of the text that, in his opinion, were unclear, ambiguous or stylistically weak. We scheduled the penultimate session for the small-group translation test, and the final session was reserved for a review of the test and our joint assessment of the classes' performance, the individual students' perception of their own learning and the students' recommendations for improving the course in the future.

The atmosphere during the following six sessions was business-like, yet relaxed. The groups selected their own working areas in the room to which they returned throughout the course. They generally began working the moment they arrived, which was often before the official starting time for the class. To a great extent they organized the flow of the work they would accomplish during each session on their own. I moved from group to group, providing assistance as necessary. I tried always to get involved to the extent that I was needed but to interfere as little as necessary when groups were making progress on their own. In order to meet our final deadline, and since some of the groups were making rather slow progress toward completing their rough drafts, it became necessary to help some groups expedite their discussion processes; this took place to make sure that all of the drafts would be finished by the beginning of the following session so that the interactive feedback sessions could begin. The students readily accepted my role of facilitating group organization, and I found that most of the regulatory behaviour needed to accomplish the task at hand and meet the deadline came from within the groups themselves.

The work progressed basically as planned, and we managed to complete the job on time and submit it to the client, with time left over for the required semester test and a review of our work. Not everything went smoothly, of course. The qualitative classroom data collected provided numerous insights into ways of improving the course in the future. In the following sections, I will outline some of the salient features of this class, both positive and negative, and provide some glimpses into our learning activities through excerpts from in-class dialogues.

Findings

Group make-up and student roles

The group size in our project class varied from two to five. While I originally suggested that all groups be comprised of either three or four students as recommended by Johnson and Johnson (1991), on some days a few students would be absent, sometimes leaving as few as two group members to work together on that day. In a few cases only one student was present from a particular group and would then join another group for that class session, thus occasionally yielding groups of as many as five students. The observations by the student data collectors revealed that group size and personal dynamics seemed to have a major effect on interaction within the group.

For example, on December 15, the day of the group examination, in one particular group comprised of four students, only two group members engaged actively in the translation task. The other two students remained virtually silent. Most of their contributions consisted of brief comments or sentence fragments of no more than three words at a time. Some of these utterances were spoken in such a low voice that they were virtually inaudible on the tape recordings. In several groups with four or five members, we observed that quieter students were unable to assert themselves well, and tended to be interrupted and overruled by other, more outspoken group members. While another group of four engaged in extensive private talk and joking on December 15, two of those students worked much more earnestly and efficiently on December 1 with an English native speaker when the other two group members were absent. On December 1, the two participating students included the most outspoken and the quietest member of that group. While working as a pair, the more vociferous student still dominated the discussion, doing much of the translation work and assuming the role of the organizer, and her turns tended to be longer than those of her partner. Nevertheless, the quieter student still took an active role in the discussion, presenting her point of view and negotiating solutions with the more dominant student.

A similar picture emerges from other groups. In those with more than four members, the quiet ones tended to stay in the background and leave virtually all of the discussion to be carried out by more active participants. In groups of any size where all of the group members were quite outspoken, they participated to more or less the same degree. However, the ideal group size for promoting balanced, productive interaction proved to be three or four.

Within the groups, specific communicative roles were assumed spontaneously by the different group members in the initial small group session, and remained constant throughout the project. The student observers and I labelled the roles we observed as follows: organizer, secretary, assimilator, devil's advocate, and entertainer.

Organizer

The person exercising this role initiated most of the discussion concerning problems, encouraged the group to re-focus on addressed problems after a pause or interruption, and also took a prominent role in the handling of procedural issues. Generally, the organizer was mainly the most active and outspoken member of a given group. A problem inherent in this role was the potential for an assertive student exercising it to assume dominance over the group, thereby essentially assuming the role of a conventional, knowledge-distributing teacher. This worked to the disadvantage of the other group members, putting them in the similarly disempowered position in which they tend to find themselves in conventional classes, and drastically restricted the potential for producing multiple perspectives that could lead to learning for all students. Ideally, however, the organizer served a co-ordinating function within the group and kept discussions from getting bogged down unnecessarily in details.

Secretary

The secretary summarized translated passages and wrote down rough drafts and final translations for the whole group. The person fulfilling this role was the only person who has the entire emerging text on paper in front of him or her, and was therefore in a position to monitor cohesion and coherence at suprasentential levels of the text. It was vital that the secretary realize the importance and responsibility of having this vantage point, and that he or she be prepared to observe the flow of the emerging text and raise questions when appropriate.

Assimilator-mediator

The assimilator identified new translation problems as they emerged, rephrased them and explained them in more depth and detail. The assimilator took on responsibility for outlining to newcomers, visitors from other groups, and the native speaker advisors the state of the group's progress as opportunities arose. The assimilator generally also assumed a mediating function, helping to resolve conflicts between other group members and making sure that everyone's point of view was considered.

Devil's advocate

This function involved asking critical questions related to the comprehension of the source text, focusing on differences in nuances between the original text and the emerging translation and generally critiquing translation solutions proposed by other group members. The function of critic was typically assumed by quieter members of a group. In efficient group interaction, we noticed that individuals fulfilling the assimilator and devil's advocate functions generally complemented each other, with the former recasting and explaining problems raised by the latter.

Entertainer

This function included the making of humorous comments that generally contributed to a relaxed, non-aggressive group atmosphere, a key feature of a classroom conducive to learning (Young 1991). At times, it did, however, lead to too much private talk and unproductive group work. In well-functioning groups, excessive joking and off-topic talk were kept in check by the individual exercising the organizer function.

The present study showed that participation patterns within small groups were more well-balanced if the individual members shared the roles evenly. Some co-operative researchers recommend having an initial session before the project begins during which students' consciousness of social roles within small groups can be explored. An introductory session might also be an appropriate venue for activities that can help reduce the phenomenon that Johnson and Johnson (1991:63) have called 'social loafing'. This is a situation where some students allow other group members to do the work, while taking undue credit for themselves. Johnson and Johnson suggest that 'social loafing' can be avoided by assigning roles (ibid.). It is doubtful, though, whether these roles should (1) be assigned either by the in-structor, who, as a collaborative, non-authoritarian facilitator, may wish to avoid interfering unnecessarily in group interaction, or (2) be explicitly selected by the group members themselves. This does not preclude, of course, having the students observe and investigate naturally occurring roles during an introductory prepara-tion session.

Of course, not all of the observed groups turned out to be efficient in the distri-bution of roles. For example, on December 15, the day of the group exam, one of the groups comprised three members. Two of the students did almost all of the interactive work on the text and clearly dominated the group. Kathrin, the most serious student in the group, assumed the functions of organizer and secretary. Eleonore, the other outspoken student in this group, participated to the same degree as Kathrin, although she was considerably less serious in her attitude that day and joked a great deal, which in this case had a disruptive effect on group interaction and efficiency. The third group member, Sylvia, was very reserved. She made only brief contributions to the discussion, in fact of no more than four words at a time, some of which were spoken in such a low voice that they were virtually inaudible on tape. She was interrupted on several occasions by her teammates. Here, the dis-tribution of social roles was clearly unbalanced; Kathrin was by far the most productive and the most dominant member. Eleonore's joking attitude kept the group from working more efficiently, and Sylvia, who had assumed no apparent role in the group, depended on Kathrin and, to a lesser extent, Eleonore to do the work at hand.

When this same group had been observed while revising another group's draft on December 1st, it comprised the same three members, but the pattern of role dis-tribution proved to be more balanced. Sylvia, the most reserved group member, took 15 per cent of the turns, most of which were again fairly short (between three and ten words each). This time she assumed the function of the critic, mainly asking questions concerning either the comprehension of the source text or background knowledge related to the translation. During the same session, Eleonore again as-sumed the role of entertainer, which on this day helped create a relaxed atmosphere within the group, as well as the role of assimilator, thus complementing Sylvia's assumed role of devil's advocate by attempting to answer questions Sylvia raised as the group work progressed. A group need not function in the same manner on two different days; efficiency and role distribution depend on numerous factors that are difficult, if not impossible, to control or even account for.

Peer assistance and correction

Miller *et al.* (1992:43) report that peer learning assistance "has been extremely effective in helping students to improve both group process and group dynamics". Peers can include both other members of the class who share a native tongue, as well as students whose native-foreign language combination is reversed. Having students correct each other's work can help them focus on their own translation strategies, see alternative ways of solving translation problems, and also support each other in the construction of joint knowledge about translation.

The use of native speakers of the target language in the classroom can be very helpful in a variety of ways. For one thing, they provide the teacher with more time to work closely with a group that is having difficulty. And students translating into a foreign language may not be particularly self-confident about their ability to produce English that is idiomatic or appropriate with respect to register or style. Often, a native speaker advisor, even one who is not a teacher, can provide assistance in such cases.

As mentioned above, two American exchange students participated regularly in our classroom activities during this case study. The results of the questionnaire showed that students were in overwhelming agreement that they were able to use these native speakers to good advantage; but the time these advisors could spend with each group was limited. After a few sessions, we decided to have five native speakers participate for a full three-hour session near the end of the project.

In addition, I arranged to have the eighth class session be conducted by George, a native speaker of American English who had not yet participated in any of the group's activities. This American student had relatively limited competence in German, and his role in this class was intended to be that of a native speaker reader of the group's revised joint draft, rather than that of a professional translator who could edit the students' translation. George was given the text at the beginning of the class, and I asked him to read the text out loud and to think aloud while reading, that is stop and comment, as if to himself, when something in the text seemed incongruous, poorly expressed, unidiomatic, etc. The goal of this activity was to help the students focus on problems that they, as non-native speakers, might not perceive and to sit in, as it were, on a simulated reading of their translation as a text in its own right. When asked about their impression of this session, 12 out of 19 students who responded to this question stated that they had felt frustrated, at least to some extent, by our visitor's criticisms. Most of the students who responded to this question, in fact 17 out of 19, felt that most of the problems George pointed out were due to his lack of background knowledge on the topic. However, thirteen subjects said that George's criticisms had pointed out to them a number of problems that needed work, while six students stated that they did not derive any benefit from this interaction with a native speaker at all. Most of the students seemed to see George as a hostile critic, and not as a member of the team who was trying to help them do a better job. They were defensive about the comments he made, and most were unwilling to reconsider problems that he identified. The personality and attitude of the native speaker assistant in this type of situation can, of course, have a major effect on the students' receptiveness.

Unlike this rather uncomfortable confrontation with a native speaker critic, when asked about the value of having native speakers work with them in the small group work, most students said that they felt that this was helpful or very helpful. The results of the questionnaire show the extremely positive attitude of the subjects toward working with native speakers in regular discussion sessions. All of the students agreed that working with a native speaker of English had had a positive influence on the quality of the text, and six out of the 19 said this was very true. Nine of the subjects who filled out the questionnaire doubted that they could have done a translation of similar quality without the help of the native speaker. All students said that they would like to work with native speakers in translation classes in the future for translation into the foreign language.

There were three main ways in which the students made use of our English-native speakers:

- To test the meaning or idiomatic acceptability of certain expressions in the target text
- To test the general readability of sentences or whole passages according to the expectations of the target audience
- To test the background knowledge of the native speaker, who under these conditions was seen as acting as a representative of the target audience

Whether they came to class with translated text segments they had done on their own at home or created a translation together in class, the students regularly called over a native speaker to help them feel more confident about using a particular expression. Often, the information obtained about the meanings or the usage of individual words could have been obtained as easily (and more precisely) from a dictionary:

> Tanja: So how about 'embellished'? Aufwerten ... städebaulich aufwerten.
> Christiane: I've never heard this word before, so I don't know.
> Ralph (native speaker of English): Well, it means to add something. To embellish something can mean to build upon something, to make it more attractive.
> Christiane: So it's to make it nicer?
> Ralph: Yeah.
> Christiane: Okay, so we'll leave it.

The focus here is on the potential or dictionary meaning of *embellish*. Neither the students nor the English speaker checked a higher level of meaning to make sure that the word could be used in this context. Strategies related to checking appropriateness at different levels of meaning could be introduced in an introductory session for both the students and the English-speaking assistants.

As in this interaction, the members of a group would often ask for advice or information from the native speaker (including the instructor), but without relinquishing responsibility for the final decision. In many cases, the native speaker's advice was rejected or ignored, suggesting that the students were in fact drawing on other information and their own intuitions about the appropriateness of tentative solutions to make a final decision. On many other occasions, the students already had acceptable solutions in mind and simply used the native speaker to confirm them:

> Tanja: What would you say here? Market place or market square?
> Ralph: Market place, market square ...
> Tanja: Market square sounds more like an actual place where buying and selling occur and not just the square.
> Ralph: Does this mean the physical place? ... Or does it mean the location where ...
> Tanja: Well, it's the address there ...
> Ralph: Oh, ok.
> Tanja: So it's the street.
> Ralph: I think you're right. Market square sounds more appropriate for the specific street corner or the intersection of streets where you have a market.
> Tanja: Maybe we should say, on the corner of market square.

In all of the observed groups, the group members used the native speaker as a representative of the translation target audience. They tested the native speaker's background knowledge in order to find out if they had to add an explanation to the translation.

> Britta: Um, what do you think about 'the people's bank'? Would you just leave Volksbank there, or does 'people's bank' suggest anything to you?
> Ralph: Not really.
> Britta: Yeah, I thought so. Do you know what the Volksbank is?
> Ralph: Yes, I have the general idea that it is a co-operative venture.
> Johanna: Yeah, that's it ... 'Volks- und Raiffeisenbank' and then explain it in brackets.

While the study shows that these students favoured working with native speakers because of their insecurity in producing an idiomatic text in English, the excellent quality of the translations produced without native speakers as well as the data obtained from observations of groups interacting with native speakers suggest that often the students would not have needed their help at all to accomplish the task. In fact the data reveal that most problems were solved by the students on their own, while the native speakers limited themselves to confirming what students came up with themselves, thus reassuring the students that their solutions were acceptable. It appeared that the reason for the dependence on the native speaker was a lack of self-confidence on the part of students.

As Allwright (1979:114) reports, "in-class dependence on the teaching expert undermines self-confidence in real life". Teacher-centred instruction provides a crutch or a security blanket, while leaving the students helpless in real-life situations, "like package tour customers who have lost their courier" (ibid.). In conventional classes, the students are not encouraged to judge the acceptability of their own translations, since transmissionist assumptions preclude their ability to do so.

Consequently, the students seem to want to place the responsibility for deciding 'right' or 'wrong' on native speakers. By confronting the students with transcriptions of their own classroom discourse, we can demonstrate to them their own competence as well as their unjustified dependency, thus helping them to liberate themselves from it.

Working with native speakers in class was clearly a welcome new activity for the German students, and it was obvious that small group work with the help of native speakers can have a stimulating effect on students and that it releases the teacher from the impossible task of being in several places at once. While the value of native speakers' participation may lie more in the feeling of security they contribute to the group than in the expertise they provide, this will depend on the level of translator competence of the native speaker advisors and on the training they receive as peer assistants.

The roles assumed by the English native speakers in group work varied considerably. The teacher in particular assumed a more prominent, enquiring role in discussions in an attempt to model for the students the kinds of questions one might ask oneself when trying to determine the appropriateness of a tentative solution. (In the following excerpt, one group is critiquing the draft done by another group.)

> Tanja: And they left out Bankenplatz. They just compare the town to Frankfurt, which is pretty big.
> Teacher: Does that mean there are lots of banks located in one spot?
> Students: Yes.
> Teacher: Sort of like 'the City' in London, right? The City has all kinds of financial institutions located there. Could it be the 'banking ...' hm ... what would you call it? ... sector?
> Christiane: Site?
> Teacher: Bank site. That would only be one site, though, wouldn't it? The site where one bank is located?
> Christiane: Right ...

Teacher: Well, let's see ... Banking quarter? How about 'the banking quarter', even though it sounds a bit too big.
Tanja: It's not a quarter. The whole city is called Bankenplatz.
Teacher: So are they talking about the city as a regional centre for banking activity?
Tanja: Yes, that's how I understand it.
Teacher: I see. That makes sense. So you would have the main offices of different banks located here and the branch offices in different places.
Tanja: So, 'Hanau is a regional centre for banking with a big city flair'.
Teacher: Or perhaps 'regional banking centre'. Which one sounds better to you?
Tanja: So we'll say: 'Hanau is a regional banking centre with a big-city flair'.

Even when a native speaker was not present, the students consistently worked collaboratively to identify and resolve problems they discovered in their and their fellow classmates' translations. While no specific techniques were taught to students for editing their own work or that of other groups, each successive draft was more idiomatic, more elegant and more accurate than the previous one. It would also be valuable to provide students with a standard list of proof readers' markings, which can significantly increase the intelligibility of their feedback for the students who will need to incorporate it in their drafts. The question remains of the extent to which it would be beneficial to include more directed instruction on editing and proof reading either prior to or parallel to the group work revolving around the improvement of the text at hand. This topic will be dealt with in more detail in the final section of this chapter, on the implications of the study.

Motivation and attrition

A major feature that set this class apart from other 7th-semester classes I had taught previously was that only two out of 24 students dropped out during the semester, yielding an extremely low rate of attrition. The students clearly saw themselves as being personally implicated in completing an authentic task for which they would be earning money for charity. They almost universally assumed responsibility for the job, were rarely absent, and usually informed the teacher and their fellow group members in advance if they had to miss a class. Small groups also met for extra sessions outside of class on those occasions where in-class time was inadequate to complete work on a particular passage. The students were introduced in this way to some of the real task constraints faced on a day-to-day basis by professional translators. Through the instructor they could interact with the client, asking questions about the source text and background information as necessary. They learned to draw on a variety of tools during class time and worked on resource management skills as well as toward translation skills even during class time. The learning process was one of true construction based on a healthy atmosphere of mutual respect and collegiality among all of the participants in the class.

From the perspective of the client, the quality of the text completed by the students was excellent. Our immediate contact person at the Hanau Chamber of Commerce was a woman who held a masters degree in English and who seemed very capable of judging the quality of our translation. She painstakingly reviewed each of the chapters returned by the various sub-contractors and discussed every point of contention with me over the phone. Of those eight chapters, only the text completed by the students in my 7th-semester class was found to be without fault. In the end all eight texts were published in the form of an attractive coffee table book.

The students were very enthusiastic about the project from the beginning; 13 out of 21 reported at the end of the semester that they would like to participate in other classes organized collaboratively around real translation projects. While no one in the group had ever done a translation for remuneration before, they were all willing to tackle the job at hand, despite the fact that their translation would be done into the foreign language. The support they were provided from the very beginning, including having their teacher serving as the project manager, other native speakers as language consultants, and access to the full panoply of resources and tools that professionals use, gave them the necessary confidence to undertake the job. The atmosphere in the classroom was, from the very first hour, completely different from what I had experienced in conventional classes. The class was imbued from the start with a sense of excitement, purpose, and responsibility for producing a high-quality translation. Unlike a conventional class, where I would choose a text, have students translate it at home and then critique it for and with them sentence by sentence, here the students automatically shifted their focus away from what I as the instructor expected of them, and toward the production of a professional quality translation that would meet the actual client's needs.

Implications

Preparing students for collaborative work

Peer assistance will not work effectively if students are simply told to "check each other's work". The literature on training students for peer response, particularly in the field of English as a Second Language, can serve as a starting point for preparing students to perform this important task efficiently (Berg 1999).

Ideally, students enrolled in a translation exercise class at this level would already have participated in a collaborative Introduction to Translation Studies class where they would have learned to work collaboratively and also defined for themselves the basic types of skills and knowledge they will need to complete a project translation in collaboration with other students. This would clearly reduce the preparation time needed as well as obviate the need to convince students of the value of the approach. This experimental group was not provided with an adequate introduction to collaborative group work. In particular, social loafing was too common, and roles were not adequately balanced in several groups on different occasions. The following semester, I started providing students with a full session of introductory activities to introduce them to collaborative group work as a result of this finding. Now, three years later, as more and more students have taken my Introduction to Translation Studies course, and as other colleagues begin to implement a similar approach in their lower-semester translation exercise classes, there is a large number of students in every 7th-semester class who are already prepared to work collaboratively when the class begins.

Role distribution

Whether the students are assigned to groups by the teacher or form their own groups instead, the teacher, serving as the group work facilitator, must be vigilant that the atmosphere within the group is relaxed but conducive to learning, and that small groups work collaboratively with a strong basis in trust and mutual interdependence. If there is excessive tension in a group because, for example, two group members dislike each other, the atmosphere can easily become aggressive and excessively competitive. Some students may be intimidated by other group members and will not benefit much from group interaction, or may even drop the course. A little diplomatic intervention on the part of the teacher can encourage those holding the organizer function in a group to yield the floor more to other group members, thus contributing greatly to an improvement in group dynamics. To ensure an authentic environment in the classroom, it seems best to allow roles to emerge naturally as a function of the particular combination of personalities and temperaments within each group respectively.

Naturally it can never be guaranteed that the arbitrary placement of individuals will lead to a harmonious group in which roles will automatically be assumed without the personalities of two persons clashing or less outspoken members being left out. It is the task of the instructor to be aware of the group climate, the distribution of roles, and possible problems – for example, the absolute dominance or passivity of individual group members. If such situations are noticed, he or she should intervene and modify the group composition, either by reducing the group size or putting students together who are better matched. For Miller *et al.* (1992), the teacher should remove the student from a group only as a last resort. These authors have even suggested giving tests of learning styles or cognitive styles to identify features about the individual students that may most affect group harmony. The 'free rider' effect can be reduced by encouraging the answerability of each member of the group to the rest of the group. By making it clear to the students that their success depends on the group's success and vice versa, it should be possible to reduce free ride effects significantly. Rather than distributing roles according to the teacher's choosing, it might be more valuable to have students undertake a task and then identify for themselves the roles that are naturally taken within that group. By carrying out some introductory activities of this kind, an individual group can learn to assess its own capability for functioning properly and efficiently and for taking measures to eliminate dissonance within the group. Such capabilities will clearly be a valuable part of our graduates' repertoire of teamwork skills once they leave the institution.

The bilingual classroom

Group work involving both native and non-native speakers of the target language can be beneficial for both groups. The native speakers of the source text language may well understand the nuances of the original text better than the non-native speakers. The latter, however may have a greater ability to express themselves idiomatically and appropriately in the target language.

Pym (1992) outlined a number of ways in which foreign exchange students could be drawn into a programme to mutually benefit all of the students. Through interaction in class, students can assume the role of teaching each other their respective native tongues. This type of interaction naturally also leads to an exchange of cultural values and increases understanding between young people who are training to become multilingual and multicultural professionals. In addition, it ensures that the teacher is no longer the sole arbiter of translation accuracy or idiomaticity in the classroom. This helps establish a more democratic and balanced distribution of authority and responsibility within the group.

I was quite surprised by the students' negative reactions to the think-aloud activity with our visitor George, particularly as I noticed that most of the comments that George made were indeed pertinent and did point out problems with the students' draft that helped them come up with better solutions. Two factors may have played a role in the students' rejection of George's assistance. First of all, George had not attended any of our earlier sessions and was not familiar with the collaborative nature of our classroom work. Furthermore, his approach to providing the commentary on the students' work was in fact quite authoritarian. While I did spend some time working with George prior to the session to outline an appropriate role in this simulation, following the session I realized that I should have worked more carefully with him to avoid having him adopt a conventional teacher's role in our anti-authoritarian classroom. Since this particularly unpleasant and counterproductive experience, I have made certain that all visiting advisors are carefully initiated into the underlying principles and working methods of the class before they join our deliberations.

Another factor that may have played a role was that I had failed to get the students' approval to have George participate, and had simply imposed my agenda on them, reverting in fact to a conventional teacher's role, applying arbitrary authority the students could not veto. In future, I would merely suggest to the students that we have this type of think-aloud session, and would discuss with them whether or not they wished to bring someone in, and if so, who it should be, what background information that person should be given, and how the students themselves wished to involve him or her. Students must have a major stake, not only in the actual process of learning, but also in classroom management if they are to buy into a method that purports to empower them.

Text selection and sequencing

In order to teach empowerment, it is essential to provide students with a rich variety of authentic translation tasks to accomplish collaboratively, but in doing so, we are obviously dependent on the availability of actual translation commissions and their suitability for instructional purposes. An appropriate project has to become available at the beginning of a semester, with plenty of time for the group to complete it given the constraints of having only a few hours of class per week and numerous other academic obligations that have to be met. The client must also agree to have the text translated with the collaboration of students. In the interest of providing a wide and representative selection of texts for students to experience during their training period, it may well prove necessary for teachers to simulate real translation projects, which will allow teachers and students to select texts that have already been translated to work on in class.

The range of topics to be covered over the course of a programme of studies will vary from institution to institution, depending on the length of the programme, the number of contact hours students will have in translation exercise classes, and the text types that students can expect to encounter on the market. A catalogue of text types for a given language combination can be prepared by teachers and students working collaboratively: an example in a translation studies seminar would be the students gathering data from published sources and doing their own surveys to determine what kinds of texts they need to have worked with extensively in order to be prepared to meet market demands once they graduate. Göpferich (1996) has prepared such a catalogue for teaching technical translation. In any event, it will be valuable to include real projects like the one observed in this chapter whenever possible in order to provide students with authentic work experience. If the project is a simulated one, there is no real client, and no real social partner to specify the readership, to clarify intent, to provide a real deadline for submission, or to assess the quality of the completed job. These duties are likely to again fall upon the teacher as in a conventional class, thus depriving the students of valuable sources of motivation and task orientation.

Even in simulated projects, ways to increase authenticity can be found, for example by having a colleague anonymously assess the quality of group translations, thus simulating feedback from a client. In this way, the authority of the teacher as the arbiter of a quality performance is displaced outside of the classroom, allowing the teacher and students to work and learn together more equitably. Even if a real commission is not available for a class, methods can be found to engage students in authentic projects. For example, they can be encouraged to find texts that need translation, like brochures at their hometown tourist office or local museum, or for charitable organizations. While for volunteer work of this kind no remuneration may be forthcoming, all of the other aspects of the translation can be authentic, thus providing students with a more valuable and inherently motivating learning experience.

The level of difficulty of the texts to be covered in the programme of studies represents a closely related problem that has received sparse attention in the translation studies literature to date. Göpferich (1996) acknowledges the importance of addressing whole texts, and in fact specifies a hierarchy of text types within the area of technical translation that allow students to move from the simple to the complex on the basis of the degree of concreteness versus abstraction in text types. This kind of catalogue could be devised for other translation areas like commerce, law or medicine, and as suggested above, might best be done with the collaboration of the students themselves, again to involve them deeply in the educational process.

Another way to deal with the problem of complexity is to share the work between classes at different levels. During the 1998-1999 academic year, several of my advanced classes translated a book on psychoanalysis and witchcraft as their project (Heinemann 1998). This was a particularly difficult text written by a professor of psychology for a specialized readership. The complexity of the text was too difficult for elementary students to handle. Instead of having lower division students actually translate the text, one group taught by a colleague agreed to prepare a specialized glossary covering the wide range of sub-topics dealt with in the book. While having the entire text as a frame of reference, this group was able to work on the less demanding, but no less essential skills of terminology management. This work was done in collaboration with my advanced students, which resulted in both sets of students learning a great deal from each other.

Focusing on learning

As the facilitator of learning in the observed classroom, I avoided assuming a domineering role of knowledge distributor. On the other hand, I did not simply leave the students completely to their own devices, to discover things on their own. I used the authentic situation of a real translation task as the venue for learning, that is for identifying and resolving the many levels of difficulty inherent in the assignment. The students spent numerous hours working through texts done by different groups and discussed matters of adequacy, appropriateness, style and numerous other features of text comprehension and production that translators face. While in the end, the problems were solved and the task was accomplished admirably to the full satisfaction of the client, I was still left with the impression that there is an essentially ad hoc nature to this type of project work that may well need to be modified to make classes like this one more valuable for students with less translation experience.

Leng-Lawrence and Kohls (1999), for example, have raised the issue of how to teach editing skills to translation students. Graduate translators may or may not have the luxury of an expert mentor to proofread and edit their work upon graduation. Such editing support, when it is available, is in any event an expensive and time-consuming proposition. Freelancers who work through agencies are likely to find that their work is passed on to clients directly without editing or proofreading of any kind. Therefore, students have to learn how to edit and correct their own work. As teamwork and project management have become commonplace features of the translator's work, they will also need to be able to accurately and efficiently edit the work of other translators. The perfect venue for learning such skills is not on the job after graduation, where there is little time for experimentation or tolerance for mistakes, but during the programme of studies. The focus on authentic activities in the constructivist classroom does not preclude the use of scaffolded instructional activities to help raise students' consciousness about aspects of and techniques for effective editing. For example, Leng-Lawrence and Kohls discuss ways of helping students focus on such aspects as:

- Distinguishing between interference errors as opposed to their own idiosyncratic errors
- Determining whether their own errors are grammatical or stylistic
- Learning to determine the severity of errors
- Developing good proof-reading habits
- Using word processing software to help students focus on and eradicate errors

These authors, who are in fact English as a Second Language instructors working with translators-in-training, note that proofreading for correct grammar, idiomatic usage and appropriate style is only one aspect of editing for translation purposes. Techniques also need to be developed to help students learn to proofread for coherence in meaning between the source and the target text. This is but a nascent area of research in the field of translator education, but there are thousands of translation exercise classrooms in which action research could be carried out to help find solutions and develop valuable techniques for this essential skill. It will be important, however, in the context of an empowering learning environment, to avoid relapses into the conventional dictation mode of instruction. It would be counter-productive, in my view, for teachers to dissociate the training of specific sub-skills from work on authentic texts. As Leng-Lawrence and Kohls (1999:55) have said:

We recommend, whenever possible, that exercises be derived from student-generated or authentic translations. This provides the most relevant source for identifying, tracking and correcting errors. From a pedagogical perspective, students will be more engaged in any classroom exercise where their own work (and the work of their peers) is the main focus than if they review an unrelated text with inauthentic examples.

A related concern involves the native speakers who are brought into the classroom to serve as peer advisors. In the observed classroom, these native speakers often served a prophylactic function, substantiating the students' own translation decisions. These advisors clearly need to be well chosen for their extensive knowledge of both languages involved and for their own highly developed translation skills. They also need to be initiated into the facilitation of group work themselves. This can be done in several sessions prior to the beginning of a course and can then be augmented by additional sessions as the semester progresses and as problems arise. Peer advisors clearly need to understand the nature of the facilitator's role. This understanding will naturally become more developed as a course progresses, but advisors will still need some preliminary coaching if they are to make a significant contribution to the learning process.

All in all, this observed course confirmed my faith in the value of a constructivist approach for the empowerment of my student translators. However, it also raised a number of questions concerning the extent to which I as the facilitator need to intervene in the dynamics of an authentic project being carried out in the classroom. In preparation for subsequent courses, I have experimented with introductory sessions on how to collaborate, introductory training sessions for peer assistants, and techniques for focusing on sub-skills involved in the translation process. Every class has its successes and its setbacks; questions and problems are resolved only to give way to new ones. Each subsequent wave of findings has an impact on how the next course is run. In fact, I see my own development as a constructivist teacher in terms of a perpetual process of evolution and innovation. As a facilitator, I am continually learning along with my students, and am constantly adapting my method to my evolving understandings of how best to empower my students to join the community of professional translators. The steps I employed to organize this action research project (planning, action and observation, and reflection), have become the key features of my practice as a teacher. Adopting the role of teacher as researcher is, I believe, the key to innovation in our field. We cannot simply prescribe a teaching method, no matter how noble the aims, and hope that that one act will change the face of our all too reactionary profession. Teachers who are tired of pulling old texts out of the drawer semester after semester, of sitting in front of group after group of passive students, and of dominating each and every class will need to develop, through dialogue with other teachers, administrators and students, a habit – in fact, a culture – of innovation based on perpetual enquiry.

7. Knowledge Construction and the Translator's Workstation

Electronic tools and the translator

If we accept the constructivist assumption that education should realistically reflect actual practice with respect to the tools, methods and procedures of the profession with which students are becoming acquainted, then the type of translation exercise classroom described in Chapter 6 is inherently deficient regarding several important aspects of task authenticity. First of all, how many professional translators actually write out their translations with pen and paper as students do in non-computerized classes? And how many would agree to take on a difficult new translation assignment without access to their usual array of tools and channels of communication? Today, both freelance and staff translators use computer-based workstations, complete with word processors, spreadsheets, terminology databases, translation memory, desktop publishing software, access to the Internet, and a variety of on- and off-line electronic resources. They send and receive files via electronic mail, and they surf the Internet for background information, parallel texts and multilingual glossaries. Translators today can establish and maintain long-term working relationships with agencies and direct clients they never see and who may be located in distant cities and even far-off countries.

If we consider just the most basic computer-based tool that translators use today – the word processor – , it quickly becomes clear just how significant the changeover from a paper-based to a paperless profession. The very advent of word processing as the standard means of producing text for translators (and most other text producers) in modern society has brought about major changes in the way we deal with texts, as any professional will confirm who is suddenly asked to do a translation on paper after years of working solely with a computer. We can now instantly move, copy and erase passages while removing every visible trace of earlier solutions; we can search for and replace terms effortlessly throughout even a book-length manuscript in a matter of seconds, and we can produce text directly in publishable form. It is not only the speed of these operations that has changed, but also our view of and attitude towards the emerging text itself. We can now allow ourselves the luxury of putting down tentative solutions spontaneously, without worrying as much about their viability for the final product. We know that we can go back and make changes with ease. And since we can move and delete text so easily, the emerging text on the screen is always moving in the direction of a finished product, unencumbered by the remnants of discarded solutions that would otherwise have remained on the paper to disturb the flow of work in a hand- or type-written text. Similar changes are also in evidence in the way we manage our terminology, carry out subject-matter research and communicate with our clients.

The translator's tools are very much a part of the translation process. Having students do all of their practice translations with pen and paper during training would be akin to having dentists-in-training use a manual drill, pliers and plaster of paris to repair patients' teeth. No matter how highly developed the emerging dentist's dexterity, knowledge of anatomy and awareness of the principles of modern dentistry, the results would in no way reflect the capabilities of that same dentist aided by state-of-the-art tools of the practice. Knowledge-in-action is mediated by the tools we use; thus an important part of the education of any professional must entail practical training in learning how to use the everyday tools of the profession.

The increased accessibility and reduced cost of electronic communications in recent years have made it more feasible and commonplace for large-scale translation projects to be shared among translators situated at remote locations (Reinke 1997). To complete such extensive projects under the usual time constraints, the translation work must often be divided up for the preparation of rough drafts, and then harmonized on the levels of style, terminology and formatting to ensure the submission of a uniform, coherent and cohesive text that reads as if it had been translated by a single person. The orchestration of the manifold efforts required to accomplish large-scale translation projects can be a complex process indeed, and to meet the demands, graduates are going to need skills that can only be developed through actual authentic project management. Similarly, learners must gain extensive experience and expertise in working as a member of a team if they are to be able to manage or even participate effectively in such projects professionally.

Translator education programmes that have been established since the advent of the computerized workstation in the early 1990s may well have been able to incorporate into their curricula and budget proposals the resources and tools that translators normally use in our electronic world. However, those dating back to an era when the translator was bound to hard copy rather than hardware and software tools are likely to have difficulty modifying existing curricula, re-training instructors burdened by years of paper-bound pedagogical routine, and finding the budgetary means to adapt their programmes of study to the current realities of the profession. In any event, having the necessary equipment and technical know-how is not sufficient for ensuring that students will actually acquire the computer-based competence they will need. Returning to the underlying theme of this book, I am certain that the nature and effectiveness of computerized instruction at a particular institution will depend to a great extent on the educational epistemology underlying the respective programme of instruction.

As instruction in translation-related computer-based tools is the topic of an excellent volume in this series (Austermühl, forthcoming), I will not go into detail here about technical aspects like hardware requirements and software programmes that can help the translator work more efficiently. Nor will I deal with special computer-based translation skills learning programmes, of which, in any event, only a few are currently available for institutional use (Reinke 1997). Instead, I will focus on the specific implications of an empowerment approach for introducing students to the use of the translator's workstation. I will specifically deal with two aspects of the technological classroom: (1) how to help students to constructively acquire skills for using common electronic tools for professional purposes, and (2) how to extend the collaborative environment outlined in Chapters 5 and 6 to workstation-based classrooms, focusing on achieving the primary goals of autonomy and competence through authenticity.

If we can assume the dichotomy between transmissionist and constructivist teaching approaches, we will find that the approaches taken to computer-based classes, like any other classes, can be situated on a continuum between the two extremes. From a radically transmissionist perspective, the teacher might attempt to teach computer skills to the group as a whole, that is to transfer the knowledge he or she believes they will need, progressing from the simple to the complex, from the objectively identifiable essentials to advanced skills. The students in turn could be expected to incrementally learn the steps outlined by the teacher for using the various programmes in the translator's panoply of tools. Practice might essentially involve applying the learned procedures and routines in exercises prepared by the teacher. The goal ostensibly would be to make sure that students acquire the objectively identifiable set of sub-skills that together comprise translator-relevant computer competence, which they should be able to apply to real translation tasks once they leave the institution. Autonomy would be the prize to be awarded with the diploma at the completion of the programme of studies.

Creating a constructivist computer-based classroom

From a constructivist perspective, one would also expect to see a general progression in learning from the simple to the complex, but the movement would be towards complexity as constructed by the students themselves, rather than being imposed by the teacher's syllabus. From this perspective, a rigidly-structured, atomistic approach foregoes valuable opportunities to foster independent and collaborative exploration and skill development on the part of the learners, who will need to know not only how to use the computer-based tools that are available today, but also how to continue to learn on their own as new tools become available in the future. Taking a constructivist approach, a teacher would design and foster a collaborative environment for guided exploration and authentic practice, helping students move toward autonomy from the very beginning. The preliminary proposals I will make in this chapter have the objective of sketching briefly how this latter approach can be seen as a natural extension of a social constructivist method for empowering translators in training. I am aware that I am dealing here only with the tip of an iceberg and that a wealth of other considerations will have to be the subject of future study.

How many computers are needed in the classroom?

A networked classroom with a workstation for each student makes it possible for each individual to get extensive hands-on experience actually using his or her emerging computer-based translation skills, thus ensuring the construction of active knowledge. Having a number of separate workstations in the classroom allows the teacher to carefully scaffold the learning of basic tool-acquisition skills in the earliest stages and then progressively withdraw from the focus of attention to allow the students to construct their own computer-based expertise by carrying out translation-related research, working through real translation problems, developing skills in the use of electronic tools, as well as editing and polishing their translations to meet professional standards. The very fact that each student has immediate and direct access to a complete set of electronic tools obviously promotes the integration of extensive hands-on experience in the classroom.

A relatively inexpensive alternative to the multi-workstation arrangement is to have a single overhead projector or beamer linked to one master computer. This type of system allows, but at the same time forces, the entire class to focus on a single piece of work projected on the screen, a situation that might not be very conducive to collaborative group work, where students should be encouraged to use a variety of strategies for producing multiple acceptable solutions. The whole-group focus might also drastically reduce in-class opportunities for reflective action, as a considerable amount of time could be spent passively considering work done by other students. Because of the need to acquire extensive, guided hands-on experience when one is beginning to develop computer skills, the multi-workstation classroom is indispensable in the early stages. Once they have acquired basic skills and a degree of learning autonomy that permits them to continue learning on their own and with the help of peers and tutors, learners can be expected to continue to make progress using those tools independently and collaboratively outside of class.

In actual translation exercise classes, students might initially work in small groups to produce rough drafts of different parts of a large group project. Each small group can do online research, terminology management work and enter its text into a word processor outside of class and later project it on the screen in the classroom for the purpose of eliciting feedback from the rest of the group and the instructor. Used in this way, the projector can serve as a means for drawing all of the expertise in the classroom to bear on the work of smaller groups as well as that of each individual learner. I have consistently noticed that if I personally operate the equipment in the projector-based class, students generally see it as a sign for them to slip back into their traditional role of being passive recipients of the teacher's wisdom. For this reason, I have found it most valuable to have each small group of students manipulate the equipment and organize the discussion revolving around their own work. Instead of running the show, I join the rest of the group to help provide feedback against the background of each small group's presentation of its own work.

Types of instructional techniques: from teaching to autonomy

Four scenarios for the interactional types of techniques that are possible in a computer-based classroom have been proposed in several publications in recent years (Paulson and Paulson 1994, Paulsen 1995, Reinke 1997). The various scenarios as described by these authors are:

1. **One-to-many techniques,** in which communication takes place between one teacher and a group of learners (for example in online lectures);
2. **Many-to-many techniques,** where communication takes place between learners (with or without a teacher as moderator), in the form of discussions, role-play activities, brainstorming and project groups.
3. **One-to-one techniques,** in which communication takes place between one teacher and one learner or between two learners, for example through online peer tutoring or e-mail tandems;
4. **One-alone techniques,** involving autonomous learning with the help, for example, of online databases and journals, online applications and software libraries, and news groups.

I have listed these four types in the general sequence in which I envisage using them most effectively within a constructivist framework, moving along a scaffolding continuum from initiation to full autonomy.

One-to-many techniques are the ones representing the greatest distance and arbitrary control in the learning process on the part of the teacher. In this mode, instructions and instruction must of necessity be generic and only roughly adapted to the momentary needs and stage of learning of each individual. This is likely to be the dominant technique type in a transmissionist classroom, with the teacher distributing knowledge to a whole class at one time. Attempts to directly transfer knowledge from one person to another play an insignificant role in a constructivist classroom. One-to-many techniques instead are likely to involve project coordination and classroom management features to ensure that a class is moving toward group goals and jointly constructing group knowledge. Here, the teacher functions as a facilitator, rather than an authoritarian figure, negotiating with, advising and encouraging learners, while getting feedback from the students on the progress they are making and the difficulties that arise. A one-to-many instructional technique can be a valuable opportunity for a teacher to appropriate knowledge that is emerging at different levels in the group and restructure it for the class as a whole, thus also acquiring a parallel, many-to-one dimension.

The role of the constructivist teacher can vary radically within this technique type: from being the provider of an initial impetus and instructions for learning how to use a programme in an elementary course, to the project manager whose job it is to ensure the smooth coordination of the work of a team of translators and to negotiate between them and their client. In any event, the one-to-many technique needs to be used cautiously and judiciously, primarily to get the students started in the direction of exploration and hands-on practice in novel situations, to raise awareness of emerging difficulties or imbalances within a group project, and to provide closure for a group's efforts. Anything resembling a lecture by the teacher must be followed immediately by, or interspersed with active student involvement, not only to enable them to try out for themselves what the teacher has just presented, but also to go beyond it. A teacher's or tutor's facilitating of one-to-many interventions would punctuate the many-to-many activities in which multi-level collaboration, skill learning and knowledge construction take place.

Many-to-many constructivist techniques are intended to allow students to tackle complex, authentic tasks with the assistance, but not under the control, of the teacher or facilitator, as well as in collaboration with their fellow group members and other groups. It is through these techniques that multi-faceted collaboration is designed to play an essential role in promoting the active construction of both group and individual knowledge. Many-to-many techniques should allow and promote the exchange of multiple perspectives that are essential for autonomous thought, reflective action and active learning to occur. However, while in a conventional classroom setting, communicative interaction can be marked by direct interpersonal interaction among various members of a group simultaneously, much of the interaction in the computer-based classroom will be mediated by the technological resources, and relegated to the realm of remote or 'virtual' interaction. This is communicative interaction at a distance, in the absence of many of the normal discourse and information-carrying cues like gestures and body language. Here, many-to-many interaction is likely to give way to one-to-one communication, with pairs of students communicating via email or networked chatting functions. For this reason, I have found it indispensable to reserve conventional classroom space for many-to-many activities so that groups of students can actually sit together and discuss their work in face-to-face dialogue.

From our constructivist perspective, **one-to-one** techniques can be sub-divided into 1) mentoring/tutoring activities, or opportunities for individual students to work closely with a mentor to develop their own knowledge; and 2) dyad collaboration, or opportunities for two students to work together to complete joint tasks and at the same time pursue their own, individual learning goals. One-to-one techniques are particularly valuable for focusing directly on an individual's personal learning goals. They allow for concentrated work on special problems in a particularly interactive and supportive environment. Once the teacher adopts the role of a learning facilitator instead of knowledge disseminator, then one-to-one techniques can lose much of their instructional delivery function and acquire instead a prompting, guiding, scaffolding quality to help learners actively construct their own knowledge of the tools and skills at hand. The constructivist teacher will need to cultivate a discourse style for one-to-one interaction to make it clear to students that learning cannot be a one-way street, but that it emerges in dialogue through mutual construction.

One-alone techniques give students the opportunity to work and learn autonomously through the mediation of tools, rather than peers or mentors. Individualized tasks allow students to apply the panoply of skills they have been acquiring collaboratively and in one-on-one instruction to their own individual work. One-alone activities are likely be a major component of constructivist classes, particularly in more advanced stages of learning, but will serve a different purpose from the their primary function in transmissionist settings. While from a transmissionist perspective, working alone serves as an opportunity to review, reinforce and practise the knowledge received from the teacher, in a constructivist setting it represents an opportunity to extrapolate from the emerging shared knowledge of the group to new situations where the learner is forced to act without the immediate support of the learning community.

While there can, of course, be no uniform sequencing of instructional types, the four basic interactional technique types presented here can be used to structure sequences of instructional tasks in a manner that reflects the spirit and goals of a constructivist educational approach. The selection and sequencing of instructional techniques will vary not only with the educational setting, but also with the stage of learning as reflected in the progression of the curriculum from the level of the initiates to that of the journeyman nearing graduation.

From novice to advanced – or from dependency to autonomy

When considering the topic of translation-related computer education at its most basic curricular level, three key stages emerge: 1) introducing students to translation-related work on the computer, 2) establishing and maintaining a collaborative learning environment within the computer-based classroom, and 3) encouraging students to move beyond directed instruction to achieve autonomy as lifelong learners and users of new technology. This sequence of stages can be seen in terms of **scaffolding** the educational process; beginning with a significant amount of teacher control and intervention and gradually, but consistently, moving through stages of collaborative work between and among students accompanied by less and less assistance from the teacher, and on to the final goal of learner autonomy. By the end of the programme of studies, graduates should be able to work independently and collaboratively without supervision using common tools of the trade, and they should also have highly developed learning skills that will enable them to learn how to use new tools as they evolve in the future.

Breaking the electronic ice

For the bulk of students who come to the university with relatively little experience in using computers for translation purposes, the first steps toward mastering multi-lingual text-processing skills on the PC can be daunting. Standard programmes like word processors, spreadsheets, databases and desktop publishing software have become highly sophisticated, incorporating features that allow the translator in many cases to produce camera-ready copy, but also requiring extensive knowledge of many complex features. Customers of translation services today can and often do expect to receive a professional quality text formatted according to their specifications. In many cases it has become too expensive to pass on a poorly designed and formatted text to a copy editor or secretary for revision – text layout is often part of the translator's work. The translator-in-training must acquire a sophisticated set of computer-based skills in order to meet the demands of his or her future employers and clients.

Just as learning how to use a foreign language can be a formidable enterprise if novices, as linguistic and cultural outsiders, are confronted with the sheer enormity of the language's structural, cultural and sociolinguistic complexity, learning how to use sophisticated new technology for professional purposes can also appear prohibitively difficult at the beginning. I suggest that the process of initiating students into the use of the translator's computer-based tools can be significantly less threatening if it is dealt with in a manner that is analogous to that of acquiring a foreign language in a naturalistic setting. Much as children 'construct' their native tongue by interacting in authentic situations, so too can our students construct their own computer-based translation skills, if we provide them with a suitable environment for doing so.

Our goal, then, will be to make students behave and feel like computer-literate insiders from the beginning, to help them acquire skills for using hard- and software without being overwhelmed by their apparent complexity. Initiation is the key term here: we need to initiate our students into the community of computer-based tool users rather than simply trying to transmit to them a sequence of isolated sub-skills.

As mentioned in Chapter 5, the introductory course in translation studies required by students studying English at the University of Mainz provides an excellent forum for offering students a brief introduction to the work translators can expect to perform on the computer. In the workshop entitled 'The Translator's Tools', one team of students introduces the rest of the class to the computer-based resources available at the university in a two-hour session in our workstation-based classroom. The students who choose to run this workshop are usually among those members of the class who are already fairly proficient computer users or who at least show great interest in the information-technology side of the translator's work. After identifying the questions they would like to answer, the group first reads several articles from the translation studies literature on the state of the art of the translator's workstation and on the acquisition of computer skills for translation students. I then encourage them to explore our local network and to consult the School's technical support team for further information and guidance as needed. I also attend as many of the small group preparation sessions as necessary to provide additional support while the group is constructing its knowledge in preparation for running the workshop.

Drawing from the current literature on the topic, the workshop team finds out what computer-related skills are required of translators on the market today. By consulting our local network and support team, they find out what tools courses are currently made available by the institution to teachers and the student body. They then work together to devise a set of brief, introductory activities to get the other students, many of whom have virtually no experience in working with computers beyond the most basic word processing and emailing tasks, to consider the value of using the various tools we have available. They generally weigh the benefits of using computers against the inconvenience of having to learn how to use them, and attempt to foster in their classmates a strong interest in continuing to learn about the translator's tools. By having students run the workshop, I demonstrate to the class that it is not very difficult to get initiated into the use of these tools and that they can indeed learn from their fellow students. This facilitates the peer work and tutoring that will be important aspects of subsequent translation exercise classes.

Project-centred classes for the learning of computer skills

It may or may not be necessary in a given institutional setting to offer special courses in the use of the hard-and software that is commonly used for translation purposes. Over the course of the past five years in which I have incorporated instruction in the use of computer-based tools into my courses in German-English commercial translation, most of my students have been able to acquire right in the translation exercise class the basic word processing, terminology management, and online research skills that I am sure they will need for their professional work. An added advantage from a constructivist perspective is that the text processing skills they learn in these classes are all directly related to actual translation work.

As in non-computerized classes dealing with general language topics, I draw on my own translation experience in computer-based classes to provide students with extensive opportunities to simulate the completion of authentic translation jobs. I usually start out the class by providing the group with a real or simulated commission, including the constraints on the task from the client's perspective. This sets the stage for the students to figure out for themselves what skills they will need to master and to what degree in order to meet the task specifications. With only 90 minutes per week of contact time, however, it has often proved difficult to cover the specialized subject matter, to deal with the host of translation problems that invariably arise, and also to cover the specific computer-based skills necessary to complete each task. Recently, a tutoring programme funded by the state government of Rhineland-Palatinate has made it possible to have an advanced student serve as a tutor in weekly sessions that run parallel to my regular classes and in which students can hone the specific computer-based skills they need to complete their translation projects.

A variety of scenarios are possible, depending on the staffing, space and funding available for computerized applications at different institutions. It might be necessary, for example, because of a lack of computer resources, to have all regular class meetings held in a conventional classroom, with tutoring sessions alone relegated to the computerized classroom. Where budgetary constraints make it difficult to offer classes on a regular basis that introduce students to computer resources, tutoring sessions during which students work collaboratively on group projects may help meet significant demand for instruction in and experience with the translator's computer-based tools. By consistently using tutors and ensuring that projects require students to learn a panoply of computer skills, it may be possible to actually reduce the need for special introductory courses to word processing, terminology management, WWW research, etc. Thus, by incorporating the learning of these necessary skills into regular translation exercise classes, we may be able to provide better instruction and actually reduce demands on the university personnel and budget in the process.

Analysis of needs

The first project of each elementary course in my computerized classroom is a needs analysis based on an activity like the one depicted in Figure 8.

A needs assessment activity provides the teacher, as well as the students themselves, with an opportunity right at the beginning of the course to find out what skills need to be acquired to complete a given project. It also places all of the computer-based skills that will be the focus of the course into a translation-specific context so that students can see the relevance of everything we will be doing in class for their professional work. This greatly enhances students' motivation to work toward mastery of computer-based skills in these classes. Following our assessment of these initial worksheets, the tutor and I agree on what aspects need to be dealt with and how the necessary competence can be fostered in the tutoring and regular class sessions. Everything that is covered in the tutoring session is directly related to translation tasks that the students are working on within the context of translation projects in my regular class.

If, for example, the students and I realize, while working on a text on financial investments, that they need to gather information on different forms of investments, I may suggest that they ask the tutor to help them find relevant information on the World Wide Web. Using an overhead projector so that the learners can observe what he or she is doing, tutors might start by demonstrating how they themselves

Semester Topic: The Y2K Problem and Commercial Affairs

Initial Assessment: What can I already do and what to I need to learn more about?

Instructions: In order for you to assess your skill at using some of the basic software functions that many translators deal with on a day-to-day basis, please complete the following assignment and place a check in the box that best describes how difficult it was for you to complete each respective sub-task. This information will be used to help the tutor determine what to focus on in initial sessions.

The overall task involves handling a number of steps that a professional translator might go through when undertaking a translation job – except for the translation work itself.

Please undertake the sub-tasks in the order given:

- Open file: o:\\utexte\kiraly\y2k_first.htm in Word for Windows©.
- Mark the section that is indicated in yellow and paste it into a blank page.
- Change the font to Times New Roman – 12 point; and change the margins to 2 cm on all sides.
- Unmark the text (remove yellow marking).
- Underline all words that you feel are especially related to the Y2K problem.
- Check for those terms in one of our networked terminology management programmes.
- Using the Internet, find one parallel page in English that you feel could help you translate the text. Copy that page onto a blank page in Word© and save it in the C:\docs directory on your workstation. Mark passages that you believe provide helpful information for translating your German text.
- Create an ASCII import file for the TM programme (using instructions in the online-help file if necessary), including all of the specialized Y2K terms you found, trans lations of them into English, and useful contextual information to ensure that the user of the glossary can be confident of its accuracy.

After saving the various files to the C:/docs folder on your workstation, create a zip file containing: 1) your downloaded Web page, 2) your ASCII import file, and 3) the Y2k.doc file that you have reformatted to: Kiraly@mail.fask.uni-mainz.de.

Once you have finished, please go through the checklist below and indicate how difficult it was for you to complete each of the above steps.

Task	No problem	Somewhat difficult	Impossible
Find and open file			
Cut and paste			
Change font and margins			
Remove yellow marking			
Check vocabulary in database			
Download WWW page			
Create ASCII import file			
Zipping files			
E-mailing zipped file			

Figure 8: A Needs Assessment for Basic Computer Skills

would go about searching for some specific information related to the topic at hand. Using the overhead projector to allow students to follow along, the tutor can log on to the WWW, use one or more browsers to search for a combination of terms that might produce a valuable array of hits, find pages with the kind of information they are looking for, and save the corresponding files to the computer. The tutor might then work offline to convert a terminology list in HTML format into a text document, reorganize and format it to make it compatible with a terminology management programme and then import the data into that programme, showing how translator can create their own knowledge base by drawing upon a variety of resources both online and offline.

From a constructivist perspective, we need to get students as quickly as possible into the practical use mode and away from conventional student roles of passive listening, observation and drill. They need to move beyond the demonstration and exercise level to use the tools they are acquiring for their own purposes. This transition is essential for the development of active, rather than inert knowledge. It is also essential that students not see the teacher's or tutor's chosen method for accomplishing a given task as the only or right way. Different techniques need to be demonstrated as alternative ways of attaining any goal, and students need to be encouraged to experiment with the various techniques presented, and if possible to come up with even better or more efficient techniques of their own.

By experimenting with the tools available, and by working with each other and seeking help from the teacher or tutor when they are having difficulties, students will start to learn the language of the technology from the inside. If they sit passively taking notes, the knowledge will simply pass from the teacher's mouth to the students' notes without becoming part of the learner's experience.

Learning the tools of the trade through collaboration

Tutoring need not be only a way to provide instructional contact hours that cannot be covered by regular teaching staff. The use of tutors in computer-based classrooms can be an excellent step towards forming a community of interactive learners in the translation exercise classroom. Tutoring sessions can provide students with opportunities to work collaboratively with others in preparation for their professional activities, where they will often be required to work together closely with a variety of other professionals, including fellow translators, clients, authors, technical experts, graphics designers and copywriters.

Tutors must, of course, be trained in collaborative working methods themselves. Just because they may have more experience in using particular tools does not make them apt for assuming tasks related to the scaffolding of learning. The tutors for my classes are chosen on the basis of their record as excellent collaborative learners who understand the value of identifying zones of proximal development and providing assistance as needed without adopting a conventional domineering transmissionist teacher's role with respect to their fellow students.

The project workshop can serve as an ideal global activity within which the translator's computer-based tools can be mastered and interpersonal working skills fostered. As in the conventional classroom, teachers can bring to the computer-based classroom real assignments or at least simulated ones that an entire group can work on. Students can also be given the assignment of identifying source language texts on the WWW that might need translating (or retranslating, in the case of un-professionally translated texts). The students can then have the task of offering their work to the respective webmaster for remuneration. This will give them the direct experience of establishing contact with potential clients and promoting their own professional services, skills they are sure to need once they graduate.

Examples of how computer-based skills can be learned in a collaborative environment

Due to space limitations, I cannot discuss here how to deal with the learning of common computer-based applications in any detail. The following brief selection of basic skills is intended only as a set of initial suggestions that I believe are consistent with a constructivist approach. It is essential for teachers to develop their own techniques that suit their own particular teaching environments.

Research for translation purposes
Translators must obviously be able to use a wide range of resources to solve translation problems. Not only mono- and bilingual dictionaries, but also encyclopaedias, specialized reference works, internal company glossaries, and parallel texts are resources that can help the translator do a better job more quickly. The computer-based translation exercise class is an excellent venue for investigating these various resources and helping each individual student determine and expand upon the array of tools that they can use to complete assignments.

A good starting point for resource investigation work might be a comparison between the utility of hard copy versus offline and online resources. The user interfaces of most commercially available resources on CD-ROM are standardized and user-friendly. It is valuable to show students that once they can use a few standard programs, they will have acquired the basic tools that will allow them to go on to learn additional programs as well. Following a demonstration of an actual search for information in an offline reference work by the teacher or tutor, for example, students can be encouraged to do their own searching, experimenting with the programs and explaining their functions to each other. The focus should remain on the overall goals of the research task, goals which should be clearly identified by the students in advance and which should be explicitly related to students' learning objectives.

If students are encouraged to work on their own translation projects in the computer-based classroom, it is easy for the instructor to focus on problems that the students actually have, rather than selecting features a priori that the students may not be ready to learn. There should also be room in the curriculum for students to pursue projects independently of the rest of the class. In an advanced class, for example, where the students have already acquired considerable mastery over the translator's computer-based tools, and have also acquired a high level of translation competence, the students could assume the task of finding a web page that needs translating (or retranslating) and negotiating with the site owner to have a contribution made to charity in exchange for a professional quality translation. By having students work on projects that they have chosen themselves, and that they know will have an impact beyond the mark on the paper, we set the stage for them to do high quality work; and it is through the doing of high quality work that learners acquire the knowledge, habits and skills for doing excellent work in their professional lives as well.

Terminology management

The management of terminology has become an extremely important sub-field of translator training due to the increased importance of terminological norms (for example within the EU) and as a result of the internationalization of business over the last few decades. Our students can expect to have to manage terminology once they graduate, whether they work as freelancers or as staff translators for a company or public administration office. There are numerous tools available for terminology management today and they are likely to proliferate in coming years. Rather than teaching students how to work with a single program that happens to be popular today, it is more valuable, in my opinion, to introduce students to principles of terminology management and help them experiment with several programs so that they will have a broad base of experience that will help them autonomously learn how to use new programs as they appear on the market.

Computer-based terminology management tools provide an excellent forum for students to collaboratively construct their own joint understandings of efficient and consistent terminology management. They can serve as a laboratory where principles proposed by the teacher or tutor can be experimented with, modified and improved upon. Rather than simply teaching the functions of a program, e.g. how to search for and enter terms in a database, how to import and export glossaries, and how to create printed glossaries, for example, it is a good idea to begin with questions related to the role and function of terminology management in the translator's work – the answers to which will help guide students' acquisition of specific terminology management skills. Students can also be given the task of finding out how certain features of a program work and explaining them to partners or the rest of the class.

In courses on terminology management at the University of Mainz, initial attention is paid to the structure of hard-copy dictionaries as dictated by the constraints of having to search in books in a sequential manner on the basis of headwords. This can lead to a discussion of more useful ways of searching for terminology-related information. I would suggest that a practical goal for a computer-based course or segment on terminology management would be to see it more as knowledge management, where contextual as well as structural information is built into the database by the translator or team of translators. This can be excellent training for ensuring that translators-in-training will always be wary of decontextualized dictionary entries, and that they will realize that it is their job to gather information from a variety of sources (multiple perspectives), to serve as a foundation for their translation decisions rather than relying on a single, narrow source.

Editing and proofreading

Learners need feedback if they are to learn from their mistakes. It need not be solely the teacher's job to provide that feedback, however. Peer assistance can also be drawn into the editing and proofreading stages of a computer-based translation exercise class to provide students with feedback, and to help those providing feedback to recognize problems in translations and thereby focus on improving their own work. Students must of course learn how to edit and proofread each other's work. Unfortunately, peer correction is a topic that has attracted little interest in the field of translator education. Word processors offer a convenient editing function which translation editors make use of and which can also be put to good use in the translation exercise class. Students can be asked to e-mail their rough translations to another member of a class or even to a student in another class or program for proofreading. Using the editing function, the proofreading student can make suggestions in the original translator's text without deleting what originally appeared there. The proofread version can then be sent back to the first student, who can be asked to incorporate necessary changes into their translation, negotiating with the proof reader if a difference of opinion arises. The revised versions will usually be better than the rough drafts and both students will have learned from the experience. The teacher will have less proofreading to do and can concentrate on editing the final version rather than the various stages leading up to it. This also encourages students to work collaboratively with their peers, thereby helping to empower them, helping them move from dependence on the teacher toward autonomy as learners.

The grammar checkers built into modern word processors are other tools that should not be ignored in the editing process. Grammar checkers can usually underline passages in a text that do not match their samples of possible grammatical sentences. While no supportive feedback is provided, the student is still given hints as to the possible location of grammatical errors. This is indeed a form of feedback that can help the learner go back and focus on sentence form, particularly when translating into the foreign language. In this way, some of the time teachers spend working on syntax can be relegated to one-alone work in collaboration with the software.

Project in website design

A graduate seminar I offered in translation studies provided a constructivist setting for a class of advanced students to develop its own Web site on Innovation in Translator Education. Starting with reports submitted the semester before by a class that had worked on 'Assessment in Translator Training', the group divided up into four sub-groups, each of which chose one of the following topics: educational epistemology, innovative projects carried out in Germersheim, foreign language learning and translator education, and innovative projects at other universities. (I originally proposed a list of eight topics, but the class decided to narrow it down to these four). Each group agreed to gather and assimilate information on its chosen topic and use it as the basis for creating a set of Web pages that would be put on line as part of a course site. Neither I, nor any of the students, had enough background in HTML editing and Web design to initiate the group into this special domain. Fortunately, we were able to draw on the assistance of an American graduate student who took on the task of instructing us to fulfill the requirement of a teaching practicum at his home university.

The small groups met in a conventional classroom for the first half of the semester. During these sessions, they shared ideas on their project topics and discussed, both in small groups and with the class as a whole, the emerging design of their online projects. Our HTML tutor arrived halfway through the semester and I first briefed him on our collaborative working style. At an initial session, the students, the tutor and I negotiated the organization and content of the tutoring sessions to come. Then the tutoring sessions began. On the basis of our joint needs analysis, the tutor began introducing us to Web design by having us program sample pages ourselves from the very first day. By the third session, all of the learners had grasped enough of the basics to allow us to begin designing our project pages with a text editor. Parallel to the tutoring sessions, we continued to hold our regular class meetings in a conventional classroom. This provided us with adequate opportunities to continue our many-to-many collaborative discussions, in which the different groups continuously revised their emerging pages and worked as a class to co-ordinate the sub-projects and link them into a single global site.

This is an example of how a course can be designed around the interests of the students and through which they can all acquire a set of skills that they are likely to need upon graduation. The seminar theme provided a basic context and an overall task that was sure to entail the focused learning of valuable computer-based skills by all the students, but in a fashion that was adapted to their respective prior knowledge and to their personal interests. Here again, the stage was set for situated learning through authentic action. The learners' obvious pride in their work, the sense of accomplishment as well as the competence with which they completed each stage of their respective projects were clear indications to me that the knowledge they were acquiring was far from inert. This was knowledge-in-action that would not only serve them individually in their professional work, but that would also remain as a record of their achievements and as a stepping stone for groups of students that would succeed them.

Conclusion: Instruction today preparing for the work of tomorrow

Given the current rapid evolution of hard- and software, many of the electronic tools in use by translators today on a daily basis may well be outdated within a few years. Speech recognition software, for example, may radically change how word processing is done. Advances in computer-assisted and machine translation may increase throughput dramatically and may also shift the focus of the work of many more translators away from translation itself to pre- and post-editing. And parallel multilingual text design may become a feasible alternative to conventional, source-to-target text translation in many more areas than it is today. The technology translators use in the future will evolve from the array of tools in use today. By acquiring a firm feel for the interplay of the computer-based tools that are used by the community of translators today, students will be well prepared to continue learning how to use the tools of tomorrow. Rather than absorbing information provided by teachers, I contend that through the consistent application of collaborative working methods and the careful design of the varieties of interactional techniques we use in our instructional activities, from one-to-many to one-alone, we can develop a micro-community of computer-users within the institution. By engaging extensively in the authentic work of the profession, the members of this community, as in all emerging professional communities, will acquire the lifelong learning skills that will ensure their ability to adapt dynamically to the tools of the profession as they evolve in the future.

In the next chapter, I would like to illustrate how the planning-action and observation-reflection sequence can also be applied to another important topic in any educational institution – the assessment of student learning.

8. Assessment and the Emergence of Translator Competence

The objectivist underpinnings of traditional assessment practices

The word 'assessment' comes from the Latin *assidere*, meaning 'to sit beside'. This, I think, is a particularly apt metaphor for constructivist assessment, which, as I will attempt to show throughout this chapter, can be seen as a process of sitting and working with students in a mutual quest for new understandings. From this viewpoint, assessment is not simply a testing and ranking process that students are subjected to periodically throughout and at the end of an educational programme to see how much knowledge they have absorbed from instruction. It is instead an integral part of the teaching/learning dialogue, the aim of which is to produce feedback for the facilitatation of new learning. To assess constructively implies that assessors are learning as well. Through assessment, teachers construe how students are constructing knowledge, which can help the teachers re-direct their instructional efforts to facilitate those construction processes. Assessment and authenticity are also intricately intertwined since assessment is something that students ultimately must be able to do for themselves. Over the course of the programme, they must increasingly be capable of determining what they already know and what they still need to learn. And by the time they graduate, learners must have internalized sufficient self-assessment skills to be able to undertake and complete professional tasks without an omnipotent teacher standing by to provide corrections.

Before going any further, I would like to define some of the key educational terms I will be using in this chapter,. While the words are surely familiar to all teachers, there is considerable variability in the meanings attributed to them. In addition to **assessment**, these terms include **evaluation**, **testing** and **marking**. I will use **assessment** to refer to the process of gathering information about the quality of students' emerging competence; **evaluation** I understand as the process of attributing meaning to the information gathered; **testing** is a scientific process of sampling performance with the goal of generalizing to competence; and **marking** is an attempt to sort performance along a scale (Azwell 1992). The importance of specifying these definitions, I hope, will quickly become apparent.

As in all educational environments, the periodic as well as terminal (end-of-programme) determination of students' progress toward learning goals is a major concern for translator education institutions. In the literature on translation studies, most contributions dealing with assessment have focused specifically on what many scholars have called 'translation quality assessment' (House 1997, Chesterman 1993,

Klaudy 1995, Kussmaul 1995) – but which I see instead as an 'evaluation' process, that is, the evaluation of information about whether or not students produce good (faithful, accurate, functional, etc.) renderings of source language texts in a target language. A number of approaches to translation quality assessment have been designed for didactic purposes in translator training programmes, including those developed by the authors cited just above as well as, for example, Kupsch-Losereit (1986), Hönig (1998), Schmitt (1997) and Nord (1994). I believe that all of these approaches have merits, and that they can serve as valuable resources for assessing the competence of the emerging professional translator.

It is not my objective here, however, to discuss the relative merits of these various translation evaluation approaches, much less to propose yet another one of my own. Instead, I would like to step back from the evaluation of source and target texts and look instead at what I have defined above as **assessment**: the process of metaphorically 'sitting with students', of gathering information about learners' progress. I hope to show that, if we expect our assessments, marks and evaluations to provide valuable information about students' learning progress to teachers, future employers and the students themselves, then our assessment (i.e. information collection) procedures must be 1) demonstrably based on deep and extensive observation of students' performance; 2) representative of the conditions and standards under which our graduates can expect to work professionally; and 3) equitable and collaborative, with students taking an active, empowered role in the assessment process. I will attempt to demonstrate how a constructivist approach can provide a basis for an assessment system that is trustworthy, authentic and fair – all characteristics of empowering educational practice.

The limits of traditional testing procedures

In order to remind ourselves of some of the situational features of a traditional assessment environment, let us look into a typical classroom where students are taking a test:

> We open the door to the classroom and walk inside. The only sound comes from the busy scratching of pens on paper, an occasional cough or the shuffling of paper. The room is otherwise eerily silent as we move past row after row of students, heads bowed over their work. A vigilant teacher paces the floor, watching for roving eyes or whispered connivance. Time drags on before the first papers are handed in. Finally free, one by one the students gather their pens and scratch paper, silently hand in their papers, and leave the room. The teacher will take the papers and head home to judge alone which answers were correct and which were not, which students performed on an average level and which ones fell above or below the mean. The results will come in the form of corrections and a final mark, to be placed on the paper and returned to the learners at a future class session.

This scenario will probably remind readers of countless tests and final examinations in which they have taken part as pupils, students and perhaps as proctors. It is clearly more a matter of 'standing over' than 'sitting with'.

Let us consider the assumptions underlying this ubiquitous testing situation. From a scientific, positivist perspective, tests are to be conducted in an 'objective' manner, with criteria of truth (right or wrong) being applied to determine accuracy and error. An ideal test will be reliable, that is repeatable with the same results; and it will be valid, which means that it will be a true reflection of what it is designed to test, presumably the learner's knowledge and/or skill in a given domain. And finally, the results for each learner should be generalizable to the set of potential performances that this learner could produce. To make tests as objective as possible, we isolate test takers from each other and from most outside resources. We often take the results of a single test to be a representative sample of performance, and we try to reduce bias by ensuring that the assessor's involvement with students and her knowledge of their earlier performance does not influence her evaluation of the performance under scrutiny. It is believed that assessment criteria should also be objective, i.e. applied uniformly to each student and each test in an equally impersonal manner.

From a constructivist perspective, a test conducted in this way, far from being 'objective', is beset by great potential for bias, limited scope of prediction and a general lack of credibility. At best, it can provide but a snapshot of a particular performance, but not a rich portrait of capability and competence. Throughout the remainder of this chapter, I will outline the key features of my emerging constructivist approach to the assessment of learning and suggest ways in which it can be applied in translator training. This discussion will focus on three main areas: 1) constructivist assessment principles that can viably replace the objectivist, scientific principles of validity and reliability; 2) the role of professional standards in bringing more authenticity into assessment practices, and 3) implications of these principles for ongoing (formative) and terminal (summative) assessment.

Principles of constructivist assessment

Guba and Lincoln (1989) pioneered the development of a systematic constructivist approach to the assessment of academic programmes over a decade ago. They illustrated how traditional assessment practices are grounded in the epistemology of logical positivism (objectivism) and how they can be evaluated on the basis of whether or not they are reliable, valid, objective, and generalizable. They then went on to propose an alternate set of criteria for judging the quality of programme assessments, based instead on the concepts of **trustworthiness** and **authenticity,** which derive from a constructivist view of knowledge-making. Other scholars have demonstrated how the findings of Guba and Lincoln can be applied to the assessment of students' learning as well (Paulson 1994), (Cole 1992), (Hipps 1993).

As suggested above, the use of objectivist yardsticks in traditional testing approaches is based on the assumptions that (1) knowledge can be measured by an outside observer; (2) it is separable from the context in which it is used; (3) a learner's true capabilities can be measured precisely by a test at one particular moment; and (4) the results of a test can be generalized to other potential performance events. These assumptions do not hold, however, within a constructivist paradigm, where there is no objective yardstick against which to measure behaviour, and where 'knowing' is not seen as the **product** of an ingestion process, but as a dynamic, intersubjective **process** in and of itself (Hipps 1993). From this perspective, any test represents no more than a momentary snapshot of some surface features of a unique constellation of personal and situational factors revolving around an ever-evolving and multi-facetted individual. It would thus be absurd either to attempt to replicate a given performance (in order to demonstrate reliability) or to suggest that one test is a true measure of that person's competence (to establish validity). The results of a one-shot test cannot be generalized to other potential performances, each of which would similarly be embedded in a unique constellation of situational factors. And, as I hope to have demonstrated throughout the earlier chapters of this book, no outside observer can objectively determine another individual's capabilities. We can obscure but not refute the fact that observation by nature entails a subjective, and never an objective viewpoint.

Guba and Lincoln's (1989) concepts of **trustworthiness** and **authenticity** are designed to take the inherently elusive and multifarious features of performance into consideration to ensure that assessments will be credible, valuable and fair. Trustworthiness refers to the quality of an assessment that allows stakeholders in the educational process (students, potential employers, parents, and faculty) to consider an assessment as a well-substantiated and believable depiction of the learner's capabilities. Authenticity refers to the degree to which an assessment takes into account the multi-dimensional situational factors that impinge on the assessment process.

The constraints of space in this volume allow me to do no more than briefly sketch my understanding of some of the implications of this constructivist approach to assessment for translator education. I hope the following discussion will serve as a starting point for a much-needed dialogue in our field on how to assess the learning of emerging translators in ways that are fair and credible – ways that can contribute to the empowerment of our students as they go through the metamorphosis from novices to experts.

First, I would like to outline the basic characteristics of trustworthiness and authenticity as discussed in the literature on constructivist assessment, and also suggest a few ways in which these concepts can be seen to apply specifically to assessment in translator education.

Trustworthiness

As proposed by Guba and Lincoln (1989) and discussed by Hipps (1993), the principle of **trustworthiness** comprises four components: credibility, transferability, dependability and confirmability. These concepts parallel the positivist scientific criteria of validity, generalizability, reliability and objectivity, but are based on constructivist assumptions regarding the multi-faceted, dynamic and intersubjective nature of knowledge construction.

Credibility asks assessors to establish that they have adequately represented the learners' constructed realities. Guba and Lincoln (1989) propose several tools for ensuring that assessments will be credible for stakeholders. Here, as throughout this section, I have applied their concepts for programme assessment to learning assessment:

• *Prolonged engagement* entails observing a learner over a long period of time, rather than basing an assessment solely on the results of a test given on one particular day. Students' periodic and terminal grades should not be based solely on their performance on single tests taken at the end or mid-point of a period of study; ongoing assessment takes the dynamic nature of knowledge construction into consideration, thus contributing to a more credible picture of a learner's capabilities for action.
• *Persistent observation* means that an assessor will be adequately engaged with a student to be able to see learning success and failure from a deeper perspective, and not solely as a function of the superficial snapshot of performance or internalized knowledge that a given test purports to provide. Persistent observation clearly goes hand in hand with prolonged engagement.
   Small-group work provides an ideal setting for teachers to interact closely with students, and these encounters can provide a much stronger basis for stakeholders to see an assessment as credible than could possibly be the case in a teacher-centred transmissionist classroom, which provides for relative-ly superficial interaction between the teacher and the individual members of the class.
• *Peer debriefing* involves having a teacher review his or her assessment findings with a peer, that is, another teacher or a supervisor. This provides the assessor with an additional perspective upon which to judge a learner's capability and helps ensure that personal bias will not be a significant factor determining a learner's success or failure. The open nature of constructivist learning environments can promote interaction between teachers, which can in turn pave the way for effective debriefing. In practical terms, peer debriefing may prove to be a daunting task in terms of manpower and time. However, team teaching and the use of tutors to facilitate scaffolding provide opportunities for interactively observing learners' progress, and thus for collaborative assessments.
• *Progressive subjectivity* refers to an assessor's monitoring of his or her emerging

understanding of a student's capabilities to ensure that assessment findings are not dictated by his or her own biases. This concept explicitly acknowledges that the assessor comes to each assessment situation with preconceived notions that invariably change with experience over time. Reflecting on one's changing impressions of a student's capabilities, perhaps by keeping a journal over a longer period of time, can help assessors keep track of their own dynamic viewpoint.

• *Member checks* are opportunities for assessors and assessees to discuss their respective perspectives on a given assessment situation. By discussing tentative assessment findings with the learner, teachers can gain important new insights into the motives behind a given performance, thus helping them to re-evaluate those findings. Such discussions also contribute to the credibility and fairness that students perceive in the assessment by giving them a dialogic voice in the process.

In a translator education environment, rather than simply handing back graded papers and pointing out errors that the students have made, it is valuable to have individualized post-assessment meetings between teachers and learners to clarify misunderstandings and to draw assessment into the teaching/learning process. Such sessions can allow learners to focus on the very specific points where they are having difficulties, and can also help teachers scaffold instruction for each individual learner. Like peer debriefing, member checks, if done on a regular basis for all students, would obviously be a prohibitively time-consuming process. However, if done on a periodic basis or if reserved for students whose performance is inadequate or borderline, member checks could be incorporated into many assessment systems.

Transferability deals with the extent to which judgments made concerning knowledge and skills displayed in one situation is applicable to other situations. Rather than seeing a test score as a definitive, generalizable measurement of a student's knowledge in a domain or capabilities for performing a skill, a constructivist assessor will constantly be aware of changing situational constraints. One tool to promote transferability is 'thick description', which involves providing extensive information about the contexts of assessment, which in turn helps stakeholders determine the extent to which those contexts are similar to or different from professional performance contexts. As Hipps (1993) so aptly states, "authentic assessments are valued because their performance is valued in the real world".

Dependability issues relate to questions of whether the enquiry process is documentable and consistent with good assessment practices. Dependability is promoted by making the enquiry process open to public inspection.

Confirmability means that the assessment-related data (constructions, assertions, facts, etc.) can be tracked to their sources, and that the logic used to assemble the interpretations into structurally coherent and corroborating wholes is both explicit and implicit in the assessment reporting process.

Guba and Lincoln (1989) propose an auditing process to ensure the dependability and confirmability of assessments. Secretive assessment practices and lack of accountability can only contribute to a perception of arbitrariness in traditional assessment practices. Maintaining a paper trail of the many factors that enter into assessments and making the process open to public scrutiny can be a powerful way for teachers to ensure that the institutional assessment process can be trusted by all of the various stakeholders to produce valuable assessments of students' emerging professional capabilities. It also means that teachers will be accountable to learners, to the institution, and to potential employers for the assessments they make.

Authenticity and fairness

As stated above, Guba and Lincoln developed the trustworthiness criteria of credibility, transferability, dependability and confirmability to parallel the positivist criteria of validity, generalizability, reliability and objectivity. In addition, they also proposed the criteria of authenticity and fairness, which have no counterparts in the scientific testing paradigm, but which are of key importance from a constructivist perspective.

Guba and Lincoln define several types of authenticity, which go beyond the task authenticity I have discussed in previous chapters: (1) awareness of the constructions one holds (ontological authenticity); (2) an awareness of the constructions of others (educative authenticity); (3) the call to action resulting from a study (catalytic authenticity), and (4) the ability to act for oneself or one's group in the political arena, empowerment (tactical authenticity). Task authenticity refers essentially to the situational affinity between the performances assessed and the skills, knowledge and capabilities that stakeholders can reasonably expect learners to need in professional life. Guba and Lincoln have included this aspect under transferability in their trustworthiness criteria, and I will return to it later in this chapter. Ensuring ontological, educative, catalytic, tactical and task authenticity means turning a unidimensional test – a snapshot of the superficial, directly observable results of a performance – into a holographic multi-dimensional enquiry into values, perspectives and implications for action.

Guba and Lincoln saw two primary ways of demonstrating the authenticity of an assessment: (1) collecting stakeholder testimony, and (2) reviewing the audit trail. First, members of stakeholder groups, including teachers, students and perhaps representatives of the profession serving in an advisory capacity, can be interviewed about the extent to which assessments were fair, how they contributed to deeper understanding, and how they were empowering. Assuring the authenticity of assessments implies a concern for the consequences of assessment practices. We not only need to correct and mark students' tests, but also to find out what happens to students after the assessment process. In ongoing assessment throughout the programme, do students use the results of the assessment as constructive feedback to further their learning? Do employers believe in the value of institutional assessments and take them as credible predictions of how graduates will be able to perform in professional settings? And to what extent do teachers draw implications from the assessments they make for subsequent teaching?

The final feature of authentic assessments, and one that is of particular importance from a constructivist perspective is **fairness**. The fairness criterion ensures that all constructions and values be presented in a balanced way, and that stakeholder groups negotiate meanings and actions from equal positions of strength. This takes assessment out of the exclusive purview of teachers and administrators, and draws students and employers into a constructive dialogue on the implications of the results for remedial action. It is the fairness criterion that ensures that students are not disempowered as they are by a traditional 'snapshot' approach, where the purported (yet unattainable) objectivity of the assessor and the testing situation obscure an enormous potential for bias and inauthenticity.

A role for professional standards: the example of DIN 2345

A question of particular importance for constructivist education is how task authenticity can be ensured in the assessment process. In order to develop trustworthy, authentic and fair assessments, it is essential to draw the standards for expert performance in a given professional community into the educational institution's assessment policies and practice.

In 1998, the Deutsches Institut für Normung e.V. (a private institution that develops widely accepted technical and industrial standards in Germany) published a standard covering translation contracts (DIN 2345). Developed by the DIN in conjunction with representatives of the translation industry, the standard covers various features of translation situations that can and should be covered by contracts between the client and the translator. Both translators and customers of translation services can voluntarily agree to abide by the standards. Translators and translation agencies can also apply to the institute for certification, which allows the use of the DIN seal and serves to inform other parties to translation contracts that one is committed to compliance with the standards. Similar standards have been proposed, for example, in Italy (UNI 10574), and the Dutch Association of Translation Companies has adopted the *Taalmerk* (language mark) certification system based on the DIN standards.

As DIN 2345 now stands, it is not designed specifically to govern translation quality, but rather, the conditions under which translations are assigned, undertaken, completed and accepted between parties to contracts for translation services. As it is still a new phenomenon in the translation industry, however, the standard will surely undergo considerable change as the result of the emerging dialogue between the translation industry, professional associations and educational institutions. I suggest that incorporating the DIN standard into our curricula can contribute to the overall credibility of our assessments, which interface with industry particularly through the reporting of summative evaluation results. By beginning to work with the standard as it emerges, students, teachers and administrators can participate in the dialogue that is dynamically creating industry standards; otherwise, we will be presented with a *fait accompli*. I also suggest that it is not only, or even primarily, translation scholars or institutional administrators who need to develop a voice for education in the development of a professional standard, but also students and teachers working with it in their actual teaching, learning and assessment activities.

The DIN standard for translation contracts

Let us take a closer look at the aspects of translation situations that are covered by DIN 2345 (DIN 1998). The standard covers six main areas: (1) the source text, (2) co-operation between the participants in the translation assignment, (3) selection of the translator, (4) organization of the translation process, (5) the target text, and (6) review of the translation product.

Source text
The client is responsible for ensuring that the source text is technically and linguistically accurate. He should inform the translator of any errors, and is responsible for clarifying them and for responding to the translator's queries about the text.

The translator must determine prior to and during the translation process the extent to which the necessary terminology is available or must still be prepared, and the extent to which he or she must learn more about the topic of the translation in order to complete the job.

The translator's tasks in this connection include reading the source text; reviewing his or her own terminology; reviewing terminology provided by the client; reading the documentation provided by the client; undertaking further research as necessary; and, as needed, clarifying other questions with the client or other experts.

Selection of the translator
The client is to ensure that only qualified translators will work on the assignment. The criteria for the selection of translators comprise: the translator's qualifications (training and experience); translation competence; technical equipment available; ability to meet the deadline; translation certification in the event that a certified translation is needed.

Organization of the translation process and agreements between client and translator

The client should request a bid, verbally or in writing, from the translator. This request for a bid should either include the source text itself or adequate information about it. In return, the translator should make a bid on the assignment, also verbally or in writing. The actual awarding of the assignment should generally be made in writing, and should be confirmed by the translator in writing as well.

The client and the translator must agree on deadlines for the receipt of the source text, all documentation agreed upon for background information; and the receipt of the translation by the client. They must also agree on the medium and means for transmitting the source and target texts. If the client expects special hardware or software to be used, a special agreement must be made to that effect. This also holds true in the event that the client wishes special services, including, for example, the preparation of terminology to be submitted to the client, graphic design, printing, or review by a third party. The parties must explicitly agree on a price for the required services.

Clients must provide the translator with appropriate and adequate support with respect to: specialized literature and terminology, parallel texts, background information, and opportunities to view any relevant operations (tour the factory, see the product, etc.). The client must also name a competent contact person who will be responsible for answering questions the translator may have.

To promote high quality, it is recommended that the client report back to the translator on the translation and the fulfilment of the contract.

The target text

The target text must meet the relevant linguistic standards of the target language. It must also reflect the complete contents of the original text. Unless otherwise agreed, the translator is to translate things like footnotes, appendices, tables, etc. It is the translator's responsibility to inform the client of any deletions from or additions to the original. The client's wishes will be the determining factor in the formal layout of the translation.

Formal aspects like numbering within the text, as well as the arrangement of tables and figures are to be taken over from the source text, whereas symbols, units of measurement, formulas and equations are to reflect the norms of the target language. Clearly identified notes from the translator concerning the target text are to be included in an appropriate form (for example in an attached document, footnotes or typographically emphasized).

Translation review

Before being submitted to the client, every translation must be reviewed with respect to the following criteria: completeness; factual and terminological accuracy in accordance with the assigned text function; appropriate use of the target language; adherence to agreements made with the client; and the appropriateness of translators' notes. The translator and client can also agree to have the translation reviewed by a third party.

A role for the standards in teaching

Every feature of this standard can be drawn into the planning of learning activities to help create realistic and fair working conditions that will help prepare students to face the constraints of the professional world and, at the same time, to demand fair working conditions from their employers and clients (empowerment). Within the educational setting, the responsibility of students (the translators) has traditionally been to perform as directed by the teacher (the client). Yet, if they are to act as responsible and autonomous professionals, they will have to play an active role in negotiating working conditions that will allow for the highest possible quality, professionalism and job satisfaction. What is perhaps most striking about the stipulations of the DIN standard is precisely the high degree of negotiation and co-operation they suggest between the client and the translator. In my view, these features would make an ideal initial framework for an equitable working relationship during, as well as following, the educational programme. Here are just a few thoughts about each of the five main sections and how they might relate to instructional activities:

• **Source text**
The teacher (acting as the client), must treat the original text as a potentially fallible artifact, a tentative product of communicative intentionality that will initiate students' research, translation and text production work. Students must be encouraged to develop an eye for clarity, precision and accuracy in the source text. And they must be given opportunities for developing a voice that will allow them to ask essential questions about the original text that will allow them to produce a high-quality translation of it. The teacher must provide special terminology if he or she has it; and students must be able to use that terminology if provided, or seek it in other resources if it is not. Both teacher and students must be prepared to negotiate to ensure that the source text is imminently translatable and that the necessary terminology is agreed upon in advance.

• **Selection of the translator**
Tasks must be assigned in accordance with the students' level of competence and experience. The question of text difficulty must also be a matter of negotiation between student and teacher. As a professional, the translator must have the right to turn down a job that he or she is not prepared to tackle. Students should have the same right.

- **Organization of the translation process and agreements between client and translator**

A 'contract' should be set up between the teacher and the students, a contract based on mutual willingness to abide by the agreed-upon standards. This contract can specify the same kinds of features of the translation process that exist in professional translation work, from hard- and software to be used to deadlines, and special services required. If the classroom task is a real project, then of course the price should be negotiated in advance as well. The teacher will be responsible for providing helpful documentation to facilitate the production of an excellent translation. This may also entail helping students to find outside documentation as well, for example on the WWW. In addition, the teacher (or perhaps a designated tutor) should be available to provide additional information as the work progresses. For example, instead of having students translate texts alone at home, they can have them collaborate in workshops, where the teacher will move from group to group, answering questions and providing assistance as necessary.

- **The target text**

"Meeting the linguistic standards" of the target language of course covers an extensive range of features, including, for example, grammaticality, cohesion, coherence, textual conventionality and idiomaticity. But typically, these are features that translation teachers have long been very good at dealing with. The proleptic feedback discussed in Chapter 7 is my preferred way of dealing with these aspects of quality, but I think there is a great deal of room for eclecticism here, with each teacher finding the right mixture of prescription and constructive description to help students make progress in the linguistic domain.

- **Translation review**

Students must (learn to) review their own and each others' work to ensure that they have indeed met the other criteria agreed to in the teacher/student contract.

In my view, the use of a set of standards like DIN 2345 can provide a convenient framework for the development of instructional activities; a framework that is also justifiable on grounds of task authenticity. The standards can help guide teachers toward truly effective instruction, and students toward expertise, competence and empowerment.

Implications of professional standards for assessment

While assessment criteria to date have for the most part emphasized the linguistic and functional relationship between the original and target text, they have generally failed to ensure fair and feasible conditions for achieving a satisfactory relationship between the texts. I suggest that an appropriate starting point for the revamping of assessment policies would be to draw nationally accepted professional standards like DIN 2345 into ongoing and terminal assessment procedures as well as into instructional design. Essentially, this would mean establishing a contract in the exam situation as well as between the assessor, acting as the client, and the student, acting as the translation service provider. Each party would commit themselves to the stipulations of the contract. This would allow evaluation criteria for students' performance to be developed on the basis of the extent to which students actually meet their contractual obligations. But it would also provide fairness safeguards for the students, ensuring for example that they have adequate recourse to terminology, reference material and other relevant information in the possession of the assessor. The criteria for evaluation would be known by all stakeholders in the assessement process. Teachers would be accountable for their evaluation decisions, and students would have the opportunity to demonstrate how well they can fulfil the obligations of a professional translator under equitable working conditions that are recognized by the profession itself. The increase in trustworthiness, authenticity and fairness of an assessment approach based on recognized standards over current practice would be no less than phenomenal.

Applying constructivist principles and professional standards

The assessment criteria discussed in the first part of this chapter and the type of professional standards just presented can serve as a basic framework for evaluating the efficacy and authenticity of current assessment systems and for designing alternative ones. These criteria and standards can be seen to apply both to ongoing and terminal assessment, often referred to as formative and summative assessment respectively.

Formative assessment is the term used in the literature to characterize teachers' periodic assessments of students' progress over the course of a programme. Formative assessment is generally used to provide teachers and students with information about the learners' progress toward the goals set by the educational system, but can also apply to goals the students set for themselves. The results of formative assessment traditionally include corrections of students' errors and a global mark to rank each student with respect to the others in the group. **Summative** assessment refers to terminal evaluations of a student's degree of success in completing the overall programme. This type of assessment is designed primarily to assist other stakeholders in the educational process – for example potential employers – to determine the suitability of a given candidate for employment. Corrections will also be indicated on summative assessments, but it is usually only the global ranking marks that are publicly reported, for example on students' transcripts.

Holographic assessments versus 'snapshot' marks

Here, I would like to give an example of a formative assessment report taken from a totally different educational setting – in fact an elementary school – but which, to my mind, goes a long way toward meeting the constructivist assessment criteria of trustworthiness, authenticity and fairness discussed above. Figure 9 includes excerpts from my son's second-grade mid-year evaluation, which was written by his teacher to inform him, his parents and the school administration about his progress in school up to that point, and particularly during the first half of the respective school year:

Geschwister-Scholl School, Germersheim, Germany
Mid-Year Academic Assessment

Overall Assessment
During the second half of the school year, Yann continued to get along well with his classmates and was always willing to help his fellow pupils.

He shows great interest in classroom activities. He always thinks through the tasks assigned to him in a very thorough manner, confidently determines what needs to be done, and completes them in an independent manner. During our Monday morning group gathering, Yann continues to pay attention to others and to talk openly about himself. He has a large vocabulary and extensive background knowledge, and he enjoys sharing his experiences and ideas in this forum as well as in other classroom activities. Yann learns very quickly and can understand and perform new tasks even without being thoroughly briefed in advance ...

...

Compared to his performance during his first year of school, Yann seems to be unfocused less often during independent work sessions. He now works more quickly and in a more concentrated manner. When working on his personal weekly learning plan and on multi-stage tasks, he demonstrates assiduity, endurance and perseverance; as a result, he can often undertake optional activities after completing his required tasks. Yann can also read and comprehend even longer texts with ease, including ones with which he is unfamiliar. When reading familiar texts aloud, he is always careful to read with feeling.

Figure 9: Excerpts from a mid-year second-grade assessment (Germany)

The actual assessment report is more than twice this length, but the sample statements are representative of the overall report. When I, as the child's parent, read such a report, I feel that I am getting a remarkably clear impression of the teacher's understanding of my son's performance in school and of the progress he is making toward goals set for him by the institution. I know quite a bit about his ability to work well with other students, his attentiveness, his proficiency at math, his difficulties with manual dexterity and his attitudes towards school, the other students and the various academic subjects. I know something about how well and how thoroughly he does his homework and how he approaches new tasks. I also see how he has progressed over time with respect to these various dimensions.

No grade is to be found on the assessment, and no reference is made to how my child is doing compared to the other children in the class – there is no mention at all of the group average or norm. The impression I am left with after reading the assessment is that of a subjective but informed personal appraisal, and one that is based on continuous observation of my son's performance and progress over an eighteen-months period. Am I not considerably better informed as a stakeholder in my son's education by this assessment report than I would have been by a series of letter grades purporting to quantify my child's skills, accomplishments, capabilities and rank in class? My son's teacher reads each child his or her assessment aloud, providing the child with an opportunity to discuss it and its implications for further learning. The assessment is not seen as the end of a process or even of a stage of learning; it is a multi-faceted picture, a holograph, of a relationship between the evaluator, the child and the scholastic environment as seen from the teacher's perspective. Instead of quantifying the results for ease of comparison, or to provide a semblance of objectivity, she presents an overtly personal and subjective, yet credible interpretation of the child in the classroom situation.

In the school my son attends, qualitative assessments of this type are the norm in the first and second grade. Numerical grading begins to complement qualitative assessment reports starting in the third grade, completely replacing them by the fifth grade. The question arises as to whether performance and competence actually become more quantifiable as pupils get older. Or is this shift toward objectivist values justified perhaps by an increased appearance of efficiency and a societal interest in convergent behaviour as pupils move on to higher levels of schooling?

Coming back to translator education, Schmitt (1997) found that translation teachers at a conference in Leipzig came up with radically disparate assessments of student translations, with marks covering almost the entire range from 'excellent' to 'very poor' being awarded by the various teachers for each translation that was assessed. Schmitt's proposal for dealing with this lack of inter-rarter reliability involved a very rigid assessment system based on features of the translation product. In my view, his experiment actually supported my argument that assessment cannot be objective, and that it cannot be reduced to the reporting of simple marks. By forcing a rigid catalogue of criteria upon evaluators, we might come up with greater inter-rarter reliability, but that will not bring us closer to a God's eye view, to greater objectivity. Let us now look at this problem from the perspective of the graduating student who receives a diploma and perhaps a transcript that reports the results of the institution's summative assessment process. Figure 10 is an excerpt from the final diploma of a translation student who has completed a four-year programme of studies at a German university to qualify as a professional translator.

The Examination Covered:

A special field in accordance with Section of the regulations for final examinations

Written examination
in the student's special field (Law)   Mark   1.7

Oral examination in the student's special
field (Law)   Mark   1.3
                                                        Overall   very good

...
Major foreign language
Translation of a general language text from the
student's native language into the major
foreign language   Mark   2.3

Translation of a general language text from the
student's major foreign language into the
native language   Mark   2.7

Figure 10: Excerpt from a translator's diploma (Translation D.K.)

Let us consider what this assessment tells the potential employer about the exit-level skills or the competence of the student in question. The report is divided into areas of expertise that include, for example, general language translation from the native tongue into the major foreign language, with a reported mark of 2.3 for the translation of a single text. There is, unfortunately, no information included on the diploma that indicates what a grade of 2.3 means with respect to any other possible grade or what criteria it is based upon; nor does it say who awarded this grade of 2.3, what experience or credentials the evaluator had that qualified him to determine the proficiency of this or any other student, or what measures, if any, were taken to ensure that one can reasonably assume that the mark awarded actually says something credible about the student's ability to translate from his or her native tongue into the foreign tongue in a plausible range of professional situations.

If we take into account the conditions under which the test was taken (in isolation, using pen and paper, without external resources, probably without a translation

brief and surely without the possibility of negotiating with the client), we must admit that the grade cannot tell us anything at all about how well the individual can
use much of the information and many of the resources that professionals would
refuse to work without. Nor does it tell us how well this individual can function as
part of a team or how well he or she has acquired life-long learning skills that will
serve them as they move to a new level of learner autonomy outside of the sheltered
world of the university. Can the translation of a single text without advance preparation, without computer-based tools, without access to reference works or the chance
to negotiate with a client really tell us anything credible at all about a translator's
competence?

A major problem here is that the common practice of awarding marks to characterize the teacher's evaluation of a performance attempts to reduce the multi-faceted
dimensions of the assessment process to a uni-dimensional alphanumeric label that
purports to reflect objectivity, but that in fact loses all value because of its inherent
lack of trustworthiness, authenticity and fairness. From a constructivist perspective,
we need thick description, verbal characterizations of the many facets of the assessment process, from the explicit defining of the task and criteria for success down to
the reporting of our assessment results. Certainly, providing such thick descriptions
of the conditions and results of an assessment situation requires more effort on the
part of the teacher than the simple assignment of marks, but the potential gains in
the credibility and overall value of our assessments are surely worth the trouble.

Collaboration in formative testing

The primary goal of periodic tests as part of ongoing assessment is to inform students and their teachers about the students' progress towards membership in the
professional community, including their ability to use common tools of the trade,
and their ability to work in conjunction with other community members to achieve
common goals. From a constructivist perspective, the assessment of an individual's
state of competence is intricately and inextricably bound up within the process of
constructing it in situation and in conjunction with others. Thus, it is essential that
formative assessment provide insight into the learning progress of both individuals
and teams of learners as they construct knowledge and skills, and apply them in
authentic situations.

An assessment situation where students' marks are determined by their score
ranking within a group is called 'norm-referenced' testing. From a constructivist
perspective, norm-referenced testing is patently unfair because, rather than helping
all students meet high standards of competence, it imposes labels ranging between
'mediocre' (average) to 'failure' on the lower half of each group of test takers.
Norm-referenced testing imposes competition rather than collaboration as the ground
rule for test takers, as each individual must strive to finish higher than every other
student in the ranking results. However, as Johnson and Johnson (1991) have made

abundantly clear with the results of their extensive meta-investigation, co-operative forms of learning are both more efficient and effective than either individual or competitive forms. In addition, we cannot expect our students to learn with and from each other if they are regularly pitted against one another in testing situations, vying for the prized top end of the bell curve. And consequently, we can hardly expect them to learn to work collaboratively as valuable team members if teaching and testing emphasize isolated individual work and competition above values of co-operation and sharing of skills and knowledge. Thus, providing students with opportunities to work collaboratively on tests can provide insight into the knowledge a group is building and also into the ability of each individual to work as an effective team member.

Rather than merely placing labels of relative success or failure on a learner's competence or amassed knowledge, formative assessment should inform teachers about the effectiveness of the teaching leading up to the assessment, and should serve as a guide to help them refocus their subsequent teaching efforts.

In professional life, revisions to the first draft of a translation are often necessary and can be seen as a natural part of the communicative negotiation process rather than a sign of lacking competence. When fresh graduates begin working in a company, they will often do their work for some time under the tutelage of an expert mentor, who will help the newcomers improve their translation performance to meet the standards required by the company. Thus, rather than providing the traditional labels of poor, average, good or excellent to a learner's performance relative to that of others, assessment can be seen as a co-operative activity engaging the assessor and each learner with a view toward achieving excellence. The emphasis is not on errors – faulty solutions – but instead on decision-making processes that are gradually becoming more expert. This perspective, emphasizing not what is deficient but rather what is good about learners' work, provides encouragement, incentives and new opportunities for learning.

If assessment is to be an integral part of the teaching/learning process, opportunities must be provided for students to go back and revise their work, thus learning directly from the assessment itself. A useful technique for using assessment feedback to enhance learning in the academic setting is to provide constructive (proleptic) feedback on every draft while refraining from assigning marks until the quality of the student's translation has reached an acceptable level. Or alternatively, depending on time constraints, a teacher can offer to review one or more drafts submitted over the course of several classes, giving a mark only on the last revised version. Instead of ticking off 'errors' in the drafts, the teacher can provide information about the impact of students' tentative solutions and perhaps hints for helping them find more viable ones.

Co-operative revision work among students can be a particularly fruitful teaching technique. By proof reading each other's work, all students can learn through the mutual negotiation of problems, strategies for solving them and adequate solutions. Either individually, in pairs or in small groups, students can make use of the teacher's proleptic feedback rather than corrections as the starting point for the re-thinking process.

A note on translation quality evaluation

As I indicated at the beginning of this chapter, because of space constraints, I do not wish to enter into a detailed discussion of the various systems that have been devised for evaluating translation quality. This is an aspect of assessment that has received considerable attention from translation scholars and that has been subject to considerable hot debate. However, the importance of task authenticity for assuring trusthworthiness in assessment suggests that, from a constructivist perspective, viable solutions to the quality evaluation problem are likely to be found, not in the ostensibly 'objective' criteria to be found in the many evaluating schemes proposed to date, but in the professional standards themselves and real-world quality criteria, that is, ones that hold within the world of professional translation work. As discussed above, professional standards like DIN 2345 can be used to establish criteria for the quality of the overall translation job. But when it comes to the quality of a translation itself, the highly subjective nature of any observation (and thus evaluation) process suggests that rigid error categorization systems are unlikely to be very viable.

In attempting to develop real-world criteria for translation quality evaluation, I keep coming back to the question of time. When, in the course of my freelance translator work, I pass translation tasks on to colleagues, my determination of the value of that colleague's work in practical terms will be based on how much time I have to spend making necessary changes to meet my own criteria of acceptability before I can send the job on to the client. The less time I have to spend editing, the better the job. In the same vein, Klaudy (1995:202) claims that, "the only correct criterion for quality assessments of students' translations is the amount of time required to transform them into print-ready texts". In providing feedback on students' translations done for classwork, the teacher may well want to indicate problematic segments and provide hints on solving problems, which will distort the time factor. But in formal assessment situations, the teacher may instead make the necessary changes and indicate why they had to be made. The final marks on individual translations often reflect the qualitative difference between various versions. For example, a text with several minor mechanical problems is easily and quickly corrected, whereas more severe translation problems such as inaccurate renderings or incorrect usage require more time for assessment and will consequently result in a lower mark.

The time factor is, of course, subjective. Some teachers will take more time to edit papers than others. It will thus be up to each individual teacher to determine how much time he or she is willing to invest in the editing process while still giving the student a satisfactory mark. And we should certainly not assume that all teachers have the same editing competence. Thus, the assessment problem becomes a dialogic one, with the competence of the teacher interfacing with that of the student. Here, there is no suggestion of objectivity in the evaluation procedure, but there can also be no claim against this approach for arbitrariness. It does, however, embody an acknowledgement of the intersubjective processes underlying real-world translation work.

Figure 11 is an example of a collaborative test and the assessment standards I have used in a translation exercise class and which I believe at least crudely meet the constructivist assessment criteria of trustworthiness, authenticity and fairness discussed above. Prior to taking the test, the group had collaboratively completed a series of related translations over the course of the semester. The students in this particular group also took a similar test individually in a subsequent class session.

The test was presented to the students as an authentic task characterized by features of professional translation work. The students were permitted and encouraged to use any and all appropriate and available resources to complete the job, and the task was set up in such a way that the students would have to work efficiently and co-operatively as a team in order to meet the designated deadline. The criteria for assessment were provided in advance. Marks were awarded to meet the university's requirements for scalable evaluation results, but the qualitative value or meaning of the respective grades was explicitly indicated so as to provide students with useful feedback concerning their performance. I also provided every group with the opportunity to revise its work in the event that a minimum level of acceptability was not reached on the first draft (corresponding to a mark of 2.0 on the above scale). In fact, only one group had to avail itself of this option, but in the end, every group decided to revise its translation in order to learn from its mistakes.

Collaborative tests naturally cannot replace individual assessments. Stakeholders in the educational process, particularly potential employers, also need to be informed about the competence of the individual working alone. Measures can be built into co-operative testing situations that emphasize the accountability of each learner within the team, for example having each student ultimately be responsible for the final version of a clearly defined part of the task. Anonymous questionnaires can also be used to elicit information from the different group members about the degree to which each individual contributed to the process of producing the translation to be assessed. Different forms of assessment need to be developed to complement each other and provide useful information on various levels about students' emerging competence. The picture created in this way will not be more objective, but it will surely be more authentic and trustworthy.

SEMESTER EXAMINATION

Group Task

Your task as a group is to translate four German texts into English for a tourist agency specializing in tours to exotic places. Please think of the work you are doing in terms of a sample translation on the basis of which the agency will decide whether or not to give the group regular, paid work in the future.

Each text is approximately 160 words in length. It is suggested that you divide up into four small groups, with each group assuming overall responsibility for the completion of one text. (You may organize the work differently if you choose). In any event, you are encouraged to work collaboratively both within and between groups (e.g. for proof-reading purposes).

General language monolingual and bilingual dictionaries have been provided, along with four notebook computers and German and American encyclopaedias on CD-ROM. You may also ask the instructor up to three specific questions per text concerning idiomatic usage.

All four texts are to be handed in on the disk provided at the end of the 120-minute session. Texts are to be saved in RTF format. No special formatting will be necessary, but please remember to leave a blank line between paragraphs.

Individual tasks

Each individual will be responsible for making the greatest possible contribution to the production of a publishable, professional-quality translation. You may divide the work up any way you like.

Assessment criteria

Your translations will be assessed by a professional translator (not the instructor) who is a native speaker of English and a near-native speaker of German. She will make only necessary changes in your texts to bring them up to what she believes to be of publishable quality, and will then assess your work according to the following basic scale. The most important criterion for determining the quality of your work will be the time the evaluator needs to edit your work and bring it up to professional standards for acceptable professional translation work.

1.0 An excellent quality translation effectively fulfils the advertising and informative functions that can be projected for the target text on the basis of the brief. English usage is correct and idiomatic throughout, and the register is well suited to the text type and the readership. No more than a few superficial language errors appeared in the text; it was possible to correct them within a few minutes and with a minimum of effort. No translation errors per se appeared in the translation. The group should definitely be offered similar work in the future.

2.0 A good translation that effectively fulfils the advertising and informative functions that can be projected for the target text. English usage is generally correct and idiomatic throughout, and the register is well suited to the text type and the readership. Some minor language errors appear in the text, requiring some revising. In addition, there may have been one or two minor translation errors in the text. The group would be worth contacting as a second choice for work of this type in the future.

3.0 An acceptable translation with a moderate number of language and or minor translation errors, requiring fairly significant work to rectify. Usage may not have been idiomatic throughout. It was possible to correct the translation without an excessive amount of effort or extensive rewriting. This group should be kept on file for future work, but only if adequate proof-reading assistance can be provided.

4.0 A barely acceptable translation requiring extensive corrections of language and/or translation errors. Considerable time and effort were necessary to correct and/or rewrite passages. This group would need to improve considerably before being considered for paid work in the future.

Figure 11: An example of a collaborative semester test

The portfolio as a supplement to marks

While periodic assessment primarily serves the needs of teachers, the educational institution and the students themselves, potential employers of graduates have a particular interest in the assessment process and results at the conclusion of a student's programme of studies. Students need to leave the institution with the results of credible assessments that provide valuable information about the degree to which they can perform the kinds of work that will be required of them as language mediation professionals. As discussed with respect to the diploma presented in figure 10 above, a listing of one-shot examination results in the form of single quantitative test grades does not provide much useful information. From a constructivist perspective, clearly no single test can realistically represent the many facets of translator competence.

More authentic and trustworthy would be a selection of translation performances, for example in the form of a portfolio. Students could collect a set of their best translations or perhaps of their semester test translations completed over the course of their programme of studies. This portfolio could be submitted to the university in partial fulfilment of the degree requirements, to be complemented, if necessary, by traditional final exams. It could also be presented to potential employers who could then assess it according to their own professional criteria. The concept of the portfolio as a constructivist assessment tool, which has already been applied to a wide variety of learning domains, should be thoroughly explored and developed for use in translator education as well. One aspect of the portfolio that is particularly attractive is its capacity for linking formative and summative assessment through a third type, called ipsative assessment. This third type refers to the learner's ability to evaluate his or her own progress and emerging expertise over the course and upon completion of the programme of studies. While there is likely to be general agreement among translation teachers that, at least by the end of the programme of studies, each learner needs to be able to assess the quality of his or her own performance, ipsative assessment is, for the most part, ignored in institutional assessment policies and procedures. Yet, from an empowerment perspective, ipsative assessment is the kingpin in the entire assessment process. In order to take control of and become responsible for their own life-long learning processes, students must develop a strong capacity for independently assessing their own strengths and weaknesses. For example before accepting a particular translation job, they must be able to assess whether or not they will be able to complete it on time and to professional standards. They must also learn how to review their own work, to determine for themselves whether a translation job they have completed is indeed accurate, complete and functional before returning it to the client.

Upon graduation, there will be no teacher (and rarely any other competent authority) around to check for fidelity, accuracy, style, or adherence to norms and conventions. Graduate translators must become empowered to assess the quality of their own work. They must know when their own translation is ready to send off to a customer and when it still needs work; they must be able to determine how long a given translation will take to complete in order to meet ever-shorter deadlines; they must also be able to decide quickly and accurately whether or not they can even complete an offered assignment with the time and resources available. Becoming an autonomous professional entails in no small measure these internalized abilities of self-assessment.

Conclusion

Assessment in translator education goes far beyond the assessment of translation quality. I hope to have demonstrated in this chapter that, while the quantification of evaluations may have some superficial face value within our institutions and society as a whole, upon closer scrutiny it is doomed to fall short of minimal standards of authenticity and credibility. The constructivist principles I have discussed – trustworthiness, authenticity and fairness – can be seen as a philosophical basis for a consistent empowerment approach to assessment. Anchoring tests in realistic translation situations and using credible professional norms of editing time for their evaluation can help provide the necessary authenticity to result in trustworthy assessment procedures. The integration of portfolios as a standard feature of formative and summative assessment in translator education can serve as a suitable framework for all of the sub-features of the trustworthiness criterion: prolonged and persistent observation, peer debriefing, progressive subjectivity, member checks, transferability and dependability. Providing opportunities for extensive collaboration in formative testing acknowledges the shared quality of knowledge that is fundamental to the social constructivist viewpoint. Collaborative assessments can also help ensure that students and teachers give appropriate consideration to the importance of teamwork in professional translation activities.

The work presented here on constructivist assessment is clearly tentative and exploratory in nature. As in every other aspect of translator education, innovation in this domain will depend on the collaboration of others. I hope that teachers and students at other institutions and in other countries, with different working conditions and perhaps facing different professional norms and standards, will join in a dialogic quest for improved methods of assessment that will bring translator education and professional practice closer together.

9. From Dead Bodies and Talking Heads to Holistic Second Language Acquisition in the Classroom

Language acquisition – A holistic enterprise

Foreign language learning indisputably plays an important role in the education of professional translators. Ideally, claim some scholars, students should enter university-level translator education programmes already having a solid grasp of the foreign languages they will translate into and out of. In reality, of course, this is not always practical. In Germany, for example, most students enter translator education programmes directly after completing secondary school, where they have typically studied one or two of the so-called "school languages", English and/or French, for between seven and nine years. Some may even have had a few years of Spanish or Russian. If, however, they choose to study Dutch, Arabic, Portuguese, Chinese, modern Greek or Polish, for example, all of which are offered as major or minor languages for translation studies at the FASK, students usually have little choice but to begin learning the language upon entering the translator education programme itself. These students will be expected to become 'competent' users of the foreign language as well as 'competent' translators out of (and conceivably into) that foreign language over the course of their programme of studies.

The foreign language competence that translators need can be seen as comprising two basic sub-competencies: 'communicative competence' and 'metalinguistic competence'. For example, the guidelines for 'Professional Training and the Profession', drawn up by the German national association of interpreters and translators (BDÜ) as desiderata for the competencies of graduates of translator education programmes, describe the foreign language competence that translators can be expected to have in precisely the same terms as it does their native tongue competence:

> (3.2.1) The first-language skills required include the ability to master and correctly use that first language in a manner appropriate to the style, subject-matter and addressee and in the appropriate cultural register, as well as the ability to discuss language (metalinguistic competence). ...
> (3.2.2) The foreign language skills of graduate translators and interpreters must match the first-language skills described in Section 3.2.1, whether or not the foreign languages in question are offered as school subjects. (BDÜ 1986:109)

In other words, one might characterize these sub-competencies in terms of **knowing how to use** language and **knowing about** language. The second of these competencies has traditionally been the focus of instruction in foreign language education, based on the assumption that language tools can (and must) be learned as a set of artefacts apart from and prior to their actual application in authentic communicative settings. As Legutke reports, despite the emergence in the 1980s of the 'communicative' paradigm in the foreign language teaching field, with great emphasis placed on lively and authentic social interaction in the classroom, the reality in actual foreign language classrooms tends to be rather dismal. Nowadays, he says "one can observe a disquieting progression of lifelessness in language classrooms on both sides of the Atlantic" (Legutke 1993:309). Legutke's depiction in the same passage of our students as "dead bodies and talking heads" is a particularly apt description of language learners in teacher- and syllabus-centred classrooms, where much time is spent following the teacher's agenda for transferring and absorbing knowledge. The teaching-learning experience is presented by teachers and accepted by students as a process of mental gymnastics involving transmission, memorization, drill and regurgitation, where learners are seen as learning robots, rather than as the multi-faceted human beings they are, with a physical, emotional and social as well as a cognitive dimension.

From the perspective I have been presenting throughout this book, a major factor underpinning the reluctance to accept the communicative paradigm that dominates mainstream academic discourse on foreign language learning is to be found in the deep-seated objectivist belief in the transferable nature of knowledge – a belief shared by teachers from the primary through the tertiary level of education and across a wide range of subject areas. Teachers who have been inculcated from their earliest institutional learning experiences with the belief that knowledge can (and must) be packaged and transmitted can hardly be expected to readily accept the principle that foreign language learners can and should learn to communicate by actually communicating in authentic situations.

Our day-to-day experiences with language tell us that language use has an important physical, emotional and social as well as an intellectual dimension. We know intuitively that our mood, motivation, gestures, tone of voice, intonation and rhythm and even our use of personal space can carry meaning. As Douglas Robinson states in *The Translator's Turn* (1991:13), we often react intuitively, even viscerally to language in use:

> Our bodies often react to language use that seems different, deviant, somehow 'wrong', with anxiety signals: there is a twinge in the chest, or a slight constriction of the throat. Most people do not know the rules that would allow them to define the triggering usage as "wrong" in any systematic, grammatical sense. But it *feels* wrong. It clashes with the body conditioning that they have for that usage or that context, with the ideosomatics of syntax, semantics, stylistics. "Bad grammar" feels wrong.

This viewpoint is supported by the "somatic marker" hypothesis formulated by the neuroscientist Antonio Damasio to help explain the interplay of emotions and logic in reasoning (Damasio 1994:174):

Somatic markers are special instance feelings generated from secondary emotions. Those emotions and feelings have been connected, by learning, to predicted future outcomes of certain scenarios. When a negative somatic marker is juxtaposed to a particular future outcome the combination functions as an alarm bell. When a positive somatic marker is juxtaposed instead, it becomes a beacon of incentive.

Damasio's book *Descartes' Error* sets out to refute Descartes' mind/body duality, and to demonstrate the key role that emotions and the body play in ordinary cognitive processes. In the best Cartesian tradition, the cognitivist educational environment, however, neatly separates the mind from the body and the emotions, focusing almost exclusively on the first while virtually ignoring the latter. There is a deep-rooted reluctance on the part of the foreign language profession to accept the fact that, of all the subjects that children and young adults study in school and university, surely none is more profoundly dependent on the interplay of the body, emotions, social intercourse and the mind than foreign language learning.

From a translation scholar's perspective, Douglas Robinson (1991:16) notes that:

Part of learning a language well is watching what native speakers' bodies do when they speak it: how they move their mouths, how they gesture and shift their weight, how they stumble over words, where and how they pause, how they use stress for emphasis – in general, how they stage their speech. But even that will not be enough if it is done mechanically, if you simply observe native speakers' bodies and mimic them. You have to do more than watch; you have to intuit, sense what their bodies are doing inside, sense how they *feel* when they speak.

This surely comes as no surprise to anyone who has learned a foreign language on the street, as it were, in day-to-day interaction with native speakers within a real language community. There is clearly a socio-cognitive apprenticeship process at work here, as the non-speaker of a language is slowly and gradually drawn into the community of language users. Here, in an authentic social setting, the individual constructs the language of the community through collaborative interaction with peers and more knowledgeable others. Learning on the street is inherently an authentic, personal experience for each learner; it is intricately interwoven with the learner's current needs, desires, emotions and stages of psychological as well as linguistic development. The overt teaching of formal rules has as little place in this natural scenario as drills, overt correction or testing for the memorization of linguistic structures do. The second language is structured by the individual on the basis of intuition and feel; the language becomes part of the learner as the learner becomes part of the language community.

The belief that foreign languages must be taught as a set of mental artefacts also persists in the face of overwhelming evidence to the contrary from first language acquisition. We are all aware that children throughout the world acquire the ability to use their mother tongue for extensive communicative purposes within the first few years of their lives without formal instruction and without an inkling of descriptive (or prescriptive) language rules. Within the first few years of life, significant mastery of the mother tongue is achieved in all cultures through experiential interaction with the environment mediated via communicative interaction with members of society. The rules of the mother tongue are not memorized, drilled, or tested; they are constructed by each individual in unique, personal, experiential communion with society and, through that society, with the physical world.

Children are not born as members of a particular culture; the process of acquiring their native tongue coincides with the process of acculturation into that society. Of course, in many cultures, children do acquire written language comprehension and production skills as well as meta-linguistic competence in schools. However, the informal process of intuitive construction of the oral/aural, socio-physical communicative system is extremely well-developed for native speakers before they enter school. It is there that they learn how to use the written form of the language and how to describe language structure on the basis of the system they have already constructed for themselves. There is nothing at all magical or mysterious about the much-touted faith in 'native tongue' language competence. Being a native speaker means nothing more than having constructed one's own language system through a process of authentic acculturation. It means having an extensive, dynamic set of viable intuitions about the accuracy and appropriateness of everyday language use that has been negotiated directly through the acculturation process. Naturally, the fact that first language competence tends to be better developed than second language competence, even if the latter is acquired in a natural, acquisitional setting, does not at all vitiate the viability of acquisition by non-infants. The mother tongue obviously represents an obstacle to the acquisition of a second language as it is closely linked to the learner's primary experiences and persona. In the case of the first language acquirer, there is no pre-existing system of symbolic representation – the very basis for thought in Vygotskian terms – to interfere with the construction of the system. The pre-existing native tongue does not prevent acculturation in a second language community; but it does make it more of a challenge.

My constructivist depiction of non-institutionalized natural first and second language acquisition can serve as a model of classroom acquisition as well, although this might well be disconcerting to those who have only experienced foreign-language learning as talking heads on dead bodies in a transmissionist classroom. The implication of Robinson's somatic view of language learning is not only that we must sense what natives feel when they speak (which applies particularly to comprehension), but that we must also have a *feel* for the language ourselves if we are to express ourselves authentically. We must have a somatic relationship with the language forms we are acquiring and we must develop a *Sprachgefühl* for appropriateness, accuracy and the effectiveness of the linguistic medium we use to project each intended message. Linguistic structures have no objective, fixed meanings. They acquire meaning in and through the real-life situations experienced by each individual.

As Robinson goes on to explain, cognitive awareness of language must indeed develop as well, even in natural language acquisition settings. But the somatic, visceral, intuitive feel for a foreign language is the foundation upon which cognitive meta-linguistic knowledge is built. Language teaching that ignores the somatic aspect, particularly at early stages, blocks rather than promotes acquisition:

> Foreign languages begin to take on reality, not through cognitive understanding – though that must certainly follow – but through our somatic responses to them. And, of course, one of the surest ways to obstruct the learning of a foreign language is to teach it (usually an idealized standard form of it) through inert grammatical rules and vocabulary lists, all in isolation from real-use situations. Language taught like this is disembodied *langue*, not richly somatic *parole*. 'Classroom' German or French *feels* abstract, lifeless, both to the second-language speaker who speaks it and to the native listener who hears it. As a result, even if the speaker makes him- or herself understood, the native listener will feel uncomfortable in the conversation. The foreigner will sound like a cleverly programmed robot. The words will feel like cardboard in the speaker's mouth: no life, no feeling. (Robinson 1991:15)

The result is a foreign language pasted onto a native tongue persona, an artificial and lifeless system of artefacts that is better suited to furthering miscommunication than successful communication. Another result is that the sterile atmosphere of the classroom, the lack of personal (physical, emotional and social) interaction on the part of learners, can hardly contribute to motivation for learning, to a positive or well-rounded self-concept, or to an authentic, collaborative environment. Far from being more efficient, disembodied learning shuts down the physical, emotional and social channels for multi-faceted acquisition that human beings naturally bring to learning situations. This holds true for adults as well as for children. Being active in the classroom, experiencing the physical and social environment through different modes, receiving positive feedback, feeling good about what one is doing in the classroom and about the progress one is making: these are all factors that are extremely important for effective learning.

Referring to significant findings in research on adult education, Brundage and MacKeracher (1980, quoted in Sainz 1994:135) cite a basic set of principles that reflect the personal, multi-channel nature of adult learning:

1. Adults learn best when they are involved in developing learning objectives for themselves which are congruent with their current and idealized self-concept.

2. The learner reacts to all experience as he perceives it, not as the teacher presents it.
3. Adults are more concerned with whether they are changing in the direction of their own idealized self-concept than whether they are meeting standards and objectives set for them by others.
4. Adults do not learn when over-stimulated or when experiencing extreme stress or anxiety.
5. Those adults who can process information through multiple channels and have learnt 'how to learn' are the most productive learners.

These principles emphasize the autonomy of the adult student in the broadest sense of the word. University students are adults; they are not disembodied brains capable of soaking up desituated theory and rules and applying them flawlessly in situation. The focus of learning must be appropriate to the learners' personal needs, desires and goals. Learners must be involved in the decision-making processes regarding their own learning objectives, which are indeed more important to them than those of their teachers. The stress and anxiety of the conventional competitive classroom is not conducive to adult learning. It is the task of the institution to ensure that students learn how to learn autonomously, that is, how to use the natural multi-channel perceptive and learning skills that they have all used so successfully to master their native tongue.

The physical, emotional and social realms are generally understood by teachers and administrators as having little place in the classroom, and thus the classroom becomes a dreary, lifeless place where *langues vivantes* are studied as if they were *langues mortes,* and where the learners' powerful non-cognitive communicative tools are left outside the classroom. There is in fact grudging acknowledgement on the part of translation teachers and programme administrators that learning about language forms cannot replace acquiring a modern language through communication: students are encouraged to spend time abroad, actually applying the language skills they are expected to have learned in the classroom. There is great reluctance, however, to draw the social, the emotional and the physical sides of students' selves into the classroom itself, to see the somatic and interactive sides of communication as the fundamental basis for native speaker-like language behaviour. To focus on language learners as the multi-channel acquirers that they are, to take their physical, emotional and social channels of meaning making into consideration in the classroom may well seem like a gargantuan task for individual teachers, particularly trained as they traditionally have been to teach the syllabus, rather than to facilitate the learner's journey on their way to joining a new language community.

To give an example of the situation that we are faced with in our English department at the University of Mainz, a situation that I expect will not differ radically from that at similar institutions elsewhere, I would like to consider the example of the placement test that we give entering students to assign them to appropriate levels for the remedial courses we offer in English as a foreign language. I have chosen at random several questions that appeared in the test administered in the fall of 1997, in order to give an idea of the type of knowledge required.

The test was divided into four main parts: structure and written expression, vocabulary, grammar and reading comprehension. The questions were all of the fill-in-the-blank or the multiple choice variety.

Structure and written expression*: Choose the word or phrase that is appropriate to complete the sentence:*
If one of the participants in a conversation wonders_____, no real communication has taken place.
(A) what said the other person   (B) what the other person said
(C) what did the other person say   (D) what was the other person saying

Vocabulary: *Identify the word or phrase that is closest to the meaning of the original sentence.*
When one is unfamiliar with the customs, it is easy to make a blunder.
(A) a commitment (B) a mistake (C) an enemy (D) an injury

Grammar: Past tense, present perfect or present conditional? *Insert the correct form of the verbs given in brackets at the end of each sentence:*
If I .... my hair blue, my skin .... whiter.   (to dye; to look)

The native speaker of English who reads these sentences can fill in the blanks intuitively and instantly. There is no need to look up rules in some internal grammar book; we resituate each sentence, perhaps projecting before our mind's eye fleeting images of imaginary situations in which they could be used and that are in fact reenactments of communicative situations we have already experienced. These and the other questions on the test do not assess the extent to which grammar rules have been correctly memorized. If we had to actually describe the grammar rules involved in the first and last questions, it would be a time-consuming process in which, starting from the intuition that a particular solution is correct, we would invent grammatical rules to provide a meta-linguistic explanation for the decision we have already made. While this might be useful for purposes of displaying academic knowledge, it is normally not very useful in practical situations. Anthony Pym (1991) has said that translational competence per se essentially involves two parts: (1) being able to come up with a set of viable alternatives for a translation problem, and (2) being able to efficiently choose the most viable among them. Is this not also the case in language use? When speaking, we choose repeatedly from an extensive array of linguistic variants, including phonetic representations, grammatical structures, lexical items, etc. Yet in most cases we produce speech that is extremely fluid, having chosen from a myriad of linguistic pools and strung the elements together in a linear fashion. In the examples given above, what is effortless and intuitive for the native speaker becomes a rule-recall puzzle for the non-native with limited experience in the use of English in real situations. It is disconcerting to note that at the testing session in question, in which 224 new students participated, the average number of errors out of a possible 86 responses was 40.

We must keep in mind that this is not a representative sample of students beginning their studies at German universities; these were all students who had chosen to pursue a career as language professionals and who had been successful learners of English through years of secondary school study. What these results suggest to me is that whatever students are doing in their English classes at school may not be helping them very much to acquire native-like intuitions of how to use the English language. The test reveals the fallacy that underlies transmissionist approaches to teaching foreign languages in that it tests for *Sprachgefühl* rather than for accurately learned rules. Language teaching tends to proceed under the assumption that disembodied and decontextualized teaching **about** language can lead to an intuitive feel for the language. However, if we take students who lack basic intuitions about the acceptable use of English, and provide them with several additional semesters of instruction of the same disembodied type at university, we should not expect them to acquire those intuitions during their programme of professional studies any more than they did in school. More of the same type of instruction is surely not the appropriate treatment for a lack of communicative competence following eight years of secondary school instruction in the language.

Let me cite another example that involves a language which students generally begin studying at university in Germany, students who study Spanish in our translator education programme must pass a vocabulary test in their third or fourth semester. The test consists of a list of Spanish words taken from a book that covers a basic 2,000-word vocabulary of Spanish as a foreign language. The terms are presented without context, and the students are required to indicate the precise equivalent of the term in German as listed in the book. (The use of a synonym not listed in the book is counted as an error.) The vocabulary list is to be memorized by the students at home. While students must attend lecture courses on Spanish grammar, there are no conversation classes, either required or optional; there is no discussion, no simulated use of the language – only rote memorization, pure and simple. Here again, we see how the institution attempts to bypass the fundamentally experiential basis of natural language acquisition by turning the learning of vocabulary – under natural circumstances a multi-channel, experience-based activity – into a purely cerebral exercise. Given the constraints of the learning and testing situation, how can the students of Spanish do anything but attempt to paste the Spanish labels onto their richly somatic German interpretation of the world? Has thought been given to the message that this type of vocabulary learning sends to translation students about the nature of translation, i.e. that knowing a foreign language is knowing the foreign labels for German concepts, and that to translate is simply to transcode?

We should not wait for language teaching in secondary schools to change its orientation radically and to adopt the communicative paradigm that dominates the academic study of foreign language teaching. The reactionary influences on secondary education are simply too stifling for such a change to occur from within. As representatives of institutions specialized in the education of language professionals, we should instead be leading the way toward innovation in language teaching. If we are ever to break away from the somatically starved transmissionist foreign language classroom, we must be prepared to experiment, to try out new techniques and to reject pedagogical paradigms as they prove incompatible with our mission to produce language professionals for the 21st century. As it is our job to ensure that our graduates are communicatively as well as meta-linguistically competent speakers of the foreign languages they study, it is also our obligation to ensure that the foreign language education we offer them meets the demands of the language mediation professions.

Sprachgefühl, a feel for language, cannot simply be extracted by teachers from experience and then transmitted to the dead bodies and listening heads of foreign language learners. Learning a foreign language means learning how to use it so that it feels right; it entails the development primarily of communicative, rather than meta-linguistic competence. Not only do teacher- and syllabus-centred, non-communicative approaches not contribute to the development of native speaker-like intuitions, they actually inhibit it. In order to serve as a tool for authentic communication, language needs to be **acquired**, that is constructed authentically and somatically, whether it be in a natural setting or in the classroom. There should be plenty of opportunities for cognitive learning as well, but the basic language acquisition activities must involve the use of language to interact with other members of a community within a shared environment. In the next two sections of this chapter, I will outline two methods for promoting second language classroom acquisition which I feel exemplify a constructivist view of learning and teaching: AVSG methodology, which was developed in France in the 1970s, and the Natural Approach, created by Tracy Terrell and Stephen Krashen in the US at about the same time. It is not my intention to promote one published method or another, but instead to demonstrate the congruence of communicative language teaching with a constructivist approach to translator education. The reader may be familiar with other methods that have a strong affinity with this approach, including, for example, Community Language Learning, Total Physical Response, and Suggestopedia. The scope of this book does not allow me to go into detail concerning other methods, but the reader is referred to the now classic work by Earl Stevick, *Teaching Languages: A Way and Ways* (1980), for a thorough treatment of such methods.

Initial steps towards a constructivist second language classroom

My personal views of teaching and learning, especially in the domain of language studies, have of course been greatly influenced by my own experience with language teaching approaches as a learner and teacher. Having failed to acquire even a smattering of French in five years of transmissionist instruction in elementary and secondary school, or of Spanish in two years of high school instruction, I again tried my hand at French during my last year at university. I continued to take French courses the following year while pursuing a master's degree in International Affairs. Then, in 1977, I found myself in Lyon, France, teaching English as a *lecteur d'anglais* at the Institut National des Sciences Appliquées (INSA). At that point I had had no training whatsoever as a language teacher. *Lecteurs* were hired by INSA to serve as native-speaker tutors to give engineering students the opportunity to practise their language skills with native speakers. There was no specific training provided for new teachers; the old hands gave us a few tips on what to do in class (essentially designed as communication practice classes), and that was it.

My teaching experiences in Lyon would have been a rather insignificant episode in my career had it not been for the fact that, parallel to my regular employment at INSA, I had the great fortune to get involved with a group of local language teachers who were working with a new method called *All's Well,* a second-generation 'audio-visual structuro-global' method developed at Crédif in France and published by Didier. When a one-week introductory training seminar was offered in Lyon, I signed up, hoping to pick up some tips on what to do in my conversation classes. What took place in that week-long seminar has helped guide my thinking on foreign language learning and my educational practice and research ever since.

When we arrived for the first seminar session, the 20-odd participants, some French, some American and some British teachers of English, found ourselves in a carpeted room without chairs, tables, pictures or anything at all but a reel-to-reel tape recorder. There was also a person called the *animateur,* whose role was much like that of the facilitator I have discussed in Chapter 4. He introduced himself briefly and then, without further ado, asked us to stand around the sides of the room. We were then asked to choose a spot somewhere at eye level on the opposite wall. Then, accompanied by soothing background music, we spent the next five minutes or so walking back and forth across the room. We first walked slowly, eyes focused only on the spot ahead of us. We then chose another spot and walked back. We also tried walking backwards across the room, then with our eyes shut, then moving our outstretched arms in circles as we walked. This was the first of several hours of activities during which we spoke very little, but moved and interacted a great deal. During a group discussion at the end of the morning about what we were experiencing we came to realize that what may have originally seemed like silly gimmicks were in fact initial steps toward re-acculturation, toward becoming members of the community of *All's Well* teachers. We were beginning to explore the space in which we would form a community of learners for the duration of the seminar. These steps proved to be essential for our understanding of how acquisition can be fostered in a classroom setting – essentially by *reinserting the physical and emotional factors involved in natural learning* that tend to be ignored by transmissionist teaching approaches.

Over the course of that week, in addition to working with the audio-visual course materials of the English course, we experienced numerous exercises for working on relaxation, concentration and perception, movement, mime, gestures, and space utilization – as well as language per se. While most of the seminar participants were at times puzzled and occasionally embarrassed by these non-academic activities at the beginning, within a few days the underlying structure of the method was becoming self-evident. Looking back on the seminar and the method now, I see them as eminently constructivist in nature. Starting out as separate individuals seeking to join the community of *All's Well* teachers, we formed a social group through a multi-faceted sequence of interpersonal activities. The *animateur* did not attempt to teach us anything; instead he set the stage for activities through which we would learn. We received no instruction, but were instead put into situations where we could experience the approach for ourselves, where we could see the importance of working collaboratively, where we could use our natural physical, emotional and social dimensions to interact naturally with others, to relax when we were under stress, to concentrate when we were distracted and to communicate non-verbally when we were at a loss for words.

The *All's Well* teaching materials themselves, which we also explored collaboratively over the course of the week, consisted of a sequence of audio-visual filmstrips, a workbook and audio tapes. The stories upon which the filmstrips were based were used to provide initial input for learners' personal construction processes. The cartoon characters in the films speak at normal conversational speed and exhibit a panoply of gestures, moods and attitudes. The stories followed a progression of interpersonal as well as linguistic complexity. The initial presentation of the filmstrips is intended to be global – with no dissection of the language used. Later analytical activities focused on sharpening awareness of supra-segmentals. These included, for example, walking while characters spoke and stopping when they paused; tapping a tambourine to the rhythm of a chunk of discourse, and following an intonation curve with the whole body. Learners were dissuaded from using their mother tongue in class because it was felt that this would interfere with the somato-cognitive construction of the new language. They were not, however, forced to speak English upon command. It was understood that students need time to process input and that they will speak when they are ready to do so. Our seminar, and indeed the *All's Well* classes we went on to teach, were not simulated communities; they became real communities. There was no room for dead bodies and talking heads; the learners and the *animateurs* saw each other as whole people bringing their own backgrounds, needs and abilities into the classroom. The principles of second language acquisition upon which the *All's Well* method was designed form a coherent approach that closely parallels the constructivist philosophy I have been discussing throughout this book.

To provide an overview of this approach, I will let the authors of the method speak for themselves to outline its basic principles. In the following section, I have included excerpts from the introduction to the *All's Well* teacher's manual (indented), followed by a few comments of my own on the implications of these principles for classroom practice.

Constructing communicative competence

> Communication of course is much wider than words and expressions; it includes the body, the time and space that surrounds each of us. A foreign language is a living, moving entity ... From the very start the foreign language must envelope the student ... Language is not the manipulation of tongue, teeth, hard and soft palates ... Language is the whole body. When we express ourselves we use affective melodies, intonations, pauses, rhythms, gestures, facial expressions and physical movements. It is "I" who am speaking, both body and spirit.

Rather than sitting passively in rows listening to a teacher, students need to use all of their senses to explore communication through the foreign language. Activities that get students to explore communication by, for example, moving, gesturing, and drawing can encourage them to use all of the dimensions of perception and learning with which they are naturally endowed. The native tongue has no place in basic second language acquisition classrooms. By leaving it outside the class, even adult students have the opportunity to become acculturated in a community through the use of a new language. Students need to be bathed in the sounds and movements of the new language. The native tongue is a distraction and a hindrance to second language construction.

> To ask students to produce exactly the same quality and quantity in their language expression as they have received in their language comprehension is tantamount to asking them to speak in words that are not yet their own. ... comprehension is the basis upon which students will be able to build their expression.

Comprehension is always greater than expression, and this fact needs to be respected in the second-language classroom. Rather than being fed grammatical rules or lexical items, which they are to memorize precisely and sequentially, students need to be given time to structure the language for themselves and at their own pace. The 'teach-memorize-regurgitate' technique of transmissionist learning approaches must give way to providing comprehensible input that naturally paves the way for personal language construction. Production will occur when the learner is ready.

> To learn a foreign language, the students must first learn how to learn. ... In their own native language the students will automatically use the right melodies and gestures to accompany their enunciations. When it comes to learning a foreign language, however, we find that there is a conviction that physical involvement is not necessary and, secondly, a certain embarrassment when expressing oneself in front of others. A precondition to effective language learning seems to be that adults must again learn the use of their body in the second language.

Adult learners need to be put back in touch with their bodies and emotions. While they may initially resist because of years of talking heads-and-dead-bodies learning in school, helping them re-appropriate their dormant somatic faculties will be invaluable for ensuring acquisition of the second language.

> Audio-visual teaching has the task of bathing the student in a variety of language sounds and linguistic data, but it is the student who has to organize them, it is the students alone who can structure the language for themselves ... There are innumerable different ways to organize and structure; we could even say that each individual has his or her own unique, personal way to do it.

The deductive application of descriptive rules to language use is disruptive to the acquisition process in the early stages (just as it would be for small children learning their native tongue). Acquisition is inherently inductive in nature. It involves hypothesis generation, testing and revision, and the gradual construction of a personal version of the second language. At a more advanced stage, the *learning* of a small set of portable rules can indeed contribute to the construction process. However, extensive reliance on rule presentation and application at the beginning results in an excessive emphasis on the cognitive domain, effectively excluding somatic interaction with the new language. By providing extensive comprehensible input and a supportive learning environment that is conducive to experimentation, authentic interpersonal experience and personal structuring, the teacher can set the stage for natural acquisition to occur. Just as small children acquire much of their native tongue competence through interaction with their peers, who also have only limited competence in the language, so can second language acquirers be expected to acquire a new language to a great extent through interaction with their peers in the classroom.

What we have done for many generations is adopt an approach 'from the simple to the complex', completely forgetting about the first and most important procedure which leads us from the global to the structured, simple elements. The most serious effect of having forgotten the first step of global to structured is that we have forgotten the individual.

Perception is a global phenomenon, and the natural progression for either first or second language acquisition is **global → analytical → global**. For this reason, students should first be confronted with the complexity of authentic language embedded in context. Each learner will analyze and structure the language individually, and each one will require different kinds and amounts of assistance from the teacher. The classroom setting must provide adequate space, time and support for this individual construction process. Putting students in situations where they will naturally explore the foreign language through peer interaction provides the teacher with the time needed to identify the zone of proximal development of individual students and to provide assistance as necessary.

The fact that the *All's Well* method did not manage to survive the onslaught of the so-called *notional-functional* approaches that swept western Europe in the late 1970s and early 1980s does not by any means cast doubt on the validity of the approach. It was an expensive method requiring a significant amount of preparation for every class and a strong personal commitment on the part of the teacher. As the authors remind readers of the teachers' handbooks on a number of occasions, at least one training seminar was strongly recommended for prospective *All's Well* teachers – another significant cost factor. With transmissionist methods, all of the material to be focused on is in a book. Little preparation is required, little personal involvement with the students, and no commitment to a holistic educational philosophy.

Over the course of the three years following that initial *All's Well* seminar, I had the opportunity to apply the method with many groups of adult students, primarily in university-run continuing education classes for engineers and private-school classes for business executives. In 1980, I left France and the method behind. But upon returning to the US to pursue graduate study in second language education at the University of Illinois, I found the essence of the *All's Well* principles that had become my guiding lights as a language teacher echoed in the 'communicative competence' revolution on the other side of the Atlantic. It would not be until six years later, when I returned once again to the University of Illinois, this time to complete my doctoral studies, that I would become involved with the Natural Approach. The 'communicative competence' movement, however, which began with Sandra Savignon's now classic dissertation (1971), had already ushered in a new era in second language teaching in North America. In 1996, Erwin Tschirner, a co-author of *Kontakte*, the Natural Approach course for German, noted that "the Natural Approach ... has become one of the most widely used communicative methodologies in foreign language departments across North America" (1996:50).

Communicative competence and communicative language teaching

In the US, the decade of the 1970s was a watershed for language teaching approaches that focused on naturalistic, experience-based, classroom-centred second-language acquisition. In particular, the advent of the notion of 'communicative competence' marked a modern theoretical breakthrough in the age-old debate between language teaching methods that focus on the rule-based learning of language structures, and those that attempt to involve the whole learner in the student-centred creation of a personal second language competence.

In 1980, Canale and Swain published a landmark article on the nature of communicative competence and its implications for second-language acquisition in the classroom. They discerned three basic components of communicative competence: grammatical competence, sociolinguistic competence and strategic competence. In Canale and Swain's terms (Canale and Swain 1980:29):

> We understand communication to be based in sociocultural, interpersonal interaction, to involve unpredictability and creativity, to take place in a discourse and sociocultural context, to be purposive behaviour, to be carried out under performance constraints ... and to be judged as successful or not on the basis of behavioural outcomes.

If we see this depiction of communication as being clearly in line with contemporary views of professional translation as a communicative process, then the implications that Canale and Swain draw from it for foreign language instruction can be seen as particularly appropriate for the teaching of foreign languages to future professional translators. In Canale and Swain's words, "exposure to realistic communication situations is crucial if communicative competence is to lead to communicative confidence" (ibid.:28).

In Savignon's (1983:45) view, on the other hand,

> ... it may be that *communicative confidence leads to communicative competence* ... communicative confidence in language learning may be like learning how to relax with your face under water, to let the water support you. Having once known the sensation of remaining afloat, it is but a matter of time until you learn the strokes that will take you where you want to go.

A synthesis of these viewpoints suggests that communicative competence and communicative confidence are intricately interrelated – supporting each other as the learner gradually becomes a member of the speech community of the second language:

The relationship between competence and self-confidence is mutually advantageous. Competence allows confidence to develop, which leads to emotional support for effort to master new skills and knowledge. Competent achievement of this new learning further buttresses confidence, which can now again support and motivate more extensive learning. This can result in a spiralling dynamic where competence and confidence grow in continued support of one another. (Wlodkowski 1993:56)

A naturalistic method

The Natural Approach was developed in the mid-1970s as a method for use in introductory foreign language classes at American universities. The goal is to develop communicative rather than simply grammatical competence. After publishing an initial article outlining his approach, Terrell began working with Steven Krashen, who had just come out with his Monitor Model of classroom acquisition. While the two were in some disagreement about certain aspects of acquisition, for example regarding the distinction between conscious and sub-conscious learning and the value of teaching grammatical rules, they shared a common core of principles that can be seen to be compatible with the *All's Well* principles outlined above, and that have consistently been applied in the development of Natural Approach methods (Tschirner 1996):

- The foreign language is taught and learned as discourse, with a focus on authentic interaction rather than on the exemplification of language usage.
  The students' native tongue is seen as disruptive and is all but excluded from classroom interaction.
- The content of classroom interaction focuses on the needs and interests of the students and the foreign-language environment.
- The primary forms of classroom interaction are pair- and small group-work.
- Perception precedes production; both are seen and treated as independent skills.
- Care is taken both in perception and in production to ensure that words and phrases are properly stored.
- Affective factors receive particular attention.
- The use of media plays a major role, both for affective and socio-cultural reasons, and in order to place special emphasis on listening comprehension.

Tschirner (1996) emphasizes the fact that a special merit of the Natural Approach is that it is based on the findings of research in second language acquisition. He also stresses that the Natural Approach and the popular methods to which it has been applied have evolved consistently and significantly over the past two decades in response to new research findings.

In the Natural Approach, instruction involves the almost exclusive use of inter-action in which the focus of attention is on communication, rather than on the form of the language. Terrell's view is that grammatical competence will essentially take care of itself if learners are motivated to interact communicatively. The interaction in a Natural Approach classroom will revolve around topics that are of personal interest to the students, and on aspects of the foreign culture. The teacher and the students in a Natural Approach classroom speak only the second language in class. The teacher's primary task is to put students in situations in which they will work collaboratively to discover the foreign culture through the medium of the foreign language, thereby acquiring the forms necessary for initial foreign language instruc-tion at the university level. The emphasis is on the acquisition of basic language skills, with comprehension coming before expression, and oral/aural skills preced-ing use of the written language.

The role of affective factors is as important in the Natural Approach as it is in the *All's Well* method. Here, Krashen's concept of the 'affective filter' comes into play. He hypothesized that the more stressful the learning situation, the less able learners are to acquire the features of the foreign language. This view has been supported by recent research on second language acquisition which:

> ... has shown that the body produces one type of hormone when a stressful situation is seen as a challenge (eustress) and a different type of hormone when the stressful situation is seen as a threat (distress) to a person's capabil-ity to function and the stressor appears inescapable. Thus the emotional response of the individual to a specific situation plays a determining role in that person's cognitive functioning – either to fight, resist, or avoid the learn-ing situation or to be open to new opportunities. (Ferro 1993:32)

The Natural Approach teacher thus helps students create an environment that sup-ports acquisition, encouraging the development of a community in the classroom, avoiding overt correction of form, while promoting meaningful and enjoyable inter-action among the learners. The physical facet of language acquisition is addressed through the recommended use of Total Physical Response (TPR), a technique de-veloped by James Asher. TPR essentially involves following commands in the early stages of foreign language learning in order to activate motor memory to somatically grasp the potential meanings of foreign language structures, just as infants do as they begin to acquire their mother tongue.

I hope that this cursory overview of the *All's Well* method and the Natural Ap-proach has shown the essence of what I would call fundamentally constructivist types of classroom foreign language acquisition. I would now like to move on to demonstrate the relevance of this type of instruction for students studying to be-come professional translators.

Implications for translator education: why learning is not enough

> Somatic response is too unpredictable to be "adequately" theorized, that is, rigorously and universally systematized. There seems to be an unwritten rule among translation theorists, in fact, that for theory somatic response is the kiss of death.
>
> (Robinson 1991:18)

The wealth of articles, monographs and conferences on translation studies over the past two decades is marked by a virtual absence of contributions dealing with the role of second language learning and teaching in translator education. This lack of research and discussion could suggest that there is basic agreement that translator education institutions are doing an adequate job of teaching foreign languages. I contend, however, that the still pervasive pedagogical view of translation as an inter-lingual transcoding process has perpetuated the stranglehold of transmissionist teaching approaches in translator education and has inhibited fruitful debate on the applicability of communicative teaching methods to translator education.

My informal surveys of students at the FASK in Germersheim have revealed that, at that institution, non-communicative methods are used for the teaching of all introductory-level language skills courses in those languages that can be chosen as major or minor subjects for a degree. These courses involve the direct, contrastive teaching of vocabulary and grammar rules, extensive rote learning, and early translation practice, ostensibly to provide students with the basic linguistic tools they will need in order to translate professionally between this foreign language and their native language. If the outcome is to be competent, self-confident language users, however, this type of approach is at odds with the overwhelming body of second language teaching research generated during the last two decades, which points to an urgent need for truly communicative and student-centred foreign language instruction. The tidal wave of research, teaching approaches and published methods for 'communicative' language teaching that has swept the language teaching profession in the US since at least the early 1980s has left the FASK – and many other translator education institutions as well – untouched.

The mastery of the foreign languages in which students will specialize as translators is essentially considered to be separate from the acquisition of translation skills per se. Yet the assumptions underlying instructional events revolving around the former will surely affect how students perceive the latter. For example, in our foreign language programmes, the dissection and compartmentalization of knowledge in the foreign language domain is pervasive. Students who study English, for example, must attend a set of disconnected basic or remedial courses with titles like vocabulary and style, phonetics, grammar, and speech production. For languages that students begin studying at university, teaching methods tend to be strikingly uncommunicative, based on extensive rote memorization, the virtually exclusive use of frontal teaching and norm-based testing.

If translators needed only an intellectual knowledge of language forms, perhaps a transmissionist, grammar-rule-and-vocabulary-list approach to foreign language instruction would be sufficient. However, if we adhere to the contemporary consensus view from the scholarship in translation studies that professional translation is an act of communication, then it is clearly appropriate to consider the applicability of teaching methods and approaches that are geared toward the development of authentic communicative competence, and not just metalinguistic competence. In fact, it can be argued that translators need the full spectrum of communicative competence in both the source and target languages if they are to achieve deep and efficient comprehension of original language texts and if they are to break away from surface structures to interpret and express text-based messages confidently and efficiently through the medium of a different language.

In *The Translator's Turn*, Robinson (1991:xii) makes a strong case for linking the intuitive socio-somatic nature of language to the translator's craft:

> It seems undeniable that translation is largely an intuitive process. Good translators choose words and phrases by reference not to some abstract system of intellectualized rules, which most of us have never internalized in the first place, but rather to "messages" or impulses sent by the body: a given word or phrase *feels* right. Intuitively, not just for the translator but for all language users, sense is not cognition but sensation.

A feel for the foreign language can thus be seen as a basic precondition for professional translation activities. It is in their initial basic foreign language courses in the translator education programme that learners can be expected to start developing a professional translator's attitude toward language use and toward translation itself as a communicative, intuitive, personal and somatic activity. Through our very teaching methods, we language teachers demonstrate to our students our own understandings of how language works. If we teach language as a set of artefacts, and translation skills as objectifiable, transmittable strategies, we can expect our students to develop a translator's self-concept that sees their own role as that of insignificant bilingual scribes, mechanically transcoding from one language into another.

Presumably, our primary goal is to help them become competent, self-confident, autonomous professionals for today and life-long learners for tomorrow. If so, they will have to depend to a great extent on the learning skills they acquire at university to continue to grow as professionals once they leave the institution. We will have to teach them, by example and through our convictions, that they will come to each new translation situation as unique individuals with their entire, personal, experience-based repertoire of problem-solving strategies and heuristics.

> Translators are never, and should never be forced to be (or to think of them-
> selves as) neutral, impersonal transferring devices. Translators' personal
> experiences – emotions, motivations, attitudes, associations – are not only
> allowable in the formation of a working TL text, they are indispensable.
> (Robinson 1991:260)

By teaching basic language skills on the basis of an intricate interplay of physical,
emotional, social and cognitive factors, we can guide future professional translators
from the beginning of their studies toward an understanding of translation that is
shared by translation professionals. Translation, like language use, cannot be efficient or satisfying if every decision must be taken on the basis of rules. In Robinson's
words (ibid.:17):

> Translation succeeds best not when the translator has obeyed every cognitive
> rule – performed a painstaking textual analysis and planned his or her re-
> structuring out carefully in advance – but when he or she is most sensitive to
> the feel of both the SL and the TL words. To the extent that it makes sense to
> talk of translational equivalence at all, in fact, it is a matter not so much of
> minds – analytical correspondences – as it is of bodies, of feel. Equivalence
> between an SL and a TL word or phrase is always primarily somatic: the two
> phrasings feel the same.

One of the most elegant definitions of translation competence per se is the two-
component 'translational competence' proposed by Anthony Pym (1991:541):

> 1.   The ability to generate a target text series of more than one viable term
> ... for a pertinent source text.
> 2.   The ability to select only one definitive target term from the series, quickly
> and with justified confidence.

> Together, these two skills form a specifically translational competence to the
> extent that their union concerns translation and nothing but translation. There
> can be no doubt that translators need to know a fair amount of grammar,
> rhetoric, terminology, general knowledge and strategies for getting paid cor-
> rectly, but the specifically translational part of their practice is strictly neither
> linguistic nor commercial. It is a process of generation and selection, a deci-
> sion process that should take place almost automatically.

From Pym's perspective, translation is clearly not a matter of knowing the correct translation equivalents for source text terms, expressions and constructions.
It is a process of projecting alternative solutions and then choosing from among
them, or as Chesterman (1997:15) has described it, "The picture that emerges is of a
repeated, cyclical process, switching back and forth constantly from hypothesis-
generation to hypothesis-testing".

Just as, in Vygotskian terms, the child internalizes speech to create thought, we can hypothesize that translation students are able to internalize the collaborative verbal process of solution generation and selection. The essential language knowledge basis for both collaborative and individual translation must be intuitive – a feel for the language based on personal experience and structuring. As Damasio (1994) says, the number of possible scenarios in a decision-making situation is immense, and in his view, it is the somatic markers that allow decisions to be made quickly and efficiently by pointing viscerally to optimal solutions.

For constructivist translator education to function well and to lead to professional competence and confidence, the preparatory language training must lead learners in the direction of a somatic relationship with the language. The translation project approach outlined in Chapter 4 provides an exteriorized forum for engaging in this process collaboratively. In the small-group setting, different participants propose various solutions to a translation problem and the group together must decide on a solution. If most of the learners in a group are lacking a strong *Sprachgefühl* for one or the other of the languages involved in a translation activity, the group will not be able to come up with the necessary intuition-based alternatives from which to choose collaboratively. The negotiation process in the translation work itself can certainly contribute to the strengthening of intuitions, but it must be based on a solid basic feel for the language from the outset.

A foreign language course that is based primarily on the overt teaching of language structures and that does not provide students with extensive opportunities for authentic communication in the classroom neglects and even obstructs the students' natural acquisitional abilities; it also ignores the fundamental nature of translation as a communicative activity. By relegating real communicative experience with foreign languages to summer courses and stays abroad, we erroneously attempt to bypass the visceral, collaborative and experiential stage of language acquisition that is the fertile ground for the development of the native speaker intuitions we associate with native language competence. No amount of grammar instruction or rote memorization of vocabulary can make up for the deep affective feel for a language that comes through communication by means of that language. By helping our students approach the foreign language in a more natural manner, we are sure to help them become more competent and more self-confident foreign language users. There is every reason to believe that they will have a better feel for the language and a deeper appreciation for the culture and its people, having themselves been actively drawn into the formerly foreign speech community.

Implementing truly communicative foreign language instruction in translator education programmes would be an excellent first step towards turning translator education into a practice-oriented enterprise. It would encourage students to begin taking responsibility for their own learning; it would help them understand from the beginning that translation is a communicative, interpretative process much more than it is a process of recoding. It would help create a spirit of community within the institution and break the mould of the transmissionist model of teaching, with students no longer being treated like empty vessels that need to be filled with knowledge.

Case studies in classroom second language acquisition

Introduction to Latvian

An exchange programme between the University of Latvia in Riga and the FASK of the University of Mainz was initiated in 1995 with the aim of assisting the former in setting up a translator education programme. It was planned for a number of instructors from Riga to come to Germersheim for one semester each to see how translators are educated in Germany, and also to offer courses of their own. FASK instructors would in turn travel to Riga for brief stays to teach intensive courses in translation studies and to discuss instructional and curricular matters with their Riga counterparts. It was decided that Dr Z was to be the first exchange instructor to visit Germersheim from Riga for a longer stay during the summer semester of 1996 and I was asked to propose courses she might teach. I felt that a good way to build a bridge between our two universities was to get students interested in the Latvian language and culture, so I suggested an introductory course in the Latvian language. However, given that students already have the choice of a wide range of languages in Germersheim, I was concerned that not many would be interested in a language of such limited diffusion as Latvian.

Having planned to offer an undergraduate seminar in second-language acquisition studies during that semester, I thought it would be a good opportunity for the participants in that course to be required to attend classes in a language that would be completely new to all of them. This would not only provide them with a laboratory within which to study second language acquisition, but it would also be a way to ensure that a fair number of students would find their way into the Latvian language course. As I had had some experience and success teaching Spanish with the Natural Approach at the University of Illinois, and because this approach is related to Krashen's controversial theory of language acquisition, which would lend itself to study in my seminar, I proposed that Dr Z teach an introductory course in the Latvian language using the Natural Approach over the course of the semester. She informed me that she had no experience using the approach and that she was, in fact, a rather traditional teacher who believed in the drilling of grammar rules and who basically liked to be in control in the classroom - two features that do not bode well for a Natural Approach class. Nevertheless, she expressed her willingness to give it a try.

It turned out that Dr Z would only be able to remain in Germersheim for the first six weeks of the semester – clearly not long enough for the students to get an idea of how the Natural Approach works or to acquire very much Latvian. I therefore found myself twisting the arms of her successors to take up where Dr Z left off and to continue with the Natural Approach course until the end of the semester. Neither Dr Z nor Ms V, both from the University of Latvia, had had any experience using the Natural Approach and neither believed it was an appropriate way to introduce translation students to Latvian, particularly given the fact that we would have only one and a half hours of class per week. For all practical purposes then, our semester-long course in Latvian using the Natural Approach class lasted for only nine contact hours, until Dr Z returned home. As the two other teachers clearly felt extremely uncomfortable with the approach from the moment they took over the course, we agreed after two classes that they would switch to what they called the 'eclectic' approach they used for Latvian and German courses at their home university. They did not specify at the outset what this approach would entail, but rather than have the course collapse completely, I gave them free reign to teach it as they saw fit.

The key features of the course as planned with Dr Z, based on Natural Approach principles, were to be the following:

- Teacher talk was to be solely in Latvian and would be geared toward providing the students with comprehensible input (i and $i+1$) continuously adapted to their level of comprehension as they progressed.
- The teacher would assume the role of an initiator and supporter of communicative experiences rather than that of a transmissionist teacher. Her main tasks would be to provide the students with a) opportunities for acquisition by creating real communicative situations in the classroom, and b) comprehensible input and feedback for the students to work with.
- The students' affective filter would be kept low by having the teacher provide non-judgmental support throughout the class, by avoiding metalinguistic explanations, and through the creation of a collaborative learning environment in the classroom.
- Acquisition of the phonological, syntactic, semantic and pragmatic systems of Latvian would be fostered by avoiding contrastive linguistic explanations and by creating a desire and a need to communicate spontaneously on the part of the learners with their emerging Latvian skills.
- Reading and writing would be delayed until the learners had acquired a grasp of the aural/oral language through listening and speaking.
- Learners would be allowed to delay speech production until they were ready to speak.
- A variety of modes of interaction would be incorporated into the class to keep students focused on the input and to help them make experiential associations with Latvian lexico-semantic elements. Students would be encouraged to interact actively with each other and with the teacher, to be involved in role-playing activities, language games, and pair work as well as small and large group work.

- Elements of Latvian culture would be presented in context to foster the students' interest in the language, culture and people of Latvia.

The very diverse impressions reported by two of the teachers of the introductory course in Latvian illustrates the difficulties inherent in using a non-traditional method that challenges the teachers' most fundamental assumptions about language learning. In the July 1996 issue of *Pulvertornis*, the newsletter for the Germersheim-Riga exchange programme, the teachers reported on their experiences in Germersheim, including their reactions to the Natural Approach class:

> Dr Z:
> I was teaching Latvian with the Natural Approach – something I had never done before and, moreover, that I did not believe in. But it works!
> Dr S:
> It was difficult and strenuous for me as the teacher because the 'writing' mode of perception was absent. It took some time before the students understood their own learning capabilities. Some of them became frustrated with learning. It was difficult for me to deal with the students as if they were little children. As not all of the available modes of perception were used, knowledge was not permanently stored. ... Of course, it is debatable whether one should devote so much time to such an old method in a university-level translator and interpreter training programme.

This last comment by Dr S is particularly interesting because it reveals just how difficult it can be for teachers with deep-seated objectivist views about language teaching and learning to work with constructivist approaches. In my view, it is the incompatibility of these two underlying perspectives that can often lead to frustration and utter failure in the implementation.

Diaries kept by the students, in which they record their personal learning experiences throughout the course, revealed an almost unanimously positive response to the learning situation while Dr Z was teaching, and an almost universally negative response to the remainder of the course, taught by Dr S and Ms V using their 'eclectic approach'. The brief explanations in the diaries do not permit an in-depth analysis of the reasons for this difference in attitudes towards the two parts of the course, but they do suggest that the primary attributes of the Natural Approach – the development of a collaborative community in the classroom, an affectively propitious environment for acquisition, an emphasis on students' needs and interests, and the absence of form-focused activities – were the key elements that made virtually all of the students feel that they were starting to acquire Latvian during the initial part of the course. The change in the students' attitudes toward Latvian and the class was radical following Dr Z's departure. Their diary comments revealed that this change was clearly due to the elimination of the supportive community, the abrupt raising of the affective filter through teacher- and form-focused teaching, the disruptive influence of the written form, and the boring, impersonal nature of classroom activities.

The 'eclectic approach' used during the second part of the course turned out to be transmissionist instruction in sheep's clothing. The students were regularly divided up into groups, not to allow them to interact personally or to explore means of Latvian expression while undertaking inherently interesting collaborative activities, but to have them drill grammatical structures and memorize vocabulary items. Games were played, not as an integrated part of the instructional approach to provide opportunities to experiment with the language in a positive affective environment, but as a simple diversion from the form-focused, impersonal stress of the 'real' instructional activities.

The Latvian course ended that semester with virtually all of the students reporting that they had stopped making progress with Latvian when the teachers changed. Unfortunately, only three students returned to the Latvian course that fall semester, out of the 22 who had participated in the spring. Having studied various teaching approaches during our seminar, all of the students realized, however, that their Latvian class had not been an example of the Natural Approach, even though Dr Z came close to providing the essential characteristics of a classroom acquisition environment during her six-week segment of the course. The frustration that came out of the 'eclectic' classroom and the unquenched curiosity about the kind of language learning experience that the Natural Approach might offer led to the next FASK experiment with acquisition in the classroom.

Acquiring Spanish in the Classroom

When a student at the FASK (Gelies 1997) decided to write her master's thesis on the effects of the Natural Approach on student's attitudes, three of the original participants in the Natural Approach class for Latvian who had also participated in my undergraduate seminar on second language acquisition agreed to offer a course in Spanish, their mother tongue, to students at Germersheim for a nine-day intensive session during the spring break of 1997. The prospective participants were informed of the nature of the course before signing up: they would be 'living' Spanish for those nine days. The research questions for the master's thesis involved the students' attitudes toward the Natural Approach itself as a language teaching method, and their attitudes toward the Spanish language and culture. Sixteen students signed up and attended the course for the approximately 50 hours of instruction.

The level of the participants' communicative competence in Spanish at the outset varied widely. Some had begun studying Spanish at Germersheim, some had just completed their third semester and had never been to a Spanish-speaking country, while others had already spent up to nine months in Spain. The course itself was an integrated programme of communicative language activities involving a variety of situational and functional topics, including games, role playing activities, sketches, reading and whole-group discussions, all carefully adapted to the interests of university-age students. Most afternoons ended with a dance session, during which the participants learned and practised the traditional Sevillanas. On one day, the students were divided into groups, with each group being responsible for teaching the rest of the class for one hour.

The most important goals of the course were to make the students feel comfortable speaking Spanish, help them develop their capacity for self-correction, and encourage them to assume responsibility for their own progress. The primary tool for accomplishing these goals was the development of a true community in the classroom, with each student feeling supported by the group and linguistically uninhibited in front of the teachers and the other students. The multiple channels of perception and learning that are available in natural language acquisition were automatically incorporated into the design of classroom activities. These produced numerous opportunities for students to interact with the native speakers and each other – in Spanish, of course. Rather than focusing on the forms of the foreign language through the presentation of rules, contrasting structures, drilling and exercises, all activities were designed around authentic interaction between the participants through the medium of the emerging second language. The absence of explanations in the students' native tongue and the requirement of accomplishing tasks collaboratively ensured that students had to make use of a variety of visual, gestural, auditory and spatial cues to make sense of the input and turn it into intake. For example, one activity involved having small groups simulate the workings of tourist information offices to put together presentations on the different regions of Spain. Working with authentic source-language information materials, they had to create their own image of the region, discuss important characteristics, etc.

The reactions of the students to an anonymous questionnaire following the course provide some insight into the value they saw in this pedagogical approach:

Q: How did the course affect your attitude toward the Spanish language?

> A: *I think I am much more motivated than I was before and I no longer have as many inhibitions about speaking Spanish. I now feel the desire to learn more so that I can express myself better and more quickly.*
>
> A: *I find it easier to speak Spanish now, and my reading and writing skills are better, too. In particular, my listening comprehension and my grammatical knowledge improved. (I just can't remember dry, boring theory.)*

Q: What is your impression of how the course affected your relationship to other course participants?

> A: *We formed a community; we worked with each other and never against each other. And we got to know each other much better in the course of the two week period.*

Q: What was the relationship between the teachers and students like?

A: At the beginning, there was some distance between the teachers and students. This soon turned into a warm, friendly relationship. The atmosphere was very pleasant.

A: Excellent! The teachers were more like partners; real friendship evolved among us. With their lively manner and perpetual good mood, they were always able to motivate us very much. By the end of the course, I had no more inhibitions about speaking with them in Spanish.

Q: How do you feel about the classroom activities you experienced during the course?

A: At the beginning I wasn't very enthusiastic about playing games, but since the group worked so well together, I changed my mind about them. They addressed all of our senses.

A: The class was a lot of fun and was also multi-faceted. Everything was fun, particularly the games in which we had to use the language quickly and spontaneously. We learned a great deal by actually using the language.

These comments are indicative of the overall response to the course. Gelies found that all of the participants were pleased with the progress they made in Spanish over those nine days. She found, in fact, that the course itself, and the communicative, student-oriented approach underlying it, was directly responsible for a dramatic increase in the students' motivational intensity. During those nine days, these students, who had previously been subjected to semesters of depersonalized, form-focused instruction, found themselves being drawn into the community of Spanish speakers. These students were not experiencing **foreign language learning**; they were experiencing **second language acquisition** in the classroom.

The pedagogical similarities between the *Natural Approach* and *All's Well* are striking. While the course materials used in the methods differ radically, the creators of both methods clearly shared a constructivist view of second language acquisition. The essence of this view can essentially be expressed in a few simple axioms:

1. Regardless of what we as teachers do in the classroom, students will structure their own language.
2. A living knowledge of a foreign language can only come through authentic communicative interaction by means of the language itself.
3. The psychological, emotional, physical and cognitive constraints and needs of adult learners need to be taken into consideration at every step of the learning process.
4. Knowing a language means, first and foremost, having a feel for (rather than a theoretical knowledge of) accuracy, appropriateness and communicative effectiveness when we perceive the language in use and when we express ourselves by means of it.

5. For the development of communicative competence, there is no replacement for personal experience with the physical world and the social environment through the medium of that language.
6. The acquisition of a language is a collaborative activity *par excellence.*

These axioms also reflect the approach underlying the "whole-language movement" which has emerged as a major pedagogical trend guiding elementary and secondary school language teaching in Australia and New Zealand (Goodman and Goodman 1990). Unlike the Natural Approach and SGAV methodology, proponents of this movement refer directly to the writings of Lev Vygotsky for inspiration and justification. The notions presented by Goodman and Goodman outlining the whole-language approach parallel the principles I have proposed throughout this book for translator education, including the second language learning component. These notions are paraphrased below (Goodman and Goodman 1990):

• Language, both written and oral, is most easily learned within contexts of use. Learners acquire the ability to control linguistic processes if they encounter holistic, relevant and functional language in the accomplishment of real purposes.
• A major task of the language teacher is to involve learners in relevant functional activities and experiences that will stretch their capabilities. Teachers should mediate learners' transactions with the world, supporting learning, but without controlling it. They should help learners find opportunities to encourage them to collaboratively address a variety of problems that are important and meaningful to them.
• Authentic activities in which language serves in real and functional ways are always stressed.
• Rather than being learned by imitating teachers or learning de-contextualized rules, it is invented by each individual, and it is adapted to social conventions in the context of actual language use.
• Whole-language teachers are leaders in the classroom; they do not abdicate their authority or responsibility. They lead by virtue of their greater experience, their knowledge, and their respect for their pupils. They know their pupils, monitor their learning, and provide support and resources as they are needed. They understand that there must be collaboration and a relationship of trust between themselves and their pupils if an effective learning atmosphere is to be created.
• Rather than intervening to control the students, the whole-language teacher mediates to empower them. Intervention presupposes that the teacher knows in advance what learning is acceptable; by intervening, the teacher determines social conventions and suppresses invention. Mediation empowers

students by increasing their self-confidence, maximizing opportunities for linguistic and social invention, and by promoting autonomy and responsibility.

A constructivist view of learning weaves its way through the discourse of All's Well, the Natural Approach, and the whole-language movement like a steel wire. Many of you will have had your own experiences with similarly constructivist methods, approaches and movements, and many will also be able to look back on your personal language acquisition experiences, either inside or outside the classroom, and reflect on the constructivist nature of those experiences. There have clearly been hotspots of constructivist language teaching for some time, and they have not been restricted to a particular age or type of learner. There is a solid basis in the language teaching literature and support from translation studies as well for applying the constructivist approach to second language acquisition for translation students.

Conclusion

I hope to have shown in this chapter that (1) foreign language *learning* alone does not constitute adequate linguistic preparation for professional translators; they must also have *acquired* the languages they work with, and that (2) acquisition can indeed be fostered in the classroom. When I present these ideas at translation education conferences, someone invariably voices the objection that our curricula simply do not allow for acquisition of this kind. The constraints of students' schedules filled with a myriad of required courses, in which knowledge is dosed out to them in digestible chunks a few hours a week, and of departmental curricula geared toward the objectivist ideals of compartmentalization and transmissionist efficiency do make it difficult even to try out alternative approaches. If, however, students and teachers can see and demonstrate the tremendous value in shifting from teaching to facilitating, from rote memorization to active participation, from dead bodies and talking heads to lively, holistic collaboration, then change will come about, and the structures of our institutions will bend to accommodate our new understandings of what it takes to educate translators today to prepare them for the challenges of tomorrow.

A Conclusion ... and a Beginning

Translator trainers would surely agree that translator competence should be the primary goal of our translator education programmes. It goes without saying that our institutional programmes should be producing graduates that the community of professional translators as well as the clients of translators' services would judge to be competent language mediators. There is probably also a high degree of consensus on what translator competence entails (which is always much more than mere translation competence), at least within particular language communities. What we do not yet have, however, is a consensus on how translator competence can be acquired or learned.

Traditionally rooted in the adjacent domains of linguistics and philology, translation studies as a field is just beginning to develop its own educational culture. There are only a handful of academic programmes worldwide that purport to train translator trainers themselves. The gravity of this deficit becomes apparent if one considers the situation, for example, in the foreign language teaching field, with its canon of theory, its enormous research base and its countless teacher training programmes around the world. Translation studies as a field of study is just starting to come to terms with what it means to acquire – and teach – translator competence. The rigid teacher-focused classroom structure as the default mainstay of teaching practice in our field is starting to be called into question. In fact, voices within the translator education establishment calling for a major change in translator education pedagogy are being heard more and more frequently in publications and at conferences. There seems to be an increasing perception that the conventional teacher- and exercise-centered classroom alone cannot equip translators-in-training with the wide range of professional and interpersonal skills, knowledge and competence they will need to meet the requirements of an increasingly demanding language mediation market.

Many of the voices calling for innovation today suggest that, at the very least, conventional instruction should be supplemented with authentic praxis-oriented work through which students can come to grips with the types of constraints and expectations they can expect to face once they graduate as language mediation experts. While heated debate will surely continue as to the respective roles of theory and authentic practice in university education, the emerging consensus view in our field seems to be that both are needed. In this book, I have outlined an approach for incorporating praxis with theory in translator education, starting with the most fundamental beliefs held by both teachers and students of what it means to know and to learn. Joining translator competence and authenticity, the concept of 'collaboration' is the third supporting column of this approach.

As I have presented it here, collaboration can be seen as a fundamental feature of effective learning environments. It can be viewed as an essential tool for our educational institutions that should have the mission of empowering learners and of ensuring their autonomy and competence as life-long learners and as members of a professional community. Collaboration, I believe, is the fundamental basis for authentic work and learning, a tool for getting students involved in the dialogue that constitutes the translator's profession, for turning inert knowledge into active, intersubjective knowing, and for introducing students to the kinds of team-work they can be sure to be involved in after they graduate. This belief in the value of collaboration also reflects an underlying approach to education as a commitment to the many facets of 'community'. These include the university as a community of learners, the professional language mediation community, the society in which our graduates will work and, not least of all, the global community we have become.

Much of education is focused on the pursuit of individual objectives, both by students and faculty members. Diplomas, good salaries, social status, personal power and control over others – these are individual goals, and certainly justifiable ones. A commitment to collaboration, however, implies that it is vital to raise our sights and to aim beyond the level of personal goals, to look beyond 'I' to 'we'. It means moving away from competition as a key focus in education, away from rigid hierarchical power structures, and towards democracy in education that seeks empowerment for all of the participants involved. The exercise of complete control by faculty over the entire educational process – from the curriculum and the lesson plan, to the criteria for the evaluation of learning, right down to turn-taking in classroom discourse – does not empower teachers in any meaningful way. And it clearly disempowers students, preventing them from assuming responsibility for their own learning, equating the development of autonomy, a key factor in professional competence, with the awarding of a diploma. We become empowered as teachers not by controlling learners, but by emancipating them. When we encourage learners to think for themselves and to depend on each other, on their individual capabilities for independent learning, and on us as guides and assistants to help them learn, we are empowering them to become full-fledged members of the communities in which they live and will work; we are helping them to build character and trustworthiness; we are promoting a culture of expertise and professionalism in our future colleagues and successors. This is empowerment for all of us: teachers, students and administrators alike.

It is not my intention to propose *the* 'collaborative', 'constructivist', or empowerment approach to translator education. Just as each translation student brings his or her own personal experience to the learning situation, so too will each teacher who believes in the value of learning-centred education develop a unique pedagogical approach and instructional techniques that are tailored to his or her local teaching situation. And no teacher will be able to do it alone. We will have to work together in dialogue with other teachers, administrators and students to develop approaches that belong to all of us as members of teaching/learning communities, and not just to a knowledge-distributing, all-powerful elite. Just as in collaborative classrooms, synergy must develop between groups and individuals working toward innovation in translator education to ensure that it is within a complex universe of community interaction that personal goals are met.

It is time, I believe, to break the stranglehold of the 'instructional performance' on our teaching practice. Instead of doing to our students what was done to us, we need to develop a true educational culture of our own, a culture of permanent innovation. And as in every mature field of study, a primary vehicle for perpetuating progress will be investigative research.

One particularly valuable way to carry out educational research is to have teachers themselves study what goes on in their own classrooms. Beginning our study of learning and teaching processes while imposing change on our individual teaching environments, I believe, can lead to a groundswell of new approaches and techniques, a plethora of practical teaching techniques and a rich dialogue for educational change. We need to start observing and effectuating change in our own classes rather than waiting for outside researchers to come and observe what we are doing. We need to identify room for improvement in our own teaching practices and to devise our own viable remedies for change that we can continuously observe and modify as necessary. Instead of stagnating in a career of repetitive pedagogical practice that treads water while the translation profession forges ahead, we need to turn our classrooms into experimental laboratories where innovation is the order of the day. The translation profession will evolve continually with advances in technology, increased globalization and changes in lifestyle and business practices. Society, and with it the translation profession, is programmed for perpetual change. To keep pace, we need to infuse our classes and our programmes with the seeds of perpetual innovation.

Classroom research is not something teachers do alone, with students serving as their guinea pigs. Instead, it is collaborative action carried out by teachers and students working together. By having students join us in research to investigate learning and teaching processes, we can instil in them the understanding that they have a stake in designing their own learning environment; thus we can encourage them to develop a sense of responsibility for their own learning and actions that will surely stand them in good stead as they develop expertise and autonomy as language mediation professionals. From this perspective, active involvement in research becomes a metaphor for the learning process itself.

While contributing to the perpetuation of innovation in educational practices, students will be acquiring valuable skills they will need as professionals later on. By participating in think-aloud protocol research, they can investigate the development of their own translation strategies. By observing what works and what doesn't in individual and in group interaction in translation exercise classes, they will be raising their awareness of the difficulties and advantages of individual, competitive and collaborative modes of work. The list of possibilities for authentic collaboration is endless.

Another valuable way to draw investigative research into the programme of studies is to see it as a metaphor for the educational process itself. Rather than having students simply perform pedagogical tasks that we devise for them with the best intentions of passing on to them our skills and knowledge, we can instead see learning as an active process of individual and collaborative research. If we can appreciate the tremendous motivation for learning and for excellence that comes from being personally responsible for one's own work and one's own learning, then we can see the value of building the curriculum and classroom experiences around authentic projects in which the learners are personally implicated from the selection of the task to the publication of the final product. It is, I believe, by meeting the challenge of real work with the support and guidance of teachers that learners can best become empowered as incipient experts, and as cognitive apprentices with a true voice in the educational process and in forging their own future.

The creation of a research culture by teachers and students together would, I am convinced, constitute a powerful force for catapulting educational practice in translator education into the 21st century. Just as students cannot expect to be handed knowledge and skills on a silver platter, neither can teachers expect empowerment to be passed down to them by the powers that be. We must begin to work together toward the development of viable educational approaches, instructional designs and pedagogical procedures that reflect the translation profession of today and that can prepare all of us for the challenges that await us tomorrow.

References

Allwright, Dick (1979) 'Abdication and Responsibility in Language Teaching', *Studies in Second Language Acquisition* 2:105-121.

------ and Kathleen M. Bailey (1991) *Focus on the Language Classroom*, Cambridge: Cambridge University Press.

Archaubault, R. D. (ed) (1974) *John Dewey on Education: Selected Writings*, Chicago: University of Chicago.

Arntz, Reiner and Gisela Thome (eds) (1990) *Übersetzungswissenschaft: Ergebnisse und Perspektiven*, Tübingen: Gunter Narr Verlag.

Arrojo, Rosemary (1994) 'Deconstruction and the Teaching of Translation', *TextContext* 9:1-12.

Austermühl, Frank (forthcoming) *Electronic Tools for Translators*, Manchester: St. Jerome.

Azwell, Tara S. (1992) 'Alternative Assessment Forms', in H. C. Foyle (ed) *Interactive Learning in the Higher Education Classroom*, Washington, D.C.: National Education Association, 160-74.

BDÜ (1986) 'Memorandum', *Corporate Language Policy* 5:103-118.

Bednar, Anne K., Donald Cunningham, Thomas M. Duffy and J. David Perry (1992) 'Theory into Practice: How Do We Link?', in Thomas M. Duffy and David H. Jonassen (eds) *Constructivism and the Technology of Instruction: A Conversation*, Hillsdale, NJ & London: Lawrence Erlbaum Associates, 17-34.

Bereiter, Carl and Marlene Scardamalia (1993) *Surpassing Ourselves – An Inquiry into the Nature and Implications of Expertise*, Chicago & LaSalle, Ill.: Open Court.

Berg, Cathrine (1999) 'Preparing ESL Students for Peer Response', *TESOL Journal* 8(2):20-25.

Bosworth, Kris (ed) (1992) *Collaborative Learning: Underlying Processes and Effective Techniques,* San Francisco: Jossey-Bass Publishers.

Bredo, Eric (1994) 'Reconstructing Educational Psychology: Situated Cognition and Deweyan Pragmatism', *Educational Psychologist* 29(1):23-35.

Brown, John Seely, Allan Collins and Paul Duguid (1989) 'Situated Cognition and the Culture of Learning', *Educational Researcher* 18(1):32-42.

Bruffee, Kenneth A. (1995) *Collaborative Learning: Higher Education, Interdependence, and the Authority of Knowledge*, Baltimore: Johns Hopkins University Press.

Brundage, D. H. and D. Mackeracher (1980) *Adult Learning Principles and Their Application to Programme Planning*, Ontario: Institute for Studies in Education.

Canale, Michael and Merrill Swain (1980) 'Theoretical Bases of Communicative Approaches to Second Language Teaching and Testing', *Applied Linguistics* 1:1-47.

Candy, Philip C. (1989) 'Constructivism and the Study of Self-direction in Adult Learning', *Studies in the Education of Adults* 21(2):95-116.

Chau, Simon C. (1984) 'How to Translate "This is a red rose": The Grammatical, Cultural and Interpretive Aspects of Translation Teaching', in Wolfram Wilss and Gisela Thome (eds) *Die Theorie des Übersetzens und ihr Aufschlußwert für die Übersetzungs- und Dolmetschdidaktik*, Tübingen: Gunter Narr, 124-33.

Chaudron, C. (1988) *Second Language Classrooms: Research on Teaching and Learning*, Cambridge: Cambridge University Press.

Chesterman, Andrew (1993) 'From Is to Ought: Laws, Norms and Strategies in Translation Studies', *Target* 5(1):124-33.

------ (1997) *Memes of Translation*, Amsterdam & Philadelphia: John Benjamins.

Choi, Jeong Im and Michael Hannafin (1995) 'Situated Cognition and Learning Environments: Roles, Structures and Implications for Design', *Educational Technology Research and Development* 43(2):53-69.

Cole, P. (1992) 'Constructivism Revisited: A Search for Common Ground', *Educational Technology* 32(2):27-34.

Collins, Allan, John Seely Brown and Susan E. Newman (1989) 'Cognitive Apprenticeship: Teaching the Crafts of Reading, Writing, and Mathematics', in Lauren B. Resnick (ed) *Knowing, Learning, and Instruction. Essays in Honor of Robert Glaser*, Hillsdale, NJ: Lawrence Erlbaum Associates, 453-94.

Cunningham, Donald J. (1992) 'In Defense of Extremism', in Thomas M. Duffy and David H. Jonassen (eds) *Constructivism and the Technology of Instruction: A Conversation*, Hillsdale, NJ & London: Lawrence Erlbaum Associates, 157-60.

Damasio, Antonio R. (1994) *Descartes' Error. Emotion, Reason and the Human Brain*, New York: Avon Books.

Dewey, John (1938) *Experience & Education*, New York: Simon & Schuster.

Dickinson, Anthony, Jean Leveque and Henri Sagot (1976) *All's Well That Starts Well – Teacher's Book*, Paris: Didier.

Dollerup, Cay and Annette Lindegaard (eds) (1994) *Teaching Translation and Interpreting 2*, Amsterdam & Philadelphia: John Benjamins.

Dollerup, Cay and Vibeke Appekl (1995) *Teaching Translation and Interpreting 3: New Horizons*, Amsterdam & Philadelphia: John Benjamins.

Dreyfus, H. and Stewart Dreyfus (1986) *Mind over Machine*, New York: The Free Press.

Duffy, Thomas M. and David H. Jonassen (1992) 'Constructivism: New Implications for Instructional Technology', in Thomas M. Duffy and David H. Jonassen (eds) *Constructivism and the Technology of Instruction: A Conversation*, Hillsdale, NJ & London: Lawrence Erlbaum Associates, 1-16.

Duffy, Thomas M. and David H. Jonassen (eds) (1992) *Constructivism and the Technology of Instruction: A Conversation*, Hillsdale, NJ & London: Lawrence Erlbaum Associates.

Dunlap, Joanna C. and R. Scott Grabinger (1996) 'Rich Environments for Active Learning in the Higher Education Classroom', in Brent G. Wilson (ed) *Constructivist Learning Environments. Case Studies in Instructional Design*, Englewood Cliffs, NJ: Educational Technology Publications, 62-85.

Engström, Yrjö (1987) *Learning by Expanding: An Activity-theoretical Approach to Developmental Research*, Helsinki: Orienta-Konsultit oy.

Ferro, Trenton R. (1993) 'The Influence of Affective Processing in Education and Training', in Daniele D. Flannery *New Directions for Adult and Continuing Education: Applying Cognitive Learning Theory to Adult Learning* 59:25-34.

Flannery, James L. (1992) 'The Teacher as Co-conspirator: Knowledge and Authority in Collaborative Learning', in Kris Bosworth & Sharon J. Hamilton (eds) *Collaborative Learning: Underlying Processes and Effective Techniques*, San Francisco: Jossey-Bass, 15-24.

Fosnot, Catherine (1992) 'Constructing Constructivism', in Thomas M. Duffy and David H. Jonassen (eds) *Constructivism and the Technology of Instruction: A Conversation*, Hillsdale, NJ & London: Lawrence Erlbaum Associates, 167-76.

Gallimore, Ronald and Roland Tharp (1990) 'Teaching Mind in Society: Teaching, Schooling, and Literate Discourse', in Luis C. Moll (ed) *Vygotsky and Education. Instructional Implications and Applications of Sociohistorical Psychology*, Cambridge: Cambridge University Press, 175-205.

Garrison, Jim (1995) 'Deweyan Pragmatism and the Epistomology of Contemporary Social Constructivism', *American Educational Research Journal* 32(4):716-40.

Gelies, Claudia (1997) *A Critical Analysis of the Effects of Collaborative Learning on the Attitudes of Foreign Language Learners*, Unpublished Diplomarbeit (M.A. thesis), University of Mainz.

Gentzler, Edwin (1993) *Contemporary Translation Theories*, London & New York: Routledge.

Gifford, Bernard and Mary Catherine O'Connor (eds) (1992) *Changing Assessments*, Boston/Dordrecht/London: Kluwer Academic Publishers.

Glasersfeld, Ernst von (1988) 'The Reluctance to Change a Way of Thinking', *The Irish Journal of Psychology* 9(1):83-90.

Goodman, Yetta M. and Kenneth S Goodman (1990) 'Vygotsky in a Whole-language Perspective', in Luis C. Moll (ed) *Vygotsky and Education. Instructional Implications and Applications of Sociohistorical Psychology*, Cambridge: Cambridge University Press, 223-250.

Göpferich, Susanna (1996) 'Textsortenkanon: Zur Text(sorten) auswahl für fachsprachliche Übersetzungsübungen', in Andreas Kelletat (ed) *Übersetzerische Kompetenz: Beiträge zur universitären Übersetzerausbildung in Deutschland und Skandinavien*, Frankfurt am Main: Lang, 9-38.

Graceffo, Uta (1996) *Constructivist Approaches to Translation Teaching: A Case Study of a 7th Semester Class in General Translation*, Diplomarbeit (M.A. thesis), University of Mainz.

Guba, Egon and Yvonne Lincoln (1989) *Fourth Generation Evaluation*, Newbury Park, CA.: Sage Publications.

Heinemann, Evelyn (1998) *Hexen und Hexenangst: Eine psychoanalytische Studie des Hexenwahns der frühen Neuzeit*, Göttingen: Vandenhoeck & Ruprecht.

Hipps, Jerome A. (1993) 'Trustworthiness and Authenticity: Alternate Ways to Judge Authentic Assessments', Conference Presentation at the Annual Meeting of the American Educational Research Association, Atlanta, Georgia.

Hoffmann, R. (1998) 'How Can Expertise Be Defined? Implications of Research from Cognitive Psychology', in Wendy Faulkner, James Fleck and Robin Williams (eds) *Exploring Expertise*, Basingstoke: Hampshire: MacMillan Press.

Hönig, Hans G. (1988) 'Übersetzen lernt man nich durch Übersetzen: Ein Plädoyer für eine Propaedeutik des Übersetzens', *FluL* 17:154-67.

------ (1990) 'Sagen was man nicht weiß – wissen, was man nicht sagt. Überlegungen zur übersetzerischen Intuition', in Reiner Arntz und Gisela Thome (eds) *Übersetzungswissenschaft: Ergebnisse und Perspektiven*, Tübingen: Gunter Narr Verlag, 152-61.

------ (1995) *Konstruktives Übersetzen*, Tübingen: Stauffenberg.

------ (1998) 'Übersetzung (therapeutisch vs. diagnostisch)', in Mary Snell Hornby, Hans Hönig, Paul Kußmaul and Peter Schmitt (eds) *Handbuch Translation*, Tübingen: Stauffenburg, 378-81.

House, Juliane (1988) 'Talking to Oneself or Thinking with Others? On Using Different Thinking-aloud Methods in Translation', *FluL* 17:84-98.

------ (1997) *Translation Quality Assessment: A Model Revisited*, Tübingen: Gunter Narr.

------ and Shoshana Blum-Kulka (eds) (1986*) Discourse and Cognition in Translation and Second Language Acquisition Studies*, Tübingen: Gunter Narr.

Jääskeläinen, Riitta and Sonja Tirkkonen-Condit (1991) 'Automatised Processes in Professional vs. Non-professional Translation: A Think-aloud Protocol Study', in Sonja Tirkkonen-Condit (ed) *Empirical Research in Translation and Intercultural Studies*, Tübingen: Gunter Narr Verlag, 89-110.

Johnson, David W. and Roger T. Johnson (1991) *Learning together and alone,* Englewood Cliffs, N.J.: Prentice Hall.

Johnson, Roger T., David W. Johnson and M. Stanne (1985) 'Effects of Cooperative, Competitive and Individualized Goal Structures on Computer-based Instruction', *Journal of Educational Psychology* 77:668-77.

Jovanovic, Mladen (ed) (1991) *Translation: A Creative Profession. 12th World Congress of FIT Proceedings*, Belgrade: Provodilac.

King, Allison (1993) 'From Sage on the Stage to Guide on the Side', *College Teaching* 41(1):30-35.

Kiraly, Donald (1995) *Pathways to Translation*, Kent, Ohio: Kent State University Press.

------ (1998) 'Pesquisa sobre o exercício de traducao em sala de aula', *TradTerm* 5(2):23-40.

Klaudy, Kinga (1995) 'Quality Assessment in School vs. Professional Translation', in Cay Dollerup & Vibeke Appekl (eds) *Teaching Translation and Interpretation 3: New Horizons*, Amsterdam & Philadelphia: John Benjamins, 197-204.

Krings, H. P. (1986) 'Translation Problems and Translation Strategies of Advanced German Learners of French (L2). Interlingual and Intercultural Communication', in Juliane House and Shoshana Blum-Kulka (eds) *Discourse and Cognition in Translation and Second Language Acquisition Studies*, Tübingen: Gunter Narr, 263-76.

------ (1992) 'Bilinguismus und Übersetzen: Eine Antwort an Brian Harris', *Target* 4(1):105-110.

Kuhn, Thomas (1970) *The Structure of Scientific Revolutions*, Chicago: University of Chicago Press.

Kupsch-Losereit, Sigrid (1986) 'Scheint eine schöne Sonne? Oder: Was ist ein Übersetzungsfehler?', *Lebende Sprachen* 1:12-16.

------ (1996) 'Kognitive Verstehensprozesse beim Übersetzen', in Angelika Lauer, Heidrun Gerzymisch-Arbogast, Johann Haller and Erich Steiner (eds) *Übersetzungswissenschaft im Umbruch*, Tübingen: Gunter Narr, 217-28.

Kußmaul, Paul (1995) *Training the Translator*, Amsterdam & Philadelphia: John Benjamins.

Lakoff, George (1987) *Women, Fire, and Dangerous Things. What Categories Reveal about the Mind*, Chicago & London: The University of Chicago Press.

Lauer, Angelika, Heidrun Gerzymisch-Arbogast, Johann Haller and Erich Steiner (eds)

(1996) *Übersetzungswissenschaft im Umbruch*, Tübingen: Gunter Narr.

Law, L., H. Mandl and M. Henninger (1998) *Training of Reflection: Its Feasibility and Boundary Conditions*, Research Report #89, München: Ludwig-Maximilians-Universität.

Legutke, Michael (1993) 'Room to Talk: Experiential Learning in the Foreign Language Classroom', *Die Neueren Sprachen* 92(4):306-331.

Leng Lawrence, Judith and Robert Kohls (1999) 'Editing Strategies for the Translation Classroom', *ATA Chronicle* 28(11):52-57.

Leont'ev, A. N. (1981) *Progress of the Development of the Mind*, Moscow: Progress Publishers.

Light, Paul and George Butterworth (eds) (1992) *Context and Cognition. Ways of Learning and Knowing*, Hemel Hampstead, Hertfordshire: Harvester Wheatsheaf.

Lörscher, Wolfgang (1991) 'Thinking-aloud as a Method for Collecting Data on Translation Processes. Empirical Research in Translation and Intercultural Studies', in Sonja Tirkonnen-Condit (ed) *Empirical Research in Translation and Intercultural Studies*, Tübingen: Gunter Narr Verlag, 67-78.

Mackenzie, Rosemary and Elina Nieminen (1997) 'Motivating Students to Achieve Quality in Translation', in Kinga Klaudy and János Kohn (eds) *Transferre Necesse Est*, Scholastica, 339-44.

McTaggart, R. (1991) 'Principles for Participatory Action Research', *Adult Education Quarterly* 41(3):168-87.

Mercer, Neil (1992) 'Culture, Context and the Construction of Knowledge in the Classroom', in Paul Light and George Butterworth (eds) *Context and Cognition. Ways of Learning and Knowing*, Hemel Hampstead, Hertfordshire: Harvester Wheatsheaf, 28-46.

------ (1994) 'Neo-Vygotskian Theory and Classroom Education', in Barry Stierer and Janet Maybin (eds) *Language, Literacy and Learning in Educational Practice*, Clevedon: Multilingual Matters, 92-110.

Miller, John P. and Wayne Seller (1985) 'Transmission Position: Educational Practice', in John P. Miller and Wayne Seller (eds) *Curriculum Perspectives and Practice*, New York: Longman, 37-61.

Miller, Judith E, John Trimbur and John M. Wilkes (1992) 'Group Dynamics: Understanding Group Success and Failure in Collaborative Learning', in Kris Bosworth (ed) *Collaborative Learning: Underlying Processes and Effective Techniques,* San Francisco: Jossey-Bass Publishers, 33-44.

Moll, Luis C. (ed) (1990) *Vygotsky and Education. Instructional Implications and Applications of Sociohistorical Psychology*, Cambridge: Cambridge University Press.

Neubert, Albrecht and Gregory M. Shreve (1992) *Translation as Text*, Kent, Ohio: Kent State University Press.

Newman, Denis, Peg Griffin and Michael Cole (1989) *The Construction Zone: Working for Cognitive Change in School*, Cambridge: Cambridge University Press.

Newmark, Peter (1973) 'Twenty-Three Restricted Rules of Translation', *The Incorporated Linguist* 12(1):12-19

------ (1991) 'The Curse of Dogma in Translation Studies', *Lebende Sprachen* 3:105-108.

Nord, Christiane (1988) *Textanalyse und Übersetzen: Theoretische Grundlagen, Methode und didaktische Anwendung einer übersetzungsrelevanten Textanalyse*, Heidelberg: Julius Groos Verlag.

------ (1994) 'Aus Fehlern lernen: Überlegungen zur Beurteilung von Übersetzungsleistungen', in Mary Snell-Hornby, Franz Pöchhacker and Klaus Kaindl (eds) *Translation Studies: An Interdiscipline*, Amsterdam & Philadelphia: John Benjamins, 363-376.

------ (1996) 'Wer nimmt denn mal den ersten Satz? Überlegungen zu neuen Arbeitsformen im Übersetzungsunterricht', in Angelika Lauer, Heidrun Gerzymisch-Arbogast, Johann Haller and Erich Steiner (eds) *Übersetzungswissenschaft im Umbruch*, Tübingen: Gunter Narr, 313-28.

------ (1997) *Translating as a Purposeful Activity: Functionalist Approaches Explained*, Manchester: St. Jerome Publishing.

Paulsen, M. F. (1995) 'An Overview of CMC and the Online Classroom in Distance Education', in Zane Berge and Mauri Collins (eds) *Computer-mediated Communication and the Online Classroom, Vol. III: Distance Learning*, Cresskill, NJ: Hampton Press.

Paulson, F. L. and P. R. Paulson (1994) 'Assessing Portfolios Using the Constructivist Paradigm', Paper presented at the Annual Meeting of the American Educational Research Association in New Orleans, LA, April 4-8, 1994. Washington, D.C.

Perkins, David N. (1992a) 'What Constructivism Demands of the Learner', in Thomas M. Duffy and David H. Jonassen (eds) *Constructivism and the Technology of Instruction: A Conversation*, Hillsdale, NJ & London: Lawrence Erlbaum Associates, 161-66.

------ (1992b) 'Technology Meets Constructivism: Do They Make a Marriage?', in Thomas M. Duffy and David H. Jonassen (eds) *Constructivism and the Technology of Instruction: A Conversation*, Hillsdale, NJ & London: Lawrence Erlbaum Associates, 45-56.

Phillips, Denis C. (1995) 'The Good, the Bad and the Ugly: the Many Faces of Constructivism', *Educational Researcher* 24(7): 5-12.

Pym, Anthony (1991) 'A Definition of Translational Competence Applied to the Training of Translators', in Malden Jovanovic (ed) *Translation: A Creative Profession. 12th World Congress of FIT Proceedings*, Belgrade: Provodilac, 541-46.

------ (1992) 'Why Translation Conventions Should Be Intercultural Rather than Culture Specific. An Alternative Link Model', Unpublished paper presented at the congress *Translation Studies – An Interdiscipline,* held in Vienna, 9-12 September 1992.

Reinke, Uwe (1997) 'Computergestützte Kommunikation im Übersetzungsunterricht', *Lebende Sprachen* 17(4):145-53.

Resnick, Lauren B. (ed) (1989*) Knowing, Learning, and Instruction. Essays in Honor of Robert Glaser*, Hillsdale, NJ: Lawrence Erlbaum Associates.

------ and Daniel P. Resnick (1992) 'Assessing the Thinking Curriculum: New Tools for Educational Reform', in Bernard Gifford and Mary Catherine O'Connor (eds) *Changing Assessments*, Boston/Dordrecht/London: Kluwer Academic Publishers, 37-76.

Richards, I. A. (1929) *Practical Criticism*, New York: Harcourt Brace.

Richards, Jack C. and Theodore S. Rodgers (1986) *Approaches and Methods in Language Teaching*, New York: Cambridge University Press.

Robinson, Douglas (1991) *The Translator's Turn*, Baltimore & London: The John Hopkins University Press.

Rogers, Carl (1967) *On Becoming a Person*, London: Constable.

Röhricht, Bettina (1998) *Collaborative Learning in Translator Education: A Case Study of a 7th Semester Translation Practice Class and an 'Übersetzerpropädeutikum'*, Diplomarbeit (M.A. thesis): University of Mainz.

Rorty, Richard (1979) *Philosphy and the Mirror of Nature*, Princeton, NJ: Princeton Universtiy Press.

Sainz, María Julia (1994) 'Student-centred Corrections of Translations', in Cay Dollerup and Annette Lindegaard (eds) *Teaching Translation and Interpreting 2*, Amsterdam & Philadelphia: John Benjamins, 133-42.

Savery, John R. and Thomas M. Duffy (1995) 'Problem Based Learning: An Instructional Model and its Constructivist Framework', *Educational Technology* 35(5):31-38.

Savignon, Sandra J. (1971) *A Study of the Effect of Training in Communicative Skills as Part of a Beginning College French Course on Student Attitude and Achievement in Linguistic and Communicative Competence*, Ph.D. Thesis: University of Illinois, Urbana-Champaign.

------ (1983) *Communicative Competence: Theory and Classroom Practice. Texts and Contexts in Second Language Learning*, Reading, MA: Addison-Wesley.

------ (1997) *Communicative Competence: Theory and Classroom Practice. Texts and Contexts in Second Language Learning*, Reading, MA: Addison-Wesley. Second Edition.

Schmitt, Peter A. (1997) 'Evaluierung von Fachübersetzungen', in Gerd Wotjak and Heide Schmidt (eds) *Modelle der Translation /Models of Translation*, Frankfurt am Main: Vervuert Verlag, 301-32.

Schön, Donald (1987) *Educating the Reflective Practitioner*, San Francisco: Jossey-Bass.

Seymour, Richard K. and C. C. Liu (eds) (1994) *Translation and Interpreting: Bridging East and West*, Honolulu: University of Hawaii.

Snell-Hornby, Mary (1988) *Translation Studies: An Integrated Approach*, Amsterdam & Philadelphia: John Benjamins.

Spiro, Rand J., Paul J. Feltovich, Michael J. Jacobson and Richard L. Coulson (1992) 'Cognitive Flexibility, Constructivism, and Hypertext: Random Access Instruction for Advanced Knowledge Acquisition in Ill-structured Domains', in Thomas M. Duffy and David H. Jonassen (eds) *Constructivism and the Technology of Instruction: A Conversation*, Hillsdale, NJ & London: Lawrence Erlbaum Associates, 57-75.

Stevick, Earl (1980) *Teaching Languages. A Way and Ways*, Rowley, Mass.: Newbury House.

Stierer, Barry and Janet Maybin (eds) (1994) *Language, Literacy and Learning in Educational Practice*, Clevedon; Philadelphia & Adelaide: Multilingual Matters.

Tirkkonen-Condit, Sonja (ed) (1991) *Empirical Research in Translation and Intercultural Studies*, Tübingen: Gunter Narr Verlag.

Toury, Gideon (1992) "Everything has its Price': An Alternative to Normative Conditioning in Translator Training', *Interface: Journal of Applied Linguistics* 6(2):66-76.

Tschirner, Erwin (1996) 'Spracherwerb im Unterricht: Der Natural Approach', *FLuL* 25:50-69.

Tudge, Jonathan (1990) 'Vygotsky, the Zone of Proximal Development, and Peer Collaboration: Implications for Classroom Practice', in Luis C. Moll (ed) *Vygotsky and*

Education. Instructional Implications and Applications of Sociohistorical Psychology, Cambridge: Cambridge University Press, 155-72.

van Lier, Leo (1989) 'Classroom Research in Second Language Acquisition', *Annual Review of Applied Linguistics* 10:173-86.

Vienne, Jean (1994) 'Toward a Pedagogy of Translation in Situation', *Perspectives* 1:51-59.

von Glasersfeld, Ernst (1988) 'The Reluctance to Change a Way of Thinking', *Irish Journal of Psychology* 9(1):83-90.

Vygotsky, Lev S. (1994) 'Extracts from *Thought and Language* and *Mind in Society*', in Barry Stierer and Janet Maybin (eds) *Language, Literacy and Learning in Educational Practice*, Clevedon: Multilingual Matters, 45-58.

Wadsworth, Yolanda (1998) 'What is Participatory Action Research?', Paper 2. Available online. http://www.scu.au/schools/sawd/ari/ari-wadsworth.html.

Wertsch, James V. (1991) *Voices of the Mind. A Sociocultural Approach to Mediated Action*, Cambridge: Cambridge University Press.

Wiggins, Grant P. (1993) *Assessing Student Performance*, San Francisco: Jossey-Bass.

Wilson, Brent G. (ed) (1996) *Constructivist Learning Environments. Case Studies in Instructional Design*, Englewood Cliffs, NJ: Educational Technology Publications.

Wilss, Wolfram and Gisela Thome (eds) *Die Theorie des Übersetzens und ihr Aufschlußwert für die Übersetzungs- und Dolmetschdidaktik*, Tübingen: Gunter Narr.

Winter, Richard (1998) 'Finding a Voice – Thinking with Others: A Conception of Action Research', *Educational Action Research* 6(1):53-68.

Wlodkowski, Raymond J. (1993) *Enhancing Adult Motivation to Learn. A Guide to Improving Instruction and Increasing Learner Achievement*, San Francisco: Jossey-Bass.

Young, D. J. (1991) 'Creating a Low-anxiety Classroom Environment: What Does Language Anxiety Research Suggest?', *Modern Language Journal* 75(4):427-37.

Index